Framing Asian Studies

Framing Asian Studies

Geopolitics and Institutions

Edited by Albert Tzeng, William L. Richter
and Ekaterina Koldunova

ISEAS YUSOF ISHAK
INSTITUTE

First published in Singapore in 2018 by
ISEAS Publishing
30 Heng Mui Keng Terrace
Singapore 119614

Email: publish@iseas.edu.sg
Website: bookshop.iseas.edu.sg

*The responsibility for facts and opinions in this publication rests exclusively with
the authors and their interpretations do not necessarily reflect the views or the
policy of the publisher or its supporters.*

ISEAS Library Cataloguing-in-Publication Data

Framing Asian Studies : Geopolitics and Institutions / edited by Albert Tzeng,
    William L. Richter and Ekaterina Koldunova.
    Papers originally presented at a Conference on Framing Asian Studies,
    Geopolitics, Institutions and Networks, held in Leiden, the Netherlands,
    18–20 November 2013.
    1. Geopolitics—Asia—Congresses.
    2. Asia—Study and teaching—Congresses.
    I. Tzeng, Albert.
    II. Richter, William L.
    III. Koldunova, Ekaterina.
    IV. Conference on Framing Asian Studies, Geopolitics, Institutions and
    Networks (2013 : Leiden, the Netherlands)
DS32.9 A8F81   2018

ISBN 978-981-4786-30-0 (soft cover)
ISBN 978-981-4786-31-7 (e-book, PDF)

Typeset by International Typesetters Pte Ltd
Printed in Singapore by Markono Print Media Pte Ltd

Contents

Foreword   vii

The Contributors   xi

1.   Introduction: Framing Asian Studies   1
     Albert Tzeng, William L. Richter and Ekaterina Koldunova

I.   Contested "Asia"

2.   From Oriental Studies to Asian Studies: 21
     The Metamorphosis of the Western Mind
     Maitreyee Choudhury

3.   Geopolitical and Social Framings of Australia's   44
     "Asia Literacy"
     Kirrilee Hughes

4.   Maps as Illustrations and Logos: Geopolitical   64
     Construction of Asia and South Asia
     William L. Richter

II.   Geopolitical Framing of Western Discourse

5.   From Geertz to Ricklefs: The Changing Discourse on   101
     Javanese Religion and its Wider Contexts
     Riwanto Tirtosudarmo

6. Framing Cambodian Affairs: French and American   120
    Scholarship, Media and Geopolitics
    Gea D.M. Wijers

7. Studying Taiwan: The Politics of Area Studies in the   142
    United States and Europe
    Hardina Ohlendorf

III. Asian Studies in Former Soviet States

8. Southeast Asian Studies in Russia: Agents against   165
    Structural Limits
    Ekaterina Koldunova

9. India Studies in Soviet Lithuania: Approaching Asia from 189
    Outside the Establishment
    Valdas Jaskūnas

IV. Inter-Asian Gazes

10. Indian Understandings of Asia   211
     Brij Mohan Tankha

11. South Seas Chinese in Colonial Classifications   231
     Huei-Ying Kuo

12. Chinese Studies in Japan and South Korea: Geopolitics, 253
     Local Embeddedness and Knowledge
     Claire Seungeun Lee

Index   275

Foreword

The present edited volume, *Framing Asian Studies: Geopolitics and Institutions*, co-edited by Albert Tzeng, William L. Richter and Ekaterina Koldunova, derives from a conference entitled "Framing Asian Studies, Geopolitics, Institutions and Networks" that was organized by the International Institute for Asian Studies (IIAS) in collaboration with the Institute of Southeast Asian Studies (ISEAS), in Leiden, in November 2013.

Dr Albert Tzeng, the 2013/14 recipient of a joint fellowship between IIAS and ISEAS, was the main architect of the event in both its intellectual and organizational "framing". Albert's research on the history of Sociology as an academic institutional discipline in Taiwan, Hong Kong and Singapore served as inspiration for a discussion that he, with our encouragement, wanted to broaden in its geographical reach, its intellectual and disciplinary ranges, and in its institutional and political configurations.

The IIAS–ISEAS Fellowship Programme was an innovative undertaking developed by the two institutes. The selected beneficiaries of the programme were asked to spend six months in the Dutch/European academic setting of IIAS, and six months in the Singaporean/Asian environment of ISEAS. The programme was unfortunately short-lived. It produced only three fellowships, with Albert as the second incumbent. He was preceded by Dr Elizabeth Chandra (2012/13), and followed by Dr Lee Yong Woo (2014/15).[1]

Given the topic of the book, I should say something about this short-lived experiment of a joint fellowship programme and the spirit behind its creation in 2012. As we planned it with our colleagues from ISEAS, the joint fellowship aimed at reconfiguring the "area studies" paradigm — and the inherent danger of an imbalanced approach or "gaze"' that characterizes it — to create a new mechanism in which

"Eastern" and "Western" academic milieus, as agents and "ecologies" of knowledge production, are placed on equal footing so as to enable truly culturally cross-connected research projects.

When IIAS and ISEAS launched the initiative, the idea was to use Leiden and Singapore as convenient hubs in their respective regions. By interacting with peer colleagues in two different cultural and intellectual environments, the fellows tested the limits of their own research methodologies in a self-reflexive fashion generally not experienced in classical programmes.

The IIAS–ISEAS joint fellowship experiment was terminated too early to yield its potential for the development of a new model of interconnected and decentred scholarship beyond or above borders.[2] Today, IIAS facilitates inter-regional intellectual exchanges such as the Africa–Asia and Latin America–Asia "axes of knowledge". It is helping to create a pan–Indian Ocean network of institutions and it is at the origin of a number of thematic platforms involving scholars and educators from Asia and other regions.[3] In an academic and intellectual landscape that is ever more connected and yet increasingly fragmented and hierarchized, mechanisms such as the IIAS–ISEAS Asia–Europe fellowship can support genuinely balanced spaces of interactions and cross fertilization.

The present book focuses on academic institutions and programmes and their epistemological, social and political dynamics. Such kind of reflection on how forms of knowledge are shaped is proving increasingly critical to our understanding of what is really at stake in their deployment.

Philippe Peycam
Director, IIAS
Singapore, 1 September 2017

Notes

1. The first fellowship led to an edited volume recently published by IIAS–Amsterdam University Press, entitled *Eurasian Encounters, Museums, Missions, Modernities* (co-edited by Yoshiyuki Kikuchi and Carlien Stolte). It was during Dr Lee's fellowship that the decision to discontinue the programme in its wide scope of intervention was made.

2. IIAS and ISEAS continue to collaborate on other initiatives: a special ISEAS page on Southeast Asia features in *the Newsletter* (the IIAS periodical), a series of joint conferences on the politics of Heritage in Asia, and some co-publications.
3. For instance, the pedagogical initiative "Humanities across Borders, Asia and Africa in the World", which involves individuals and institutions from Asia, Africa, Europe and America.

The Contributors

Maitreyee Choudhury is Professor, Strategic and Area Studies, Centre for Himalayan Studies, North Bengal University, India. She studied Geography at Calcutta University, India. She specializes in area studies and Himalayan Studies. Currently she is the Director of the Centre for Himalayan Studies.

Kirrilee Hughes completed her doctorate in Asian Studies at the Australian National University in Canberra, Australia. A passionate advocate for Asia literacy, intercultural learning and global citizenship, she has held various teaching and business development roles at a number of Australian universities and is now CEO and Partner Director for AFS Intercultural Programs Australia.

Valdas Jaskūnas is Associate Professor of Indian Studies at the Centre of Oriental Studies of Vilnius University (Lithuania). His publications include the book *Visual Identities: Reception of Indian Art in the West* (2005; in Lithuanian), an annotated translation from Sanskrit into Lithuanian of Jayadeva's Gītagovinda (2012), and over twenty refereed articles on the shastric tradition of early medieval Hindu temple architecture and on critical Asian area studies. Currently he is the Vice-Rector for Studies of Vilnius University.

Ekaterina Koldunova is Associate Professor at the Department of Asian and African Studies of Moscow State Institute of International Relations, the MFA of Russia (MGIMO University). Her publications include "Russia as a Euro-Pacific Power: Dilemmas of Russian Foreign Policy Decision-making" in *International Relations* 29, no. 3 (2015).

Huei-Ying Kuo is Senior Lecturer and Associate Research Scientist in the Department of Sociology, Johns Hopkins University. She received a junior fellowship from the Social Science Research Council's Transregional Program in 2012–13 and was in 2016–17 a recipient of the William-Dearborn Fellowship in American History, Houghton Library, Harvard University. She is the author of *Networks beyond Empires: Chinese Business and Nationalism in the Hong Kong–Singapore Corridor, 1914–1941* (2014) and many refereed articles on ethnic Chinese business networks and Japan's southward advance in Southeast Asia in the early twentieth century.

Claire Seungeun Lee is Assistant Professor at the Department of Chinese Studies at Inha University, Incheon, South Korea and an affiliated fellow at the University of Massachusetts Boston. Her research areas include digital and economic sociology, international migration, and the local and global connections between China and its neighbouring countries.

Hardina Ohlendorf is a lecturer at Mahidol University International College, Thailand, and a Research Associate at the Centre of Taiwan Studies, SOAS, University of London. Prior to moving to Thailand, she worked as a senior teaching fellow in the Politics of China at SOAS and was a visiting scholar at the Institute of Sociology, Academia Sinica, with the Taiwan Fellowship. In her research, she looks at the construction of Taiwan identity in the global field of Taiwan Studies, cultural and geopolitical dimensions of Cross-Strait tourism, and Chinese identities in Southeast Asia. Her publications include "The Taiwan Dilemma in Chinese Nationalism: Taiwan Studies in the People's Republic of China" in *Asian Survey* 54, no 3 (2014).

William L. Richter is Professor Emeritus of Political Science and former Associate Provost for International Programs, Kansas State University. His authored and co-edited books include *Approaches to Political Thought* (2009) and *Combating Corruption, Encouraging Ethics* (2007). He is also author of numerous articles and book chapters on South Asian politics and security issues.

Brij Tankha retired as Professor of Modern Japanese History, University of Delhi. At present he is Honorary Fellow, Institute of Chinese Studies, Delhi. His research interests centre on nationalism, religion and Japan's interactions with Asia, and he is currently working on the intentional communities in Asia. His publications include *A Vision of Empire: Kita Ikki and the Making of Modern Japan* (2003) and (translated from the Japanese) Sato Tadao, *Mizoguchi Kenji no Sekai (The World of Mizoguchi Kenji) Kenji Mizoguchi and the Art of Japanese Cinema* (2008).

Riwanto Tirtosudarmo recently retired as Senior Research Fellow at the Research Center for Society and Culture, Indonesian Institute of Sciences (LIPI). His research covers issues of migration, urbanization, political demography, ethnicity and territorial politics. He has held visiting appointments at Brown University, the Netherlands Institute for Advanced Study in Humanities and Social Sciences (NIAS), Oxford University, Tokyo University of Foreign Studies, and the Asia Research Institute, National University of Singapore. His two latest books are *From Colonization to Nation-State: The Political-Demography of Indonesia* (2013) and *On the Politics of Migration: Indonesia and Beyond* (2015).

Albert Tzeng is a sociologist, a public intellectual, a media innovator and a policy advisor. He studied chemistry and psychology in National Taiwan University before obtaining sociology degrees in the London School of Economics and the University of Warwick. He was an ISEAS–IIAS Fellow while organizing the conference "Framing Asian

Studies" in Leiden. He became a media consultant of United Daily News Group in 2014, the chief curator of CNEX Doc channel in 2015, and the editorial director of Initium Media, Hong Kong, in 2016. He now serves as advisor to Fairwind Foundation, Taiwan Next Generation Foundation and Bleu & Books. He also taught in Tunghai University and Feng-Chia University.

Gea Wijers is a political scientist, organizational anthropologist and architectural historian. Currently, she holds a part-time postdoctoral position with the Management Studies Group at Wageningen University and Research (WUR) and runs her own consultancy (Wijers Community-based Consulting) in Amsterdam, the Netherlands.

1

Introduction: Framing Asian Studies

Albert Tzeng, William L. Richter and
Ekaterina Koldunova

"Asian Studies", whether broadly defined as the production and
dissemination of scholarly knowledge about Asia or narrowly limited to
the specific field of study named as such, has constantly been framed
by a changing geopolitical context. The term "geopolitics", borrowed
from the study of international relations, denotes a perspective of
considering power relations as embedded in the spatial structure (size,
distance, adjacency) of geographical territories. By "framing", we refer
to the process by which a configuration of contextual factors (economic,
political, cultural, historical or organizational) leads to an inclination
towards a particular pattern of knowledge.

This point is illustrated by considering the colonial roots of Oriental
or Asiatic scholarship, the war-driven migration of Asian scholars and
the dispersion of their expertise, and Cold War American investment
in both social sciences in East Asia and in "Asian Studies" at home.
The rising scholarly interest in Japan, China and India following their
growing political-economic significance in recent decades, as well as the
emergence of various "alternative discourses" and "inter-Asia dialogues"
as attempts at intellectual decolonization, provide further examples.

This framing effect is at least partially mediated by various institutions involved in the social process of knowledge production — such as foundations, professional associations, publishers, journals, research institutes, cultural societies, governments and multinational entities. These institutions operate in ways that reflect their roles, agendas and power relations within the geopolitical context, and leave their imprints, through funding and agenda setting, on their associated scholarly networks and subsequently the intellectual landscape of human knowledge about Asia.

While institutions often can be seen as mechanisms by which geopolitical priorities help to frame Asian Studies, it is important to recognize that institutions and their associated networks can also be centres of opposition to the prevailing foreign policies and their geopolitical underpinnings.

Investigating these themes further invites critical examination of the power structure underlying this knowledge: Who has written about Asia — for what and for whom? Where has Asian knowledge been disseminated and consumed? Which (institutional, societal-structural, national) interests and biases have been brought into knowledge production? Which topics have been emphasized or excluded? Even the term "Asia" as an epistemological unit is subject to question, in part for its historical roots in being associated with European perspectives for more than two millennia.

Asian Studies in Changing Contexts

Asian Studies has roots that can be traced back to the European colonial interest in Asia, or the Orient, and the indigenous intellectual attempts to resist colonial dominance through promoting forms of pan-Asianism. But as an institutionalized field of inquiry it was largely developed in the special geopolitical circumstances following World War II — the rapid dismantling of colonial empires; the proliferation of "new nations" in Asia, Africa, and elsewhere; and Cold War competition between the United States and the Soviet Union.

The Cold War confrontation of the two camps in East and Southeast Asia created strong demand for knowledge about the region, as well as the political legitimacy for the spending to meet this demand.

Scholars from both sides were sent to investigate and survey their allied countries. Institutionalized Asian Studies were rapidly developed in both the United States and the Soviet Union. Moreover, the competition for ideological domination provided the imperative to invest in education in societies close to the confrontation line.

The end of the Cold War, whether measured by the fall of the Berlin Wall in 1989 or the break-up of the Soviet Union in 1991, challenged the necessity of Asian Studies and area studies in general. In particular, the decline of United States' federal funding became a major concern of area studies centres and scholars.

But there were also issues of globalization, questions of academic priorities, and new theoretical directions (Ludden 1997). Globalization, some argued, was creating a "flat" and more homogenous world in which area-specific knowledge would become increasingly irrelevant (Friedman 2005). Traditional academic disciplines questioned the allocation of scarce resources to interdisciplinary area studies programmes. New funding initiatives and approaches brought additional challenges to what had become familiar area studies frameworks.

These post–Cold War challenges triggered debate about the future of area studies, including Asian Studies. Some writers went so far as to pronounce Asian Studies moribund and to speculate on what might be its "afterlife":

> Like those jerrybuilt temporary buildings thrown up on so many campuses during World War II, area studies outlived the original reason for its construction and has become an entrenched structure that maintains the separation of area expertise from general knowledge. (Harootunian and Miyoshi 2002, p. 6)

Nonetheless, Asian Studies — and area studies generally — appears to have survived the dire assessments of its impending irrelevance and demise for several reasons:

First, the 11 September 2001 attacks on the World Trade Center and the Pentagon marked something of a turning point by ushering in the "War on Terror" and revealing the need for language skills and area-specific knowledge. This need for Asian knowledge was repeatedly emphasized by ongoing conflicts in the Middle East, tension on the Korean Peninsula and in the Taiwan Strait, and mounting pressure in the South China Sea.

Second, the economic and political performance of Japan, China, India and other Asian countries also attracted continuing interest in studying them. In particular, the development models adopted by China and India had huge effects on their respective regions, and even on the international system, adding significance to the study of these countries and regions.

Third, with the passage of time the world turned out to be not so "flat" as some globalists had predicted. Alternative variants of regionalization, most of all visible in Asia, brought back to the research agenda the issues of the proper balancing of general and specific knowledge and of the spatial factor in world politics (Voskressenski 2017).

Finally, the prosperity of some areas of Asia demonstrated the growing influences of promoting Asian Studies — countries like Japan, Taiwan and China helping to fund studies of their respective cultures in other countries. A number of Asia-focused journals, like *Inter-Asia Cultural Studies*, have flourished, with cooperation between Asian and Western scholars as well as international collaboration within Asia. The rise of universities across an economically booming Asia in the 1990s onwards and their efforts to internationalize Asian research and education also contributed to the development of Asian Studies.

The expansion of Asian Studies in Europe, in Asia itself, and indeed throughout the world, manifests the thriving presence of Asian Studies. To paraphrase one book title, Asian Studies has become "decentred" and "diversified" (Goh 2011).

There are several institutions that play pivotal roles in maintaining networks of Asian Studies scholars. The creation of the International Institute of Asian Studies (IIAS) in Leiden and its companion International Convention of Asian Scholars (ICAS) helped to expand both European and Asian scholarly participation in Asian Studies. The biennial ICAS conferences attract around a thousand participants each year from between thirty-five and fifty-three countries. The ICAS Book Prize, established in 2004, received "approximately 50 dissertations and more than 200 books" submissions for the 2015 contest. By February 2017 it had received 330 English-language books and 126 dissertations for that year's round.[1]

Similarly, the U.S.-based Association for Asian Studies (AAS) now annually convenes an "AAS in Asia" conference at a site in Asia. The AAS itself now has more than seven thousand registered members. In 2011 the AAS held a joint conference with ICAS in Honolulu. This enlarged event attracted five thousand participants. The International Studies Association, an interdisciplinary professional network focused on international affairs, recently started a vigorous debate on Asia's possible impact on the understanding of international relations.

In short, Asian Studies appears to be alive and well, at least according to these broad measures. Asian Studies has become polycentric and more diverse. If the Asian Studies of half a century ago was framed primarily by Cold War geopolitics, present-day Asian Studies may be seen to be shaped by much more diverse, decentralized and complex geopolitics, as several of the following chapters demonstrate.

The "Framing Asian Studies" Conference

The current volume originates from the conference "Framing Asian Studies: Geopolitics, Institutions and Networks" held in Leiden, the Netherlands, 18–20 November 2013. The conference was jointly hosted by the IIAS and the Institute of Southeast Asian Studies (ISEAS) and was convened by Albert Tzeng, at that time an IIAS and ISEAS postdoctoral Fellow.

The theme of the conference grew directly out of the subject of Tzeng's doctoral dissertation, "Framing Sociology in Taiwan, Hong Kong and Singapore: Geopolitics, States and Practitioners". In that study, Tzeng traced how sociology as a Western discipline had been introduced, institutionalized and developed in the three Asian societies. It related observed patterns to regional geopolitical factors (e.g., the Chinese Civil War, the Cold War and decolonization) and the distinctive contexts of the three places.

Anchored within the broad tradition of "sociology of knowledge", Tzeng's dissertation started with a review of numerous approaches to theorizing about the social sciences in Asia — orientalism, Eurocentrism, post-colonialism, Captive Mind, intellectual imperialism, academic dependency theory and some others. However, he found these approaches limited by their built-in dualistic image of an East–West dichotomy and an inability to deal with more sophisticated patterns of multi-site knowledge flow. Tzeng therefore drew upon ideas of the "world system" (Wallerstein 1974), "network society" (Castells 1996), the knowledge network (Altbach 1998) and cultural capital (Bourdieu 1993) to propose a *world system of knowledge network* as an overarching conceptual frame for narrating the historical expansion of the knowledge enterprise from medieval European universities to a vast global network of knowledge production and dissemination.

The conference was conceived by appropriating this analytical framework to inquiries about the social framing of Asian Studies. The conference theme situated the production and dissemination of knowledge about Asia within the "world system of knowledge network". Geopolitical contexts were central to the discussion, but for this broad treatment of Asian Studies it was important to pay attention to a wider array of institutions that include both the state-centric and the transnational; and it was important to focus more on their networks than on individual actors.

The call for papers invited applicants to explore:

- The influence of geopolitical factors on how knowledge about Asia is produced and disseminated: colonialism and its legacy, wars and regional conflicts, the Cold War structure, and the "knowledge economy" competition in the new era of globalization.
- The role of various institutions in promoting and directing Asian Studies: foundations, professional associations, publishers, journals, research institutes, governments and multinational entities.
- The outlook of various knowledge networks, including both (a) macroscopic investigations on the patterns and developmental trajectory of knowledge networks measured in terms of flows of scholars/students, capital and knowledge, and (b) case studies of particular networks of institutions or people on Asian Studies.
- Critiques of the power structure underlying the observed patterns of knowledge production and dissemination of Asian Studies, including consideration of fundamental questions like: Knowledge for what? Knowledge for whom? Whose interests were represented or excluded? How relevant and appropriate is it to use "Asia" as an epistemological unit?

Altogether, 140 abstracts were received from 39 countries, of which 71 were from Asia, 36 from Europe, 16 from the United States, 10 from Australia and New Zealand, and the rest from elsewhere. Submissions from Asia mostly came from the "southeast coastal belt" that included South, Southeast and East Asia. The distribution pattern roughly reflected the geographical span of the scholarly network associated with the two organizing institutions.

Thirty-four submissions were selected to be presented in the conference — which consisted of nine thematic sessions over three days — of which eleven papers were further selected to be included in the present volume.[2] Tzeng also invited William L. Richter, Professor Emeritus of Kansas State University, and Ekaterina Kuldunova, Associate Professor of MGIMO University, to join the editorial team for this book.

The primary criterion for selection was each paper's potential to make sharp points or to raise critical questions about the interplay of geopolitics, institutions and scholarly networks in framing the outlook of knowledge about Asia. It was also advantageous to have papers that were clearly written and in a relatively complete form at the time of the conference. A minor consideration was to achieve a degree of geographical and thematic diversity as represented in the conference. The resulting volume was not intended to be a complete survey, but rather a sample of interesting case studies to advance understanding of the subject.

Most of the selected papers incorporated geopolitical factors in their analysis, while several discussed the role of particular institutions. However, the third topic, "knowledge network", received little attention and was dropped from the book title.

Structure of the Book

The chapters in the present volume are presented in four sections. The first section focuses on "Asia" as a contested subject. It not only traces the framing of Asian Studies back to the multiple traditions of Oriental Studies in Europe, but also explores the variant geographical framing of Asia. The second section explores the geopolitical framing of Western discourses on Asia. The three chapters included take Java,

Cambodia and Taiwan as examples of how scholarly or even public media representation of them in the United States or Europe have been shaped by the changing geopolitical contexts. The third section turns to Russia and Lithuania, two former Soviet states, and demonstrates how the historical trajectories of their Asian Studies also reflect their changing geopolitical positions. The final section, titled "Inter-Asian Gazes", includes three case studies on the generation of Asian knowledge within Asia.

I. Contested "Asia"

"Asia is not one", as Amitav Acharya (2010) reminds us, "there is no singular idea of Asia". The notion of Asia is characterised by "fuzziness and incoherence" and is "essentially contested" (Acharya 2010). Asia is contested in multiple ways. Like other large landmasses, Asia has been claimed and fought over for centuries by indigenous and intrusive political powers. Despite the present-day universality of a system of states, interstate boundaries continue in many places to be unresolved or challenged by ethnicity or ideology. The meaning of Asia has been contested among colonial writers, between colonizers and colonized, and among post-colonial countries. Its geographical definition is also a matter of contestation (Lewis and Wigen 1997). Is it a single entity or several (Duara 2013)? Does it make sense as a geographic concept? What constitutes the boundaries of Asia?

The three chapters in section I explore some of these aspects of contested Asia.

Maitreyee Choudhury, in chapter 2, traces the European roots of Asian Studies in English, Dutch, French, German and other traditions of Oriental Studies. Her broad historical overview of the European orientalist tradition draws upon Edward Said's critique of orientalism (Said 1978), but it also shows how Said fails to account for certain aspects of the orientalist tradition. In addition to her summary of the historical development of orientalist institutions in Western Europe, the United States, and elsewhere, she provides a more detailed study of the Oriental Society of Bengal, which was something of a prototype for later orientalist institutions.

After considering the historical orientalist background to the development of Asian Studies in the last half of the twentieth century, Choudhury looks at some of the geopolitical factors that helped to frame and reframe Asian Studies in the decades following World War II. She notes the importance of the Cold War, 9/11, the expanding numbers of Asian scholars on Asia, and other factors that have helped to explain the vicissitudes of Asian Studies over the last six or seven decades.

She argues that these changes in Asian Studies have brought about a "metamorphosis of the Western mind". Geopolitics has framed Asian Studies, but Asian Studies has in turn shaped how Europeans and Americans view Asia. If she is correct in this argument, might we speak with equal validity of Asian Studies leading to a "metamorphosis of the Asian mind"?

Kirrilee Hughes in chapter 3 reflects on Australia's "Asia literacy" programme and its relevance to our understanding of "Asia", "Australia", and area studies. Central to her discussion is the widespread "metageographical" perception that Asia and Australia are two separate geographic entities. To some extent, Asia literacy challenges the absoluteness of this notion by asserting a degree of shared identity and shared interests, based in part on geographic proximity. Hughes draws on the concepts of *metageography* (Lewis and Wigan 1997) to highlight the contestability of geographic givens, such as Asia, and *hybridity* (Ang 2001) to explore the impact of Asia literacy on Australian society.

Hughes suggests an interesting but complex interplay among geopolitics, Asian Studies, Australia's Asia literacy project, and the very meanings of Asia and Australia. The post–World War II geopolitics of the United States were important in framing the areas of today's area studies, including East Asia and Southeast Asia. The development of Asian Studies programmes in Australian institutions of higher education helped to frame the Asia literacy initiative. Asia literacy is helping to reframe both Asia and Australian identity.

William Richter in chapter 4 explores the question of how Asia and South Asia are "constructed" by something as commonplace as the maps found on covers of books and professional journals and in the logos of professional associations. Drawing on metageography, cartography and postmodern social theories, Richter argues that cover illustrations and logos reflect socially constructed "mental maps" rather than any intention of authors, illustrators or publishers to shape geographic perceptions.

Richter explores differences between "atlas" definitions and the "geopolitical" portrayal of Asia and South Asia in cover illustrations and logos. He also shows how such representations have changed over just a few decades. Processes of framing and reframing Asia and Asian Studies, he argues, are ongoing.

II. Geopolitical Framing of Western Discourses

Geopolitics began in the nineteenth century as an attempt to establish an objective geographic science of statecraft (Cohen 2002). Ironically, the "science" of geopolitics was itself shaped by the same imperial forces and motivations that gave rise to orientalism. Sir Halford Mackinder's famous "heartland" doctrine — that whichever power controlled the Eurasian "heartland" would control the world — reflected decades of British imperial competition with Russia in Central Asia. American Admiral Alfred Thayer Mahan developed a geopolitical theory of sea power that helped justify President Theodore Roosevelt's expansion of U.S. naval forces. German Karl Haushofer adapted Mackinder to create a *Geopolitik* in support of Hitler's Third Reich. American Nicholas Spykman countered Mackinder's Heartland theory with a "Rimland" theory that later became a significant basis for the application to Asia of the United States' Cold War doctrine of containment.

The recognition that geopolitics might differ from country to country (Dodds and Atkinson 2000) has led to the contemporary study of critical geopolitics (Tuathail 1996; Derluguian and Greer 2000). Like Asian Studies, Geopolitics (as a set of theories or field of study) is itself framed by geopolitics (as real and/or perceived political conditions).

We tend to speak of geopolitical eras. Orientalism developed in the era of European colonialism. Area studies developed in the Cold War era, faced major challenges in the brief period between the end of the Cold War and 9/11, and continues to evolve in the post-9/11 era. These broad generalizations, of course, mask a lot of temporal and geographic complexity. As Choudhury notes in chapter 2, the orientalism of William Jones in the late eighteenth century was very different from that in the time of Rudyard Kipling a century later. The chapters in section II explore some of this complexity.

In chapter 6, Riwanto Tirtosudarmo looks at American scholarly treatment of Javanese Islam over a period encompassing both the Cold War and the War on Terror. This is a period in which a changing geopolitics has made for a "changing context of area studies" (Bonura and Sears 2007). Indonesia is the largest country in Southeast Asia, the third-largest country in Asia and the largest Muslim country in the world. Java is a major island component of Indonesia, and Islam has been politically relevant both to democratization issues during the Cold War and, especially, to "clash of civilizations" concerns during the post-9/11 era.

Tirtosudarmo considers the writings of three American scholars whose books have been prominent in analysing and interpreting Javanese Islam to Americans and the wider world. The three are Clifford Geertz, Robert Hefner and Merle Ricklefs. Tirtosudarmo is of course cognizant of non-American scholars writing on Islam in Indonesia, but focuses on these three to discern the extent to which the changing geopolitical context is reflected in their writings.

The chapter shows connections between the categories with which Geertz analysed Javanese Islam and important Cold War issues and events, including democratization, modernization, and the anti-Communist massacres of 1965. It also shows links between the later writings of Hefner and Ricklefs and their changed geopolitical environments. However, there is also a notable continuity in analysis from Geertz to Hefner to Ricklefs. Geopolitics frames their successive studies of Javanese Islam in identifiable ways, but the categories of the earlier period are largely carried forward into the later one.

In chapter 7, Gea Wijers explores the ways in which the dynamics of geopolitics helped frame media reporting on the Cambodian situation during the Khmer Rouge takeover (1975–79) and the Vietnamese intervention (1979–89). Her chapter illustrates how social constructions such as historical relationships, the accepted media discourse and scholarship "traditions" can contribute to perceptions of Cambodian "genocide" as well as influence the resettlement of Cambodian refugees.

Comparing France, its former colonizer, and the United States in their media reporting and scholarly traditions, Wijers provides additional evidence that the subjects compiled in Asian Studies are not established in a neutral process but are affected by temporal variations in internal and external political constellations and public opinion. She illustrates this with a look at Cambodian refugee resettlement experiences in Lyons, France, and in Long Beach, California (USA), drawing on field research in both communities.

Wijers broadens the scope of Asian Studies by moving beyond its academic impact and acknowledging the role of the zeitgeist on research perceptions, output and societal outcomes. She concludes that lack of attention to the true complexity of Cambodian affairs at the time helped shape a limited view on "genocides" that exists to this day.

Hardina Ohlendorf, in chapter 7, looks at the special case of Taiwan Studies, "a relatively new field of research" that she claims "challenges the conventional models of area studies". In contrast to the long orientalist traditions preceding most other Asian Studies programmes, Taiwan Studies emerged as a distinct field of studies since the late 1980s — a time when the general legitimacy of area studies was challenged for their connection with colonialism or American hegemony. "The institutionalized academic study of Taiwan as a distinct region", she writes, "has primarily been locally driven, in a bottom-up fashion, with academics challenging the prevalent perspective on Taiwan as being part of and congruent with China." Their motivation, she found, was directly linked to the changing national identity in Taiwan.

Ohlendorf compares the development of Taiwan Studies in the United States and in Europe and demonstrates how their geopolitical connection with Taiwan intertwined with the development of Taiwan Studies in both settings. But more importantly it was the political developments in Taiwan that gave greater impetus to the development of Taiwan Studies in the West, as most academics in this field rely on research funding from Taiwan. She argues that this case represents a new mode of area studies that is motivated largely by the subject studied, and describes it as "area studies in reverse".

In her conclusion, Ohlendorf raises additional questions concerning the ethical challenges faced by Taiwan Studies researchers who directly or indirectly receive funding from the country they are studying. These questions are particularly relevant to a society like Taiwan, whose political status and identity are contested, but in a broader sense they raise issues that area studies researchers should consider in any political setting.

III. Asian Studies in Former Soviet States

Most discussions of area studies, including Asian Studies, focus on how Americans and Western Europeans view the respective regions. Much less attention has been paid to the development of Asian Studies, or of specific Asian regions, in former Soviet societies or in other "non-Western" scholarly communities.

The two chapters in this section consider aspects of Asian Studies in two former Soviet countries — Russia and Lithuania. Some works on Russian orientalism have appeared in English (Tolz 2011; Schimmelpenninck van der Oye 2010), but little or nothing on Asian Studies in smaller European countries like Lithuania. The chapters by Ekaterina Koldunova and Valdas Jaskūnas not only fill major gaps in understanding of the subject but also suggest interesting comparisons — both similarities and differences — with the development of Asian Studies in the United States, Western Europe and Asia.

The chapter by Koldunova focuses on Southeast Asian Studies in Russia and traces the evolution of this field through three broad historical periods: pre-Soviet (or Imperial, prior to 1917), Soviet (1917–89) and post-Soviet (since 1989). When Imperial Russia expanded into its adjacent territories in Central and Northeastern Asia in the nineteenth century, Russian explorers also established ties and created interest in the lands of Southeast Asia. Full development of Southeast Asian Studies came only in the Soviet period, especially after World War II (as in the United States), but came under serious threats with the political and economic challenges of the 1990s (as in the United States, but even more so). This case shows that Asian Studies in Russia, like their counterparts in the West, have also been framed by geopolitics.

However, Koldunova also demonstrates the resilience of academic institutions and scholarly networks in the changing context. They helped to weather these challenges and to adapt Southeast Asian Studies to new circumstances. Geopolitical factors frame Asian Studies, but institutions and scholarly networks also help to frame geopolitics as well as Asian Studies.

Jaskūnas looks at Indian studies in Lithuania and relates the long tradition of scholarly interest in India to Lithuania's special circumstances — lengthy periods of statelessness and of subjection to

Soviet domination. Lithuania developed an "inward orientalism", he argues, in contrast to the outward orientalism of such colonial powers as England, France and the Netherlands. Lithuanians initially found affinity with India in the Indo-European links between the Lithuanian language and Sanskrit, but also identified with India as a country subjected to foreign rule. For Lithuanians, Soviet Russia rather than India was seen as "the Other". Geopolitics framed Indian studies in Lithuania, but it was the geopolitics of a small country with a history of statelessness and subjection to foreign rule.

Jaskūnas also shows that the institutions involved in Asian Studies are also shaped by these geopolitical circumstances. Lithuanians interested in India were not fully free to develop Indian studies within their formal academic institutions, so they pursued their interests through politically acceptable channels such as the Lithuanian Society for Friendship and Cultural Relations with Foreign Countries.

IV. Inter-Asia Gazes

The final section focuses on the framing of Asian knowledge within Asia. The three studies included here demonstrate how intellectuals, administrators and scholars in selected Asian countries have viewed their Asian neighbours.

Brij Tankha, in chapter 10, looks at the evolution of Indian views towards Asia and Asian Studies, with particular focus on Indian perspectives on Japan and China. He shows how leading Indian intellectuals during the nineteenth and early twentieth centuries shaped notions of Asian identity.

Changed geopolitical circumstances following World War II, especially independence from colonial rule, helped to erode these pan-Asian identities, however. Ideas of a shared "Asianness" were further damaged as Sino–Indian relations soured in the late 1950s and broke into open warfare in 1962. Whereas the earlier pan-Asianism might have predicted a strong interest in Asian Studies following independence, the result has been much more modest. Tankha shows that the study of Japan and China in independent India has been more limited and more practical than cultural (e.g., with priorities on language study rather than learning about societies and cultures of other Asian countries). He also shows that India has been relatively slow to develop educational exchanges with other Asian countries, at least with those outside its immediate "neighbourhood" or security perimeter.

However, Tankha notes, there appears to be a recent resurgence in Indian interest in Asian Studies. It is yet unclear how strong this will be or what geopolitical factors might be at play. If and when Asian Studies become a more vibrant component of Indian academic institutions they will have a rich pre-independence intellectual tradition to draw upon.

Huei-Ying Kuo's chapter compares British and Japanese classification systems for "South Seas Chinese" — what today would generally be called ethnic Chinese in Southeast Asia. Kuo's analysis actually entails two dimensions of comparison. British practice evolved during the period of colonial rule, so Kuo employs both a temporal comparison of early British classification patterns with later ones and the cross-country comparison of British and Japanese categories. In both dimensions of analysis, she explores the social, political and geopolitical factors that help to explain the differences.

Kuo uses imperial census records and related official statements to identify and interpret British classification practices. Comparable administrative resources do not exist for the Japanese, who were not in a similar colonial role in Southeast Asia, so Kuo draws upon scholarly, journalistic and commercial sources to identify and explain Japanese perceptions. Her methodology demonstrates imaginative use of evidence from institutions (British imperial census records) and networks (Japanese scholarly and other writings) to discern geopolitical and political framing of valuable area studies knowledge.

Claire Seungeun Lee in chapter 12 compares the development of Chinese studies in neighbouring countries, Japan and the Republic of Korea (ROK). For both countries, China is a large and important neighbour. She finds interesting differences in the development of the area studies "knowledge industries", not only between the two countries but also within each country over time.

Lee notes a variety of types of geopolitical factors that have helped to shape Chinese studies in the two countries. One has been the changing political status of Taiwan and the People's Republic of China (PRC) and the timing of Japanese and Korean normalization of relations with the PRC. Another has been each country's historical role in Asia. Japan's history of imperial rule over Korea, Taiwan and parts of mainland China, for instance, gave it a much longer tradition of "Sinology" than existed in the ROK.

As some of the other chapters in this volume demonstrate, geopolitics can frame Asian Studies in complex ways. In the case of Chinese studies in Japan and Korea, Lee shows, the geopolitics of both the host countries and the area being studied have shaped the educational institutions and scholarly networks involved in area studies.

Summary

This book explores the interconnection between geopolitical context and the ways this context frames our knowledge about Asia, highlighting previously neglected cause–effect relations. In addition, the work also examines how various knowledge institutions (e.g., foundations, associations, institutes, publishers and archives) promote and shape Asian Studies. To do this the authors look at a number of cases ranging from colonial impact and Western approaches to Asia to the current state of Asian Studies in Asian countries themselves.

Going beyond simple accounts of the discipline's development, the authors seek to explain why Asian Studies and its subfields developed in the way they did and what the current implications of these transformations might be on intellectual and political understandings of Asia.

The work contributes to existing knowledge by building on the current debates on the decolonization and de-imperialization of knowledge about Asia (Chen 2010; Wang 2011). However, it proposes a more multifaceted view rather than just examining the impact of the West on the framing of Asian Studies.

Notes

1. Data provided in email communication with Doreen Ilozor at AAS and Paul van der Velde at IIAS/ICAS, February 2017.
2. At least two conference papers not included in this volume have been published elsewhere as journal articles (Barter 2015; Das 2015).

References

Acharya, Amitav. "Asia Is Not One". *Journal of Asian Studies* 69, no. 4 (November 2010): 1001–13.

Altbach, Philip B. *Comparative Higher Education: Knowledge, the University, and Development*. Westport, CT: Ablex, 1998.

Ang, Ien. *On Not Speaking Chinese*. London: Routledge, 2001.

Barter, Shane J. "Geographical Record. Area Studies, Asian Studies, and the Pacific Basin". *Geographical Review* 105, no. 1 (January 2015): 105–19.

Bonura, Carlo, and Laurie J. Sears. "Introduction: Knowledges that Travel in Southeast Asian Studies". In *Knowing Southeast Asian Subjects*, edited by Laurie J. Sears, pp. 1–32. Seattle: University of Washington Press, 2007.

Bourdieu, Pierre. *The Field of Cultural Production*. New York: Columbia University Press, 1993.

Castells, Manuel. *The Information Age: Economy, Society and Culture*, vol. 1, *The Rise of the Network Society*. Cambridge, MA: Blackwell, 1996.

Chen Kuan-Hsing. *Asia as Method: Toward Deimperialization*. Durham, NC: Duke University Press, 2010.

Chou, Cynthia, and Vincent Houben. *Southeast Asian Studies: Debates and New Directions*. Singapore: Institute of Southeast Asian Studies, 2006.

Cohen, Saul Bernard. *Geopolitics of the World System*. Lanham, MD: Rowman & Littlefield, 2002.

Das, Anup Kumar. "Mapping of University Presses in India: Pattern of Knowledge Production and Dissemination". *Annals of Library and Information Studies* 62, no. 2 (2015): 57–67.

Derluguian, Georgi M., and Scott L. Greer. *Questioning Geopolitics: Political Projects in a Changing World-System*. Westport, CT: Greenwood, 2000.

Dodds, Klaus, and David Atkinson, eds., *Geopolitical Traditions: A Century of Geopolitical Thought*. London: Routledge, 2000.

Duara, Prasenjit, ed. *Asia Redux: Conceptualizing a Region for Our Times*. Singapore: Institute of Southeast Asian Studies, 2013.

Friedman, Thomas L. *The World is Flat: A Short History of the Twenty-first Century*. New York: Farrar, Straus and Giroux, 2005.

Goh Beng-Lan, ed. *Decentring and Diversifying Southeast Asian Studies: Perspectives from the Region*. Singapore: Institute of Southeast Asian Studies, 2011.

Harootunian, H.D., and Masao Miyoshi. "Introduction: The 'Afterlife' of Area Studies". In *Learning Places: The Afterlife of Area Studies*. Durham, NC: Duke University Press, 2002.

Kratoska, Paul H., Remco Baben, and Henk Schulte Nordholt, eds. *Locating Southeast Asia: Geographics of Knowledge and Politics of Space*. Singapore: Singapore University Press, 2005.

Lewis, Martin W., and Kären W. Wigen. *The Myth of Continents: A Critique of Metageography*. Berkeley: University of California Press, 1997.

Ludden, David. "The Territoriality of Knowledge and the History of Area Studies". University of Pennsylvania, 6 December 1997 <http://www.sas.upenn.edu/~dludden/areast1.htm> (accessed 7 August 2013).

Miyoshi, Masao, and H.D. Harootunian, eds. *Learning Places: The Afterlives of Area Studies*. Durham, NC: Duke University Press, 2002.

Noor, Farish A. *The Discursive Construction of Southeast Asia in 19th Century Colonial–Capitalist Discourse*. Amsterdam: Amsterdam University Press, 2016.

Park Seung Woo and Victor T. King, eds. *The Historical Construction of Southeast Asian Studies: Korea and Beyond*. Singapore: Institute of Southeast Asian Studies, 2013.

Reid, Anthony, ed. *Southeast Asian Studies: Pacific Perspectives*. Tempe: Program for Southeast Asian Studies, Arizona State University, 2003.

Said, Edward W. *Orientalism*. New York: Random House, 1978.

Schimmelpenninck van der Oye, David. *Russian Orientalism: Asia in the Russian Mind from Peter the Great to the Emigration*. New Haven: Yale University Press, 2010

Spykman, Nicholas. *American Strategy in World Politics*. New York: Harcourt, Brace, 1942.

Stremmelaar, Josine, and Paul van der Velde, eds. *What About Asia?* Amsterdam: Amsterdam University Press, 2006.

Tolz, Vera. *Russia's Own Orient: The Politics of Identity and Oriental Studies in the Late Imperial and Early Soviet Periods*. Oxford: Oxford University Press, 2011.

Tuathail, Gearóid Ó [Gerard Toal]. *Critical Geopolitics: The Politics of Writing Global Space*. London: Routledge, 1996.

Voskressenski, Alexei D. *Non-Western Theories of International Relations: Conceptualizing World Regional Studies*. Basingstoke: Palgrave Macmillan, 2017.

Wallerstein, Immanuel. *The Modern World System: Capitalist Agriculture and the Origins of the European World Economy in the Sixteenth Century*. New York: Academic Press, 1974.

Wang Hui. *The Politics of Imagining Asia*, edited by Theodore Huters. Cambridge, MA: Harvard University Press, 2011.

Part I

Contested "Asia"

2

From Oriental Studies to Asian Studies: The Metamorphosis of the Western Mind

Maitreyee Choudhury

Oriental Studies, generally speaking, is understood as knowledge of Asian cultures, languages and people. Asian Studies, too, is concerned with Asian people, culture, history, and, predominantly, politics. Conceptually, Oriental Studies developed over a long period beginning in the late sixteenth century. The heyday of Oriental Studies was the colonial period, when a number of Eurocentric scholars set forth to interpret the mind and manners of the people living in the East. However, due to overindulgence in cultural relativism and occidental high-handedness in interpreting the Orient, Oriental Studies (in general) and orientalists (in particular) were severely criticized. A shift from traditional Oriental Studies to contemporary Asian Studies started happening after World War II, more precisely during the Cold War. Twentieth century Euro-American scholars realized that Asia was never a monolithic oriental entity. On the contrary, the continent is characterized by sharp regional differences, plural cultures and heterogeneity.

Eurocentric scholars divided the globe in two: East–West, Orient–Occident, civilized–uncivilized — and religiously maintained the difference between "us" and "them".[1] They viewed the Orientals or the Asiatics as "exotic beings", the specimens of which were to be scrutinized by the "civilized" West. Europeans came, saw and conquered much of the Orient, and felt it necessary to study the mind and manners of the Orientals, not simply to satiate their thirst for knowledge (*episteme*) but also to hone practical intelligence (*phronesis*) to administer their colonies. In the process, "Oriental Studies" continued for over three centuries, till it was remodelled and rechristened as Asian Studies, beginning in America in the mid-twentieth century.[2] In essence, Europe led in the creation of Oriental Studies while America pioneered Asian Studies.

Americans joined the league of orientalists in the nineteenth century with the formation of the American Oriental Society in 1842. Since America had no colonies at that time in the Orient, initially the approach of the American orientalists was humanistic. The North American orientalists were engaged in basic research in the languages and literatures of Asia. Traditionally, such research included philology, literary criticism, textual criticism, palaeography, archaeology and the history of oriental civilizations. However, American interest in the Orient took a sharp turn, both qualitatively and quantitatively, during and after World War II. The reference point of transformation of the Western mind, particularly American, in framing Asia may be traced to the late 1940s, when America became heavily involved, first with Japan and then the rest of Asia. America's involvement with Asia expanded soon after the war, and by the 1960s America held the dominant position in Asia, replacing Britain and France.

The production of knowledge on Asia in the context of geopolitics became a major issue in the late twentieth century. There emerged a palpable change in the Western approach to understanding Asia, by finding convergence of the East and the West rather than stressing only the otherness of Asia (Nisbeth 2003; Hobson 2004). There was also a felt need to examine Asian societies more critically through a multidisciplinary lens. The transformation necessitated a theoretically informed discipline-based approach to Asian Studies, in contrast to the humanistic approach prevalent in Oriental Studies.

Oriental Studies in Europe

Asia and Europe are linked by geography, but the prevailing cultures and civilizations in the two continents were delinked for a long period. The landmass located to the east of Europe, which came to be known as the Orient, was an imagined space, perceived by the pre-colonial and colonial Westerners as a land of tropical climes and wilderness, of plenitude and pestilence, and of exotic and enigmatic cultures. In spite of containing countries and cultures as varied as Arab, Chinese and Indian, the Orient to the Occidentals was a "cohesive whole" which was imagined to have little in common with the Occident.

The Orient was primarily a European construct which underscored the dissimilarity between the East and the West.[3] The terminology (Orient, Oriental, orientalist, etc.) came from Europeans rather than the people of Asia. Edward Said opined, "The Orient was almost a European invention" (Said 1978, p. 1). In short, Oriental Studies was a European enterprise to describe, analyse and understand Asia. According to Said, "from the end of the eighteenth century, there emerged a complex Orient suitable for study in the academy, for display in the museum, for reconstruction in the colonial office, for theoretical illustration in anthropological, biological, linguistic, racial and historical theses about mankind" (Said 1978, p. 2). Said further elaborates, "The Orientalist surveys the Orient from above, with the aim of getting hold of the whole sprawling panorama before him — culture, religion, mind, history, society" (ibid., p. 239). During colonial times, European orientalists, anthropologists in particular, wrote "primitive ethnographies" on the peoples of Asia and elsewhere. The primitive societies and cultures in the East were viewed by Western anthropologists (e.g., Morgan, Bachofen, McLenan and others) as earlier stages of social evolution in the West, and their ethnographies were used to explain the idea of progress and social change. From the approaches of the orientalists, two things are clear about the nature of Oriental Studies: firstly, European scholars viewed the Orient from a superior plane, and secondly, they tested Western theories in the Eastern context to prove their own progress and to confirm their superiority.

Said's views on orientalism were in no way beyond criticism. His book (*Orientalism*) attracted a great deal of attention worldwide and generated controversies. The "orientalists", who admittedly were not the intended audience for his book, were most vociferous against Said's interpretation of orientalism. In an "Afterword to the 1995 printing" of his book, Said admitted to having tried hard to overcome his book's reception as anti-Western (1995 edition, p. 331). It was argued by Albert Hourani (1992, letter to Said, p. 341) that ever since Said's *Orientalism* was published, the book had made it almost impossible to use the term "orientalism" in a neutral sense, to the extent of making it a term of abuse. Hourani, despite his arguments, accepted the word (orientalism) for a rather "dull" but "valid" discipline of scholarship (ibid., p. 342). Earlier, in 1979, Hourani pointed out that Said singled out the exaggerations, racism and hostility in orientalist writing but ignored numerous scholarly and humanistic achievements (ibid.). It was indeed the main allegation against Said's interpretation of orientalism. Said tried to defend himself by arguing that nowhere did he describe orientalism "as evil or sloppy, or uniformly the same in the work of each and every Orientalist" (ibid.).

Said's interpretation of the Western attitude to the "Others" was criticized time and again. It was challenged as recently as 2007 and 2008 by Warraq (2007) and Varisco (2008). Both of them tried to establish that Said employed a highly selective approach to Western writings on the Orient. They argued that Said started with the writings of ancient Greeks, and that too very selectively, who hardly represented the West, and then proceeded to imperial Britain and France, and later to modern America. It was also argued that the examples Said had chosen (Renan, Sacy) had little impact on orientalism. While Warraq defended the West by providing some correction to Said's depiction of Western intellectual history and Western attitudes towards the "Others", Varisco's focus was to take stock of all debates on Said's book and provide a critique of Said's work, with a suggestion to close the debates. All said and done, it cannot be denied that Said's *Orientalism* earned a dubious reputation in Europe and America by giving equal weight to amateurish and scholastic writings on the Orient. Scholastic Oriental Studies in the European universities started during the Renaissance with the establishment of chairs primarily in linguistics and religious studies in Cambridge, Oxford, Salamanca, Avignon, Bologna and Paris at the behest of the Church Council of Vienna (Misra 1996, p. 5). In Cambridge and Oxford, chairs of Hebrew were established as early as the sixteenth century, while the Chair of Arabic was introduced in the seventeenth century. Distinguished chair professors of that era included Edmund Castell who published lexicons of several Asiatic languages (Hebrew, Syrian, Ethiopian, Arabic, Persian, etc.) and Edward Pococke who travelled to the East before writing on the history and society of the Oriental people. Jesuit missionaries like Matteo Ricci went further east to study China.[4] Occasionally, scholars like Montesquieu, Voltaire, Diderot, and Gibbon discussed Eastern countries and found faults with their own countries in comparison with the Orient, at least in terms of religious tolerance.

The orientalists learned oriental languages and translated the literature of the Orient into English, French, German, Russian, and so on. The most celebrated orientalists were such eighteenth-century scholars as William Jones, Henry Thomas Colebrooke, Sylvestre de Sacy and August Wilhelm Schlegel. The early orientalists, most of whom were polymaths or at least polyglots, enthused a set of European aspirants who — by virtue of their Asian connections through trade, religious mission, administration or otherwise — tested their skills in writing about the Orient and were given access to the transactions of oriental societies. Consequently, there developed the notion that an orientalist could be "anyone who teaches, writes about, or researches the Orient — and this applies whether the person is an anthropologist, sociologist, historian or philologist — either in its specific or its general aspects ... and what he or she does is Orientalism" (Said 1978, p. 2). There was a group of orientalists who were engaged by the colonial rulers on the assumption that effective colonial administration required knowledge of the conquered people. Simultaneously, there were romantic orientalists who studied the Orient without the baggage of colonial biases. In the following paragraphs, the distinctive traditions of Oriental Studies of five European countries (namely, Portugal, the Netherlands, Germany, France and Great Britain) are discussed in chronological order.

Although the Portuguese were known to be the first Europeans to establish "permanent and regular relations with Asia since the sixteenth century" (Neves 2009), they had little interest in developing Oriental or Asian Studies in Portugal. Instead, Macao in Asia happened to be the most important Portuguese centre for Oriental Studies beginning in the late sixteenth century, courtesy of the Jesuit priests. The first European University in Asia, the Colégio de São Paulo, was founded in 1594 by Portuguese Jesuits, where Chinese, Japanese and other

Asian languages and cultures were studied. Portuguese interest in Asia waned in the eighteenth to nineteenth centuries due to Portugal's declining empire in Asia and increasing engagement with Brazil in Latin America. Nevertheless, "ad hoc individual works" (ibid.) on Asia were produced by occasional priests, diplomats and historians. In 1899 a magazine exclusively devoted to Asian culture and history (Chinese, Japanese, Malay, etc.) helped to revive Portuguese interest in Oriental/ Asian Studies. In the early twentieth century, Portuguese interest in China was renewed, and as a result there was a revival of Sinology in Portugal. But it was not until the late twentieth century that there was a structured academic body or school of Asian Studies in Portugal.

The Dutch, mainly the merchants and missionaries, sailed eastward to Asia on a regular basis in the early seventeenth century for trade and religious purposes. Their journals and reports reflected their efforts and keenness to understand the cultures and languages of the countries (viz. India, Sri Lanka, Indonesia) they visited. As a result, knowledge-based studies on Asia started quite early in the Netherlands. For example, Indology started there in the seventeenth century (Hart and Oort 1985). However, systematic studies on Dutch colonies in the Netherlands began around the mid-nineteenth century. The Royal Netherlands Institute of Southeast Asian and Caribbean Studies (KoninklijkInstituutvoorTaal, Land-en Volkenkunde) was founded at Leiden in 1851 with the specific objective of the advancement of knowledge on Southeast Asia, the Pacific and the Caribbean. The study of South Asian languages began with the establishment of the first Sanskrit chair in Leiden University in 1865. Subsequently, chairs of other South Asian, Tibetan and Southeast Asian languages were established in the first half of the twentieth century. The main streams of study in the institutes of Oriental/Asian Studies in the Netherlands were anthropology, linguistics, social science and the history of Southeast Asia with special reference to the then Dutch colonies of Indonesia, as well as colonies elsewhere, such as Suriname and the West Indies.

Oriental Studies took its root in Germany in the early eighteenth century. The Institute of Oriental Studies (Orientalisches Institut), University of Leipzig, started a language course in Arabic as early as 1728, under the stewardship of Professor Johann Christian Clodius. A few years later Professor Johann Jakob Reiske established the science of Arabic Studies (1774) in the same institute. The tradition of research on

Arabic philology continued in Germany throughout the nineteenth century. Contrary to the colonial mercantile orientalists, the German orientalists (e.g., August Schlegel, Friedrich Schlegel, etc.) were characteristically "romantics".[5] The eighteenth-century German scholars had a romantic interest in the languages and cultures of the people in the Near and Middle East, particularly the Arabs. They had a great fascination for the exotic East and diligently worked on Eastern art and literature as independent academic enterprises. Institutes for learning and teaching Asiatic languages started appearing in German universities in Berlin, Bonn and Tübingen. The nineteenth century witnessed a gradual transformation of German interest in Asia, particularly towards India. The romantic literary tradition gave way to academization and institutionalization of the discipline called Indology,[6] which was formally introduced in various universities by means of university chairs. The University of Berlin instituted the first chair of Indology in 1821, and Franz Bopp, Professor of Sanskrit and Comparative Linguistics, was the first official Indologist. Professor Bopp graced the chair for forty-six years, from 1821 to 1867. Similar dedication was shown by August Schlegel, Professor of Literature (1818–30), Bonn University and Rudolph Roth, Professor of Sanskrit (1848–95), Tübingen University.

In France, The first major effort to understand the Orient was made by a theoretician scholar Abraham-Hyacinthe Anquetil-Duperron (1731–1805), who, on a religious mission, travelled to Asia, as far east as Surat in India. There he chanced upon Avestan texts, the most ancient scripts of Zoroastrianism, and completed the translation of the Avesta in 1759 (Said 1978, pp. 76–77). Back in Paris, he translated the Upanishad, the ancient Hindu scripture, in 1786. With this, Asia acquired a precise intellectual and historical dimension in Europe (ibid., p. 77). However, the first French institute of Oriental Studies came into existence in 1795, i.e., after the French revolution. Formally known as the Institute national des langues et civilisations orientales (INALCO), and colloquially called Langues O (for Orientales), this institute became one of the "Grands établissements" in France. The institute was originally established as École spéciale des langues orientales vivantes, with a mission to teach living oriental languages "of recognized utility for politics and commerce" (www.inalco.fr), which underscores the colonial attitude and purpose of the eighteenth century French administration. Noted orientalist Silvestre de Sacy was associated with the institute from its inception. He joined as the chair of Arabic and later took the additional responsibility of Persian professor. Sacy was the first modern and institutional European orientalist who worked on Islam and Arabic and Persian literature (Said 1978, p. 18). A specific school for the study of the "extreme orient" called the École française d'Extrême-Orient (EFEO) was founded in 1898 at Saigon in Vietnam to carry out interdisciplinary research and training "in the civilisations of South, Southeast and Northeast Asia" (www.efeo.fr). The institute was created on the joint initiative of the Oriental Studies section in the French Academy of Inscriptions and Belles-Lettres and the colonial government of French Indochina. The main fields of study at EFEO included history, anthropology, archaeology, art history and linguistics. The school laid great emphasis on primary resources (archaeological, written and oral) and fieldwork in Asia. The French colonial administration in India and Indochina encouraged production of knowledge on the peoples and culture in the Orient, and French merchants and Catholic missionaries in the Orient were motivated to learn the "native" languages. By the early twentieth century, EFEO had branches all over Asia for the study of the archaeology, ethnography and history of all Asian civilization from India to Japan.

The British had the lion's share in the field of Oriental Studies due to their expansive empire and superordinate position in Asia. The involvement of British scholarship with the Orient and Oriental Studies was intense for over two centuries. The case of the Asiatic Society of Bengal, one of the earliest seats of Oriental Studies in Asia, exemplifies the intensity and impact of British Oriental Studies.

The British and the Asiatic Society of Bengal

The landmark Asiatic Society of Bengal was founded by the British in the late eighteenth century, drew Orientalists from across Europe and kept the tradition of Oriental Studies alive for more than two centuries. The British, having their first and foremost colony in India and determined to rule it for a long time, created a prototype society of orientalists at the then British capital Calcutta (now Kolkata) in Bengal. Founded in 1784 by William Jones,[7] a preeminent British orientalist and polyglot, the Asiatic Society of Bengal attracted the like-minded and soon became a centre of exchange of knowledge about the Orient in general and India in particular.

Interestingly, while deciding the name of the society, Jones preferred the term "Asiatic" over "Oriental" and clearly stated, "*Asiatic* appears both classical and proper, whether we consider the place or the object of the institution, and preferable to *Oriental*, which is in truth a word merely relative, and though commonly used in *Europe*, conveys no very distinct idea" (ibid., p. ix). Eventually, all such societies established by the British in Asia were named Asiatic Society, whether in Bengal, Burma, Ceylon, Malaya, Hong Kong or Shanghai. Jones's choice of "Asiatic" over "Oriental" can be interpreted as a point of departure from the Eurocentric, relativist view prevalent in the West. (It is to be noted that "Asiatic" was generally used in naming the societies, while "Oriental" was commonly used all over Europe in naming the academic institutes established in the eighteenth and nineteenth centuries, e.g., Orientalisches Institut, University of Leipzig, Germany; Institute national des langues et civilisations orientales, France; Orientalistikos Centras, Vilnius University, Lithuania; etc.)

The purpose of the Asiatic Society of Bengal was to investigate whatever is "rare about Man and Nature in Asia". The membership of the society was limited only to the Europeans, and any interested European could be a member with no other qualification than "a love of knowledge" (ibid., p. xi). But no Asiatic or "native" author, whatever merit or ability he might have possessed or acquired, could be a member, at least when the society was first established. It was later left to the members to decide on ballot by two-thirds majority whether the Asiatics/natives were to be enrolled as members (ibid.). The Englishmen found it easier to learn classical Indic languages like Sanskrit from native tutors rather than accept the latter as members of the society. It was not until 1832 that a native member was enrolled as a member of the Asiatic Society of Bengal.

The colonial bearing of the organization was made clear even at the time of its inception by offering the presidency of the society to Warren Hastings, the then Governor General of Bengal. Upon Hastings' inability to accept the offer, William Jones was nominated as the first President of the Society. In his maiden presidential address before the members of the society, William Jones, despite his wisdom, could not refrain from uttering such superlatives as, "There is an active spirit in European minds, which no climate or situation in life can wholly repress" (Jones 1788, p. i), hinting at the inferior situation and uneasy life in the Orient. But his vision was well defined and objectives clear. The society was instituted ostensibly "on the plan of those established in the principal cities of Europe" (ibid., p. ii) and Jones opined "it will flourish, if naturalists, chemists, antiquaries, philologers, and men of science, in different parts of Asia, will commit their observations to writing" (ibid.). The *Transactions of the Society* were meant to be "A Discourse on the Institution of a Society, for inquiries into the History, Civil and Natural, the Antiquities, Arts, Sciences and Literature, of Asia" (ibid., p. vii). The design was to limit literary investigation to the geographical limits of Asia, considering *"Hindustan* as a centre" extending to the north to the "empire of *China* with all her *Tartarian* dependencies and that of *Japan*", "many important kingdoms in the *Eastern Peninsula*", "the very interesting country of *Tibet*", "the vast regions of *Tartary*", "on the left the provinces of *Iran* or *Persia*", "the deserts of *Arabia*", "the once flourish [*sic*] kingdom of *Yemen*" and "further westward the Asiatic dominions of the *Turkish* sultans". The map of the plan of study was more or less complete, leaving hardly anything or any part of Asia out of the society's purview.

Unlike many later orientalists who viewed the Orient and the Orientals with disdain, Jones had a deep admiration for Asia and was exceptional in eulogizing Asia as the "nurse of sciences, the inventress of delightful and useful arts, the scene of glorious actions, fertile in the production of human genius, abounding in natural wonders, and infinitely diversified in the forms of religion and government, in the laws, manners, customs and languages, as well as in the features and complexions of men" (ibid, p. vii). At the same time he could not help remarking on how important and extensive a field was lying unexplored and how many "solid advantages" were "unimproved" in this part of the world (ibid.). During a second anniversary discourse of the society, Jones remarked, "The civil history of their (Asiatic) empires, and of India in particular, must be highly interesting to our common country: but we have a still nearer interest in knowing all former modes of ruling these *inestimable provinces*, on the prosperity of which so much of our national welfare, and individual benefit, seems to depend" (Jones 1788, pp. 336–37). In a way, he made a mix of both European romanticism and practical business sense.

The most significant outcome of the Asiatic Society of Bengal was a corpus of literary transactions, which was published in twenty volumes from 1788 to 1839 under the title *Asiatic Researches: History and Antiquities, the Arts, Sciences and Literature of Asia*. There were altogether 367 essays on such diverse subjects as antiquities, history, languages, literature, religion, manners, customs and music on the one hand, and mathematical and physical sciences, chemistry, botany, zoology, geology, geography, ethnography, economics and statistics on the other. The enquiries were extended to whatever was performed by Man or produced by Nature, as long as the investigations were well within the geographical limits of Asia.

Major advancements in Oriental Studies happened in Britain and France and were then refined by German scholars. It should be noted that there was one major difference between Anglo-French and German scholarship: While Anglo-French orientalism was linked with economic and political interests, German orientalism was almost exclusively scholarly and classical. German orientalist scholars' indulgence in romanticism and not having colonies in Asia gave a uniqueness to German literature on the Orient. To quote Said, "There was nothing in Germany to correspond to the Anglo-French presence in India, the Levant, North Africa" (Said 1978, p. 19). The Germans undoubtedly had intellectual expertise on the Orient, although German scholarship (e.g., Schlegel, Bopp, Max Muller, etc.) was primarily engaged with philology, philosophy and religion, whereas the dealings of Anglo-French Oriental societies were more akin to corporate affairs grappling with a variety of issues and subjects ranging from archaeology to anthropology and civil to natural history.

It is true that crucial and influential works on the Orient were accomplished by the Portuguese, Dutch, German and other European scholars, but the quantity, quality and consistency of British and French writing on the Orient surpassed others. According to Said, "to speak of Orientalism ... is to speak of a British and French cultural enterprise" (ibid., p. 4). He reiterates, "it seemed inescapably true ... that Britain and France were the pioneer nations in the Orient and the Oriental studies" (ibid., p. 17). The British and French had to their advantage the colonial networks for a period spanning over two centuries that facilitated their advanced positions in Oriental

Studies. But their involvement with the Orient was somewhat limited, and primarily confined within their colonial territory. Said noted, "Orientalism derives from a particular closeness experienced between Britain and France and the Orient, which until the early nineteenth century had really meant only India and the Bible lands" (ibid., p. 4). At a later stage, the Near and Middle East attained centre stage in Oriental Studies due to the Europeans' growing interest in Islam. Since a large portion of the population in Asia were Muslims, it became imperative for the predominantly Christian Western scholars to understand Islam. The interest was sustained by growing trade in the Mediterranean region and Africa. It may be mentioned that the School of Oriental and African Studies (SOAS) began as the School of Oriental Studies in London in 1916. It became the School of Oriental and African Studies in 1938. SOAS specialized in the study of Asia, particularly the Near and Middle East, and Africa. Beginning in the eighteenth century, the Europeans founded societies and associations of the learned to conduct study on the Orient at several places, both in Asia and Europe. The purpose of such societies was to collect and disseminate information about the countries in Asia. The Royal Asiatic Society of Great Britain and Ireland was founded in 1823. Similar Asiatic societies were established in France (Société Asiatique in Paris, 1822) and Germany (Deutsche Morgendändische Gesellschaft, 1845). It should not be missed that Russia and the East European countries had a strong tradition of Oriental Studies. In pre-revolution Russia, Oriental Studies followed the tradition of European romanticism. The Institute of Oriental Studies in the Russian Academy of Social Sciences, Moscow, had its origin in St Petersburg in Tsarist Russia. It started working from a museum established in 1818 and rapidly became a hub of Russian orientalists. Initially it followed the Western European tradition of Oriental Studies as far as the methodological principles and content were concerned (Misra 1996, p. 17). After the Great October Socialist Revolution of 1917, the perceptions and priorities of scholarship underwent phenomenal change in Soviet Russia, and the institute was shifted from St Petersburg to Moscow. Apart from the said institute, some of the states in the peripheries of the erstwhile USSR — for example, Lithuania — had a long-standing tradition of Oriental Studies. The Institute of Oriental Languages at Vilnius

University in Lithuania was founded as early as 1822. The Institute started language teaching in Mongol, Armenian, Turkish, Arabic and Persian. Visibly, there was preference for West Asian/Islamic languages at Vilnius. Later, some Indic languages such as Sanskrit, Bengali and Sinhalese were included.

It is evident from the works of European orientalists (viz. Ricci, Castell, Pococke, Jones, Colebrooke, Sacy, Schlegel, etc.) that orientalism emerged as the dominant paradigm of the study of the mind and manners of the "others", and Oriental Studies came to stay as the study of "languages, religion, and the habits and morals of these others under the euphemistic nomenclature of philology, comparative philosophy, and anthropology respectively" (Misra 1996, p. 13). As long as Orientals were blissfully ignorant or unaware of "orientalism", Oriental Studies progressed and ignited the passion for romanticism, first in Europe and then in America. But the likes of Said countered the Western experts on the Orient by the literary weapons the former acquired during their training in the West

From Oriental Studies to Asian Studies: The Metamorphosis of the Western mind

The whole world and mankind underwent massive transformation in almost every respect after the world wars. The world order changed, maps were redrawn and mindscapes restructured in the aftermath of the wars. The humankind that survived was never the same. Belief systems were reconstituted, thought processes renovated and even cultures reinvented. In the universities, deterministic ideas were thrown out and new schools of thought emerged. The relative positions of superior and inferior cultures were challenged both in the East and the West.

After the two world wars, the Orient, according to Gibb (1950, 1964), became much too important to be left to the orientalists. What was needed in the aftermath of wars was a "traditional Orientalist plus a good social scientist working together, and between them, the two should do interdisciplinary work. The traditional Orientalist will not bring outdated knowledge to bear on the Orient" (Gibb 1964, quoted in Misra 1996, p. 20). After World War II, with the ascendancy of America, Asia became significant for the Atlantic powers. America and the nations in West Europe could not afford to stay indifferent to the "Third World" in the Cold War era. The study of the East, which started in Europe, became essential in America for its future strategy in the international arena. The new trend responded to a new need. In the period of the Truman Doctrine and the Marshall Plan, the Americans realized that their knowledge about the peoples of the world and the areas which they inhabit was inadequate (Cahnman 1948, p. 233). Post-war anxieties about the inadequacy of American understanding of the rest of the world and geopolitical concerns compelled the United States to create academic infrastructure for specific area studies (Volkman 1999, p. viii).

There was a major upheaval in the realm of Oriental Studies when Said published his critique on the Western conception of the Orient in the late 1970s. His book created an uproar in the Western world, where, until Said, orientalism was generally understood to refer to academic Oriental Studies in the older, European tradition (Kramer 2001, p. 28). Even in America, scholars in various Asian Studies Institutes were complacent with their traditional way of interpreting the Orient. For instance, the art historians in America were still found to follow nineteenth-century European romanticism. According to Said, Oriental Studies subtly fuelled racism, and since the time of Homer, almost every orientalist was ethnocentric (quoted in Kramer 2001, pp. 27–43). Although Asia caught the imagination of the West for centuries, it was not strategically important for the West until the mid-twentieth century. The drastic developments that took place during the last five decades in the wake of the oil crisis of the Persian Gulf and sporadic yet violent warfare in Iran, Iraq, Vietnam, Bangladesh and Afghanistan thrust Asia into the world geopolitical arena. In the recent past, the Middle East became potentially one of the "most explosive regions of the world that threatened on more than one occasion to bring the major world powers into direct confrontation" (Tirtha 2001, p. 9). In East Asia, the dramatic rise of Japan as an industrial major was a big jolt to the Western, particularly American, economy. The rivalry among Japan, Korea and, of late, China to gain economic prominence endangered economic stability in the West. America's unwitting involvement in the internal problems of Southeast Asia was another glaring example of Asia's growing importance in the eyes of the Western powers. South Asia too was noteworthy, both politically and economically, for the rest of the world. The rivalry between India and Pakistan was no longer just a regional issue. India's and China's emergence in the closing decades of the twentieth century as economic superpowers drew considerable attention from the West. The population explosion in Asia and the large-scale "brain-drain" exodus of Asian people for material comforts in the West reached alarming proportions. Asian immigration, particularly from the poverty-stricken colonized countries, posed a threat to the well-being of the West. By the end of the twentieth century there was hardly any romanticism left for even hardcore orientalists. The issues that were of prime importance now included, inter alia, diasporas, labour migrations, the movements of global capital and media, and processes of cultural circulation and hybridization (Volkman 1999, p. ix). Scholars, political leaders, business houses and the media in the West shed their inhibitions, if any, to pay attention to the East, popularly described now as the Global South, that included Asia, Africa and Latin America. The globe was now divided North and South, rather than East and West.

The process of metamorphosis of the Western mind that started in the aftermath of the world wars in "framing" and understanding Asia followed a particular track till the beginning of the new millennium. The traditional practice of interpreting the history, philosophies and cultures of the Orient through the lens of European romanticism was gradually overlaid by newer strata of international relations, politics and economics aided by a multidisciplinary, capitalist approach. Even in communist Russia, the methodology to study the newly liberated countries in Asia changed drastically. According to Primakov (1983), former director of the Institute of Oriental Studies, USSR, post-war orientalists in Russia had the task of studying economics, modern and contemporary history, politics, national liberation movements and class structure. Further, to gain holistic knowledge of the countries under investigation, individual scholars working independently were replaced by teams of specialists drawn from various disciplines and possessing long-term plans of study. The trend continued even at the height of the Cold War, since the superpowers were still preoccupied with the arms race and mutual hostility.

At the sudden end of the Cold War, with the collapse of communism in Russia and the Soviet Bloc countries, the entire concept and programme of area studies — Asian or otherwise — went under temporary wrap, especially in America. After the "dissolution" of the Soviet Union, the Cold War map of "spheres of influence" lost much of its relevance, and the process of globalization through the mobility of people, ideas, technology and capital challenged traditional assumptions about areas.

But the tack changed in 2001. Asian Studies, particularly Middle Eastern Studies, once more occupied centre stage in the wake of the 9/11 attacks on the United States. The incident is etched in world history, and it is needless to elaborate on the implications of the terrorist attacks. But the events alerted academia in the United States, so complacent until then with their literary achievements. In the United States, many questioned the performance of Middle East experts, since they failed to produce policy-relevant studies (Teti 2007, p. 118). It became obvious that the tasks of such centres in the United States included, inter alia, supplying "classified" information on potential threats from the areas concerned. The centres and institutes of Asian Studies that went almost dormant for about a decade after the end of the Cold War were jolted out of slumber, and were even reproached for their non-performance in areas as vital as U.S. security and prestige. In a corrective measure, some key centres were revitalized to research all known and hitherto unknown facts about Asia, specifically about the Arab and Islamic world. Post 9/11, the strategic concerns that fuelled the emergence of Asian Studies underwent a resurgence. Apart from structural changes in such centres, modifications were made both in curricula and research foci. Numerous conferences were organized on Islam, terrorism and non-military threats in the following decade.

The other force that changed the course of Asian Studies in non-Western countries was the rise of Asian scholarship on Asia. With an upwardly mobile contingent of Asian scholars in Asian Studies in America and Europe, there came a major change in the Western perspective towards Asian Studies. The methods of Western scholars in framing certain "nomothetic" concepts and formulating hypotheses about "Asian ways" were unacceptable to Asian scholars firmly rooted in "Asian values". The universality of theories in the Social Sciences was challenged by scholars of Asian origin in the West. Said's critique of orientalism already set the momentum. The Western mind was considerably intrigued and partially influenced by the ideas of Eastern thinkers. Consequently, the modalities and methods in Asian Studies centres were reviewed. Some scholars were even sceptical of using the umbrella term "Asian Studies" as it was extremely impractical to study the continent of Asia as a monolithic whole. According to Amitav Acharya (2006, p. 4), the physical, cultural, political and linguistic diversity of Asia "makes it difficult for anyone to claim credible specialisation on more than one country". Besides, it was understood that production of knowledge on Asia was not the prerogative of only Western scholarship.

In spite of debates on "who holds the authority to judge and evaluate Asian ways", an enormous amount of knowledge of Asia was generated in the West. The tomes on Asia in university libraries were the result of personal and institutional efforts shaped by disciplinary and geopolitical interrelationships. Side by side, the "discipline" versus "area" debate continued. Post World War II, "Asian Studies" gained currency in the United States, while in Europe the term "Asian Studies" was used interchangeably with Oriental Studies. During the Cold War, Asian Studies emerged as a constituent of a new paradigm called area studies. America and the nations in Western Europe could not afford to remain indifferent towards the emerging independent nations in the "Third World". In fact, all the countries in the world, whether in the "First" or "Second" or "Third" category, became strategically involved with one or more groups during the Cold War. The newly liberated/ decolonized nations in Asia discovered their own space and sphere of influence within the Third World. The countries in the First (read capitalist) and the Second (read communist) worlds competed with each other to bring the Asian nations under their respective wings. It was essential for them to understand Asia, not in terms of simply history, language and culture, but in terms of politics, economics, law and, most importantly, military might. The nineteenth-century ideas of Indology, or Sinology, and so on, fell far short of fulfilling the demands for strategic planning. The generic concept of Oriental Studies was contested, so much so that it was sometimes seen as an obstruction to modern scholarship. Linguist relativist Benjamin Whorf (1941) noted, "The West has attained some emotional understanding of the East through the aesthetic and belles-lettres type of approach, but this has not bridged the intellectual gulf". In the wake of urgent demands for scholars and practitioners trained on Asia, the concept of area studies emerged and evolved. Area studies on Asia and its constituent states were symptomatic not only in the United States or Europe but also in the rest of the world. Consequently, a number of generic Oriental Studies centres converted themselves into area studies centres. For example, the Institute of Oriental Studies at Cambridge University became the Institute for Asian and East Asian Studies in 2007. A new kind of diplomacy emerged out of strategic necessity, prompting the non-Asian countries to start a specific area studies programme called Asian Studies, which had little in common with Oriental Studies. However, there remained one common field of study, namely, language. Asian languages were still important for the scholars of Asian Studies, for the very basic reason that without delving deeply into local texts and literature, any knowledge on the concerned area would be superficial and incomplete.

The initial reasons behind the transformation of the Western mind in framing Asia were geopolitical and strategic. Large investments were made, particularly by the United States in the 1940s and 1950s to understand Asia, especially the Far East, Southeast Asia, the Middle East and South Asia. In due course the field of Asian Studies widened and focused more on intellectual research agendas. For example, U.S. research on Southeast Asia that started with an emphasis on political and strategic issues dramatically shifted towards economic and cultural issues (Bowen 2003). Studies on South Asia, which were built on an orientalist tradition of Asian languages, religions and philosophy, shifted towards socio-political studies and were eventually dominated by "Subaltern Studies" and a broader epistemological debate on the study of post-colonial societies (Dirks 2003).

The intellectual and political views of Asian scholars living outside Asia (e.g., Edward Said) have continued to influence Western views on Asia. In parallel fashion, a handful of committed Western social scientists (e.g., Wallerstein 1996, Nisbet 2003, Hobson 2004) have helped build empathy towards Asia. Meetings of Eastern and Western intellectuals, diplomats and political leaders in international forums and international debates on emergent issues have contributed to changing ideologies concerning Asia. On a practical note, the removal of entry bottlenecks faced by Westerners in certain "closed countries" and easier access for field research in lesser-known regions of Asia helped Western researchers to redefine their notions and views on Asia.

With the call for opening the social sciences (Wallerstein 1996, 1999), multidisciplinary Asian Studies have acquired greater legitimacy. Ever since area studies scholars in the West have been "developing and legitimating new understandings and forms of knowledge which their Euro-centric or American colleagues in the social sciences and humanities are not likely to have imagined" (Szanton 2003), Asian Studies has created a platform for a new breed of scholars and specialists on the region. They framed Asia in a new light by generating fresh concepts and approaches to legitimize the "analytic value of the perspectives of the *natives* or the *other*" (ibid.). The metamorphosis of the Western mind in understanding, capturing and framing Asia has gained momentum with the acceptance of interpretations and explanations of Asian phenomena offered by Asians.

Concluding Remarks

Oriental Studies was the precursor or prototype of Asian Studies. Oriental Studies, in spite of its traditional mould and associated disadvantages, has not been discarded as a discipline, and nearly every European institute of Oriental Studies is continuing. However, with the ascendency of American power after World War II, European dominance in Asia faded, and the study of Asia has been remodelled in accordance with America's geopolitical perspective.

Asian Studies — more precisely, studies on Asian sub-regions — has not emerged from a vacuum: The Cold war and its fallout, the rise of certain East Asian powers, particularly China, the oil diplomacy of the West Asian countries and the emergence of terrorism and various non-military threats from the Asian hinterland have necessitated a recasting of the concept of area studies and a relook at Asia. Needless to say, Europe too has been influenced by the American concept of Area/Asian Studies. However, there are differences between and within the United States and Europe in the format of Asian Studies, primarily due to historical and geopolitical reasons, and also due to academic and institutional traditions.

All said and done, the metamorphosis of the Western mind also derives from contradictions posed by Asian critics of Oriental Studies and the convergence of Eastern and Western thought.

Notes

1. According to Wallerstein (1996), orientalists depend upon a binary view of the social world. The Department of Oriental Studies, Oxford University, still claims Oriental Studies is unique in introducing students to civilizations that are "radically different from the Western one" (www.ox.ac.uk).
2. The University of California at Berkeley started an interdisciplinary course under the name Asiatic Studies in 1949, which was changed to Asian Studies in 1959 (www.iastp.barkeley.edu). Even the Institute of Oriental Studies at Cambridge University became the Institute of Asian and East Asian Studies in 2007.
3. See Hay (1968). Said (1978), too, has iterated the same in his book.
4. Edmund Castell (1606–85) and Edward Pococke (1604–91) were English orientalists. Castell taught Arabic at Cambridge while Pococke taught both Arabic and Hebrew at Oxford. Pococke visited Aleppo in Syria and Constantinople to learn Arabic and to collect valuable manuscripts. Castell's great work was the *Lexicon Heptaglotton* (a dictionary of seven Middle Eastern languages) completed in 1669, while Pococke's magnum opus was the *Arabic History of Bar-Hebraeus*. Matteo Ricci (1552–1610) was an Italian Catholic priest who lived in India and China. Ricci, an established mathematician and cartographer of his time, composed the first European-style map of China in 1584 and, in association with Portuguese missionary Ruggieri, compiled a Portuguese–Chinese dictionary, the first of its kind in any European language. (See Chisholm, 1911.)
5. The age of German romanticism (1790–1830) was an age of imagination, egotism and antiquity. Romanticism included, among other things, a creative interest in ideas and themes about the primitive, the medieval and the East. In 1809, A.W. Schlegel differentiated the romantic from the antique or classical. The first generation of German Romantics (Schlegel brothers et al., Berlin-Jena group, 1790–1804) were known as early romantics, while the second generation (Brothers Grimm et al. 1805–15) or the Heidelberg group are called the high romantics. There was also a period of late romanticism (Vienna, Munich and Berlin, 1815–30). See Roe (2007).

6. Indology or Indologie is mainly associated with German scholarship. Indology is the academic study of the history, cultures, languages and literature of the Indian subcontinent and is a subset of Asian Studies.

7. William Jones (1746–94), an Anglo-Welsh philologist, was a hyperglot and a polymath. He learned Greek, Latin, Persian, Arabic, Hebrew and the basics of Chinese at a very early age and by the end of his life had mastered thirteen languages thoroughly and twenty-eight languages considerably well. In addition, he was a legal professional, a poet, a historian, a classicist and an indefatigable scholar.

References

Acharya, Amitav. *International Relations and Area Studies: Towards a New Synthesis? (with special reference to Asia)*, State of Security and International Studies Series 2. Singapore: Institute of Defence and Strategic Studies, Nanyang Technological University, 2006.

Bilgin, Pinar. "Is the 'Orientalist' Past and Future of Middle East Studies?" *Third World Quarterly* 25 (2004): 423–33.

Bowen, John, R. "The Development of Southeast Asian Studies in the United States". In *The Politics of Knowledge: Area Studies and the Disciplines*. Berkley: University of California, 2003.

Cahnman, Werner J. "Outline of a Theory of Area Studies". *Annals of the Association of American Geographers* 38, no. 4 (1948): 233–43.

Chisholm, Hugh, ed. *Encyclopaedia Britannica*, 11th ed. Cambridge University Press, 1911.

Dirks, Nicholas, B. "South Asian Studies: Futures Past". In *The Politics of Knowledge: Area Studies and the Disciplines*. Berkley: University of California, 2003.

Gibb, H.A.R., and H. Bowen. *Islamic Society and the West: A Study of the Impact of Western Civilisation on Moslem Culture in the Near East*, vol. 1, pts. 1 and 2. London: Oxford University Press, 1950.

———. *Area Studies Reconsidered*. London: School of Oriental and African Studies, 1964.

Godemont, Francois. *The New Asian Renaissance: From Colonialism to the Cold War*. London: Routledge, 1997.

Hart, Hanneke, and Marianne Oort. "Selected Bibliography of Indology in the Netherlands since the 17th Century". Paper presented at the 7th World Sanskrit Conference, Leiden, 1985.

Hay, Denys. *Europe: The Emergence of an Idea*. Edinburgh University Press, 1968.

Hobson, John, M. *The Eastern Origins of Western Civilization*. Cambridge University Press, 2004.

Huntington, Samuel P. "The Clash of Civilizations?" *Foreign Affairs* 71 (1993): 222–49.

Hussin, Nordin, ed. *The Easternization of the West: Europe Meets Asia.* Institute of Occidental Studies, UKM, Malaysia, 2006.

Jones, William. *Asiatic Researches*, vol. 1. Calcutta: Asiatic Society of Bengal, 1788.

Kramer, Martin. "Said's Splash". In *Ivory Towers on Sand: Failure of Middle Eastern Studies in America*, pp. 27–43. Washington: Washington Institute for Near East Policy, 2001.

Ludden, David. *Area Studies in the Age of Globalization.* Philadelphia: Pennsylvania University Press, 1998.

Lyall, A.C. *Asiatic Studies, Religious and Social*, vol. 1. London: John Murray, 1882; repr. New Delhi: Cosmo Publications, 1976.

Misra, B.P. "Area Studies: Policy and Methodology", Occasional Paper no. 10. Centre for Himalayan Studies, NBU, 1996.

Neves, Santos Miguel. "Asian Studies in Portugal – The State of the Art". Lisbon: Institute of International and Strategic Studies IEEI, 2009.

Nisbeth, Richard, E. *The Geography of Thought: How Asians and Westerners Think Differently ... and Why?* New York: Free Press, 2003.

Oostindie, Gert, and Bert Paasman. "Dutch Attitudes Towards Colonial Empires, Indigenous Cultures, and Slaves". *Eighteenth-Century Studies* 31, no. 3 (1998): 349–55.

Peter, J. Katzenstein. *A World of Regions: Asia and Europe in the American Imperium.* Ithaca: Cornell University Press, 2005.

Primakov, Y., and A. Baziyants. "Soviet Oriental Studies – Origin and Development". *Asia and Africa Today* 46, no. 4 (1983): 28–31.

Roe, Nicholas. *Romanticism.* Oxford: Oxford University Press, 2007.

Said, Edward. *Orientalism: Western Conceptions of the Orient.* New York: Pantheon Books, 1978.

Spanos, William, V. *The Legacy of Edward Said.* University of Illinois Press, 2003.

Stokhof, Wim. "Towards a Dutch Association for Asian Studies". Speech delivered at a study day held by Work Community Southeast Asia and Oceania, The Hague, 12 January 1996.

Szanton, David, L., ed. *The Origin, Nature, and Challenges of Area Studies in the United States.* Berkley: University of California, 2003.

Teti, Andrea. "Bridging the Gap: IR, Middle East Studies, and the Disciplinary Politics of the Area Studies Controversy". *European Journal of International Relations* 13 (2007): 117–45.

Tirtha, Ranjit. *Geography of Asia.* New Delhi: Rawat, 2001.

Varisco, Daniel Martin. *Reading Orientalism: Said and the Unsaid.* Seattle: University of Washington Press, 2008.

Volkman, Toby Alice. *Crossing borders: Revitalizing Area Studies*. Ford Foundation, 1999.

Wallerstein, Immanuel. "Eurocentrism and its Avatars: The Dilemmas of Social Science". Keynote address at ISA East Asian Regional Colloquium on "The Future of Sociology in East Asia", Seoul, Korea, 22–23 November 1996.

———. *End of the World as We Know It: Social Science for the Twenty-first Century*. Minneapolis, Minnesota University Press, 1999.

Warraq Ibn. *Defending the West: A Critique of Edward Said's Orientalism*. Amherst, New York: Prometheus Books, 2007.

Whorf, Lee Benjamin. *Language, Thought and Reality*, edited by John B. Carroll. Cambridge: MIT, [1941] 1971.

3

Geopolitical and Social Framings of Australia's "Asia Literacy"[1]

Kirrilee Hughes

One of the most salient, and longest-running, public discussions about Asian Studies in Australia is the "Asia literacy" agenda, which commenced in the early 1970s and has experienced discontinuous federal government funding through to present times. In essence, "Asia literacy" focuses on encouraging more Australian students to take up Asian languages and Asian Studies in Australian education systems. Much of the debate about Australia's "Asia literacy" has concentrated on the need for corresponding increases in education funding and other resources in order for participation targets to be achieved. This includes training and retraining programmes to boost the stock of "Asia-literate" teachers able to deliver these courses in Australian schools and universities.

To view Asia literacy in such narrow "supply and demand" terms or to focus on unmet participation targets, however, is to overlook the ways in which Asia literacy is framed by Australian geopolitical and social perspectives. Underscoring these concepts is a spatial assumption that "Australia" and "Asia" are separate geographical and cultural categories: that "Australians" cannot also be "Asians" and vice versa.

In this chapter, I argue that an analysis of Asia literacy reveals deeper truths about how Australians view "Asia" and their own geopolitical place in the world, as well as the make-up of Australian society. Asia literacy has been framed as an educational and geopolitical project aimed at "knowing Asia", which has also been equated to knowing *others*. This dismisses the fundamental concept of Australians knowing *themselves*.

In this chapter, I first present a background of Australia's Asia literacy. I then separately examine geopolitical and social framings of Asia literacy. From a spatial perspective, which can also be thought of as the "where" of Asia literacy, I draw on Lewis and Wigen's concept of "metageography" to reveal the geographical and geopolitical assumptions that underpin Asia literacy, particularly in terms of thinking about Australia as part of Asia and as a member nation of an "Asian neighbourhood". I then explore Asia literacy from a sociocultural viewpoint, which is a function of the "who" of Asia literacy. I use this perspective to analyse agency, and I consider Ang's work on "hybridity" as an alternative to the apparent "Australia" and "Asia" categories that permeate Asia literacy. Ultimately, these two perspectives of Asia literacy — geopolitical and social — demonstrate that concepts of space and place are fundamental to Australian framings of Asian Studies.

Asia Literacy: Rationale and Goals

The term "Asia literacy" was not coined until 1988 (FitzGerald 1988, p. 12); however, the aspiration for more Australians to have a deeper knowledge of Asian languages and Asian societies was first expressed in the Auchmuty Report, published in 1971. Between 1971 and the present day, a large number of official reports and documents that address Asia literacy have been released in Australia, with most commissioned by the Australian federal government.[2] The most recent of these is the *Australia in the Asian Century: White Paper*, which was published in October 2012. In this chapter it is not my intention to explore participation trends in Australia's Asia literacy programmes over this forty-year period. Rather, I focus on the range of different interpretations of the rationale of and goals for Asia literacy in Australia, from which four key points emerge.

First, since the Auchmuty Report of 1971, Asia literacy has always encompassed the learning of Asian languages in particular *as well as* the learning about Asian societies more generally. There are thus two dimensions to the content of Asia literacy: Asian languages education and Asian Studies education. In this way, Asia literacy is *more* than just "Asian Studies". Within Asian languages education, certain languages have received priority, namely Chinese, Indonesian, Japanese and Korean (Rudd 1994). And within Asia literacy there has also been an overt focus on Asian languages education, often at the expense of Asian Studies education. This can be viewed as a response to the introduction of various "Languages Other Than English" (LOTE) policies in the Australian education system and the subsequent setting of explicit participation targets for Asian languages education. In a nutshell, participation in Asian languages education lends itself to discrete measurement by education authorities, whilst Asian Studies education, which occurs across multiple areas of school and university curricula, is more difficult to quantify and consequently to report on.

Second, Asia literacy is a uniquely *Australian* term and policy initiative. Asia literacy aims to promote the study of Asia within Australia (and for the most part, not outside Australia) and by Australians. Asia literacy denotes the acquisition of knowledge about Asia by Australians and *not* by others. Agency is threefold here: Asia literacy is to be learned by Australian students, taught by Australian educators and promoted by Australian federal and state governments. It is important to note the absence of the involvement of foreign, Asian governments in the formulation of Asia literacy initiatives in Australia; of Asian educators in the teaching of Asia to Australian students; and of Australian students who may already be "Asia-literate". These questions of agency are essential to understanding social framings of Asia literacy in Australia, and I revisit them in the final section of this chapter.

Third, the two dimensions of Asia literacy — Asian languages education and Asian Studies education — are almost always defined aspirationally. In coining the term "Asia-literate" in 1988, Stephen FitzGerald encouraged Australia, as a nation, *to become* Asia-literate (FitzGerald 1988, p. 12). More recently, the National Asian Languages and Studies in Schools Program (NALSSP) proffered that "Asian languages and studies *will equip* the students of today with the skills to excel in the careers of tomorrow" and that Asia literacy *"will help* to build a more productive and competitive nation" (DEEWR 2012; emphasis added). Asia literacy, therefore, is not a status quo for which the maintenance and further development is being argued; rather, Asia literacy is a desired future state for Australian students and graduates: one that after forty years of policy work is yet to be achieved. This highlights that Asia literacy is couched as a mass-based mission for Australians and not a specialized area of study for select students. Asia literacy targets *all* Australian students.

And finally, a connection is made between Asia literacy and Australia's economic and commercial systems, as well as Australia's security and defence. Asia literacy is cast as an instrument that can be used to foster and safeguard the economic prosperity of the Australian population. The case for the economic benefits of Asia literacy has been repeatedly made since 1971. It is, for example, explicitly evident in the title of the Rudd Report published in 1994 — *Asian Languages and Australia's Economic Future* — and is most overt in the Australian federal government's recent approaches to Asia literacy through NALSSP, which emphasized that Asia literacy "is beneficial for our economy, community and individuals, creating more jobs and higher wages" (DEEWR 2012).

These four points raise important questions about the rationale and goals for Asia literacy; what exactly does Asia literacy seek to achieve and for whose benefit? In the next section, I use material gained from interviews with a number of authors of official reports that address Asia literacy to explore these questions from intersecting spatial and social perspectives. In doing so, I present a new way of looking at Asia literacy and acknowledge its metageographical foundations that attempt to separate "Australia" and "Asia" and, consequently, mask cultural hybridity *in* Australia.

Asia Literacy as a Spatial Practice

It can be argued that the essential moment of geopolitical discourse is the division of space into "our" place and "their" place, its political function being to incorporate and regulate "us" or "the same" by distinguishing "us" from "them", the same from "the other" (Dalby 1991, p. 274).

Lewis and Wigen opened their book, *The Myth of Continents*, with the following quote from 1995:

> Foreign Minister Gareth Evans was determined to put Australia on the map. Literally. He arrived in Brunei in late July for talks centred around the annual ASEAN (Association of Southeast Asian Nations) foreign ministers' meeting armed with a new map depicting the land Down Under as smack in the heart of the East Asian hemisphere.
>
> The persuasive diplomat failed to convert everyone to his world view, however. If I look at a map, I will immediately say that Australia is not part of Asia, Malaysia's Foreign Minister Datuk Abdullah Ahmad Badawi said under questioning from Australian journalists. You don't know your geography. (Hiebert 1995, p. 26, quoted in Lewis and Wigen 1997, p. ix)

Lewis and Wigen used this quote for illustrative purposes in a publication with an overt America focus.[3] Analysed from an Australian perspective, however, the ideas and assumptions presented in this quote are highly pertinent to a discussion of the metageographical assumptions within Asia literacy.

Critical geography examines the power relations underpinning geographical epistemes and structures, recognizing geography not only as an inert body of knowledge but also as a dynamic spatial practice. These power relations are present in "metageography" and "critical geopolitics", which I apply to Asia literacy in this section. Notions of metageography, geographical determinism and geopolitics lie beneath and shape the purpose of Asia literacy; they are present within the very terminology of *Australia*'s *Asia* literacy and were argued from its inception.[4] Geography itself, however, is about power: the power to organize, occupy and administer space (Ó Tuathail 1996, p. 1), as well as to *belong* to space, as evident in the claims made by Gareth Evans in Brunei in 1995.

Lewis and Wigen defined metageography as "the set of structures through which people order their knowledge of the world; the often unconscious frameworks that organise studies of history, sociology, anthropology, economics, political science or even natural history" (1997, p. ix). These structures are not just spatial representations, such as the standard seven-part continental scheme, but also constitute ideological constructs, such as global economic partitioning into "First", "Second" and "Third" worlds as well as the politico-civilizational frameworks of "East and West" and "North and South" (Lewis and Wigen 1997, p. xi). Geographical determinism is "the belief that social and cultural differences between human groups can ultimately be traced to differences in their physical environments" (Lewis and Wigen 1997, p. 42), casting geography as destiny. Lewis and Wigen argued that a subtle variant of geographical determinism "lurks behind the myth of continents", and I suggest it is also evident in the goal of Asia literacy for Australians to understand their "neighbourhood". For Lewis and Wigen, the seven-part continental system continues to be applied in such a way as to suggest that continents are at once physically and culturally constituted, that is, that natural and human features correspond in space (1997, p. 42). Having been taught that continents are the building blocks of global geography, we "slip" into assumptions that the configuration of landmasses correspond to the distribution of cultural traits and social forms (Lewis and Wigen 1997, p. 42). Within conceptualizations of Asia literacy this means the "Asian-ness" of those who inhabit "Asia", the "Australian-ness" of "Australia" and, importantly, the clear distinctions between the two.

Alongside the notions of metageography and geographical determinism, a third geographical concept important for a spatial approach to Asia literacy is that of geopolitics, or the influence of physical geographical factors on interstate relationships (Agnew 2000, p. 92). Ó Tuathail recognized geopolitics not as a concept that is "immanently meaningful and fully present to itself, but as a discursive 'event' that poses questions to us whenever it is evoked and rhetorically deployed" (1996, p. 17). Geopolitics, like geography, is discursively produced. It does not simply "happen", but is practised "by agents at discrete sites of knowledge production from where it is disseminated and enforced" (Agnew 2000, p. 98). Ó Tuathail referred to the practice of "geo-graphing" (1996, pp. 2, 10), which describes geography not as a noun but as a verb and highlights geography's power/knowledge relationship.

Asia literacy represents knowledge bounded by the spatial and political borders that constitute Asia. These borders are not "natural" as suggested by the Malaysian foreign minister, as quoted earlier in this section: "If I look at a map, I will immediately say that Australia is not part of Asia." Rather, the representation of these borders — of what does and does not constitute "Asia" — is an interaction between power and knowledge, with maps serving both to reinforce and to reproduce this relationship.[5] This process of geo-graphing is fundamental to a spatial rationale for Asia literacy, that is, for Australia to understand its neighbourhood better. Furthermore, Asia literacy can also be viewed as having a geo-graphing role itself, serving to both reflect and shape the location of "Australia" in relation to "Asia".

As a spatial practice, Asia literacy sits at the intersection of geopolitics and education; it is Australia's geopolitical position that provides a rationale for Asia literacy. Australia is part of, or in the same "neighbourhood" as, Asia, and Asia literacy provides the means for Australia and Australians to become even "closer" to Asia. This geographical reimagining of Australia's place in the world is evident, for example, in the way one report writer, John Ingleson (2010), described a "whole terminology" of "Australia's engagement with Asia" in the 1990s and the direction — in geographical terms — of Australia's future.[6] Ingleson (2010) explained the need to "shift from being a European-orientated country to one more orientated to its region", and that this "didn't mean losing our cultural roots, but it meant changing the gaze that our economic future lay with Asia". For Ingleson (2010), "Australia's geo-political location" was a factor in "what should be part of a student's education in the late twentieth century ... and the way they would live their lives". Ingleson was driven by the lack of knowledge about Asia within Australia's tertiary sector, and for him Asia literacy presented an opportunity to fuse geopolitics and education.

However, Ingleson also described Asia literacy as an attempt to destabilize the metageographical assumptions beneath Asia literacy in terms of the ideological structures of the "West" and "Asia". He commented that, "We were trying to break down the notion of the other. That there's the 'West' and this thing called 'Asia' ... we were trying to break it all down to understand the diversity of Asia" (Ingleson 2010). In attempting to disrupt these categories and pursue Asia literacy as a means of making Australia "more orientated towards its region", Ingleson also embraced geographical determinism. By breaking down "Asia" to understand its diversity, he described the relationship between

"Asia" and "Australia" as symbiotic: "Asian studies and Australian studies were two sides of the same coin ... Asia literacy was the other side of the coin of understanding what it was to be Australian" (Ingleson 2010). Ingleson's attempts to deal with the concept of "the other" reveal the difficulties of describing a relationship between two seemingly different entities: "Asia" and "Australia".

Other authors of official reports that address Asia literacy also engaged with the metageographical notion of "regions". For example, in his report, Garnaut (1989) focused on regions within Asia: the terms of reference of the Garnaut Report concentrated on "East Asia"; reference was also made to the "Western Pacific" region; and the title of his report explicitly referred to "Northeast Asia". These regions proved problematic for Garnaut, however, as he necessarily also focused on other nations outside these regions, including Indonesia. In 1990, Estela Valverde provided an alternative geopolitical view for Asia literacy by claiming that it was only Asian languages in Australia that had been assigned a geopolitical importance (1990, p. 50). She argued for greater focus to be given to Spanish, not as a "European" language but as a language of the "the lost continent on the other side of the Pacific" (Valverde 2010), and in doing so engaged with the "Asia Pacific" metageographical structure. In describing sub-regions within "Asia" and introducing the super-region of the "Asia Pacific", Garnaut and Valverde had a different focus to Ingleson, but also demonstrate a reliance on metageographical structures.

Metageography highlights "continents" as pejorative terms, but there is also a need to reduce geography to teachable categories, which is, after all, the pedagogical endeavour of Asia literacy. "Asia" and "Australia" are not mutually exclusive terms, a fact to which the current composition of Australian society attests. There is significant Asian-ness within Australia's population and citizenship, with the notion of citizenship itself another construct. This is problematic in that modern nation states, or indeed continents, are based on the spatial concept of "territory" that does not always align with the social concept of "identity".[7] Lewis and Wigen also acknowledged this dilemma in teaching geography: "it might be tempting to succumb to the postmodern mood and declare the end of metageography altogether. But metageography refuses to die. If one is to think seriously about the world, one must have recourse to a spatial vocabulary" (1997, p. 205). It is important to critically question geographical structures, yet the usefulness of the terminology to describe them cannot be denied. A "spatial vocabulary" is necessary to teach students about the world and the ways in which it is organized. This practical approach to deconstruction and pedagogy stems from Lewis and Wigen's experience as university educators in America, a position to which they refer repeatedly in their book. This approach is also relevant to Asia literacy as an educational endeavour in Australia.

In arguing for the inadequacy of "received metageographical categories" such as continents and civilizations for global human geography, Lewis and Wigen proposed alternative spaces. Their alternative is "the framework of world regions" (1997, p. 157). This framework has its origins in military strategy and the geopolitics of World War II and is defined as:

> Like civilisations, world regions are large socio-spatial groupings delimited largely on the grounds of shared history and culture; unlike civilisations, they do not presuppose a literate "high" culture, with the result that a world regional scheme can be used to classify all portions of the globe ... East Asia, Southeast Asia, South Asia, Southwest Asia and North Africa, Europe, Russia and environs, sub-Saharan Africa, Latin America, Australia and New Zealand, and the United States and Canada. Oceania and Central Asia are sometimes added to the list. (Lewis and Wigen 1997, p. 157)

Lewis and Wigen argued that a world region framework served to "break up Asia" and used boundaries based on historical connections rather than physical landforms. It is precisely a lack of historical connection, however, in addition to perceived physical landforms, which preserves Australia's segregation from "Asian" regions. While Lewis and Wigen saw these regions as alternatives to continents, I propose that they are equally problematic, particularly because it is these regions that have discursively produced "area studies" in Australia and beyond. This reinforces geography as a dynamic, creative force that has important implications for Asia literacy as an educational project. Below, I compare the interaction between metageographical practice and critical geopolitics in the United States and in Australia in terms of shaping "regions" and knowledge of them.

Geography and Education

The entry of the United States into World War II provided an immediate and important impetus for the organization of disparate "world regions" into a formal system (Lewis and Wigen 1997, p. 162). For the first time, the American military were coordinating a worldwide effort, and the subsequent search for relevant expertise revealed low levels of relevant second-language skills and cultural training within the American population. In order to address this newly emerged "knowledge gap", in June 1942 four organizations — the National Research Council, the American Council of Learned Societies, the Social Science Research Council and the Smithsonian Institute — established the Ethnogeographic Board (Guthe 1943, p. 188).[8] The board was charged with advising government "in matters of global geography" and examining "the current status of knowledge in American academia about diverse areas of the world" (Lewis and Wigen 1997, p. 163). Whilst the Ethnogeographic Board initially used the standard seven-part continental scheme, protracted military activity forced its members to devise an alternative (Lewis and Wigen 1997, p. 163). Ultimately, the result of the inadequacy of the continental architecture for strategic planning along with the irrelevancy of the territorial structure of European colonial empires was a new system of world regions, which has also become the basis for post-war "area studies" (Lewis and Wigen 1997 p. 163).

Lewis and Wigen described the new global framework as "merely a means to an end" for those funding the Ethnogeographic Board (1997, p. 166): what mattered was finding and implementing a practical, workable structure around which to organize policy and through which to enhance education about international affairs (Hall 1947, p. 9). American governmental interest in area studies only intensified in the early years of the Cold War and this further highlighted the absence of — and need for — relevant area studies in American universities. Encouraged by the Social Science Research Council and the Ford Foundation, the American federal government began to fund multidisciplinary "area studies centres" at key universities (Lewis and Wigen 1997, p. 166). This was done through Title VI of the National Defence Education Act 1958, which provided for the establishment of "language and area centres" that would teach the history, geography, economics and other disciplines of specially defined regions (Lewis and

Wigen 1997, p. 166). As defined under the original Title VI Act, these discrete "areas" included Russia (which became the Soviet Union and Eastern Europe), the Far East, Southeast Asia, South Asia, the Near East (now the Middle East), Europe, Africa and Latin America, and between 1947 and the early 1990s the number of area studies centres grew from fourteen to 124 (Lewis and Wigen 1997, pp. 166–67). Australia and New Zealand did not appear on Title VI's "area studies" map at all, further emphasizing the connection between geography, knowledge and *American* military activity and security interests.

This world regional grid acquired a life of its own outside American institutions, and its influence has spread across the globe. In Australia, it was not during World War II, but afterwards — in the 1950s and 1960s — that a federal government commitment to Asia was expressed and Australian universities began a major expansion in what became known as "Asian Studies" (Milner 1999, pp. 193–94). A "School of Oriental Languages" was established in 1952 at what is now the Australian National University (Milner 1999, p. 194).[9] The school's foundational academic emphasis was on the languages, histories and cultures of the region defined through an extensive geographic scope "from India to East Asia and Indonesia". This aligned almost exactly with the requirements of Australia's Department of External Affairs at the time, which had led the call for establishing such a school in Australia's national capital (Milner 1999, p. 194).[10] At the University of Sydney, whilst a Department of Oriental Studies had been founded in 1917, its focus was on China and Japan, and in 1955 a new Department of Indonesian and Malaysian Studies was established (Milner 1999, p. 195).[11] Between 1961 and 1971, the University of Melbourne opened a Department of Oriental Studies; Monash University established a Centre of Southeast Asian Studies; the University of Western Australia founded a Centre of Asian Studies; and a School of Modern Asian Studies was set up at Griffith University.

It was geopolitics that gave rise to "area studies" of Asia, which came to be expressed as "Asian Studies" in Australian universities, which has in turn played a pivotal role in Australia's Asia literacy agenda. These faculties and departments not only deliver Asian languages education and Asian Studies education to Australian students, they also play an important role in training future teachers for Australian primary and secondary schools. Milner argued that these new departments, centres and faculties of Asian Studies in Australian universities were established at a time when the Australian government was beginning to understand the full significance of ambitious, emerging nation states in Southeast and South Asia as well as the likely world power status of China and Japan (1999, p. 195).[12] Although the area studies system is also used within the United States, in Australia there has been a tendency to focus on either *Asian* Studies or studies of *specific* nation states in Asia. This has been enduring, and today it is either the continental descriptor "Asia" or individual nation states which are the primary units of analysis for both Asian languages education and Asian Studies education within Asia literacy.[13] In proposing an "alternative" to the continental system, Lewis and Wigen's framework of world regions is still problematic, and its practice has disseminated and enforced new sites of knowledge production. These regions are not a useful alternative to continents, and they continue to promote geographical determinism within Asia literacy.

In searching for alternatives to continents or world regions, Flint acknowledged "the time is ripe for geographers critiquing geopolitical thought to move beyond deconstruction and wrestle with ontological problems of creating alternative spaces" (2002, p. 392). He called for geopolitical perspectives which instead focus on identity, movement and the demise of "embedded statism" and the assumed "primacy of national identity" (Flint 2002, p. 392). Alternative spaces emerge from the flows of everyday practice that serve to connect states rather than structures that differentiate them. This highlights the significance of social framings and the notion of hybridity, which I explore in the next section of this chapter.

Asia literacy has been used as a spatial practice to reconfigure geographical imaginings to emphasize Australia's propinquity with Asia. This can be seen as an attempt to reproduce metageographical assumptions underscored by geographical determinism and expressed as a need for Australia to know its neighbours. While some proponents of Asia literacy see Australia as part of Asia and highlight the importance of Asia literacy in bringing Australia even closer to Asia, I argue it is crucial that Asia is also seen as part of, and within, Australia. Asia literacy has the potential to create new "alternative spaces" instead of reinforcing and reproducing dominant spaces such as "Australia" and "Asia".

Asia Literacy as a Sociocultural Practice

My discussion of Asia literacy thus far has been concerned with geopolitics, geographical determinism and the role of Asia literacy as a spatial practice. In this section I view the potential of Asia literacy as a sociocultural practice, with a particular focus on identity. Metageographical categories such as "Australia" and "Asia" are not just spatial representations or ideological structures, but also sociocultural constructs and practices. This also intersects with the goal of Asia literacy to reorient Australia towards Asia, as described in the previous section. Ang used the concept of "distant proximity", or subjective appraisals concerning "what people *feel* or *think* is remote" and not "what they think is close at hand", to describe Australia's "cause for maintaining psychological distance rather than closeness to Asia" (2010, p. 129). Australia's "distant proximity" to Asia, which Ang argued is beyond the control of governments, casts the metageographical rationale for Australia to become closer to or part of Asia as contradictory and contentious.

In the late 1970s and 1980s, languages other than English, including Asian languages, became linked to the concept of multiculturalism, which was a centrepiece of official government policy in Australia's federal political sphere at the time. The Fraser government (1975–83) introduced three legislative initiatives to reflect its new focus on "multicultural Australia": the enactment of a new national language policy, the Special Broadcasting Service (SBS) and the Australian Institute of Multicultural Affairs. The notion of multiculturalism was viewed as an outcome or by-product of increased immigration from Europe, Asia and other regions; indeed, it was "migrants" who were the primary source of Australia's newfound drive for multiculturalism. This was also connected to the dismantling of the "White Australia" policy from the mid-1960s, which restricted immigration into Australia by non-Europeans, and its formal abolition, which was formalized in the 1970s.

The first usage of the term "multicultural" in Australian federal legislation was related to languages education, with "multicultural education" defined as the "provision of special educational programmes and facilities for the purpose of teaching languages (other than the English language) spoken in overseas countries".[14] This definition does not acknowledge that these languages, which included Asian languages, were also being used *in* Australia. In a paper presented to the National Languages Conference of the Australian Federation of Modern Language Teachers Associations (AFMLTA) in 1986, AFMLTA president, David Ingram, attempted to rectify this conceptualization of languages education. He described one of the reasons for "fostering a strong languages teaching system in education" as "the vital role it plays in a multicultural society in strengthening identity, enriching cultural interaction and fostering inter-community communication and understanding" (Ingram 1986, p. 6). Ingram referred to a "preoccupation with multiculturalism" and also recognized that languages education had complementary, not competing, *intra*national and *inter*national roles in Australia.

In conceiving Asia literacy as a sociocultural practice, the term "multiculturalism" is both important and inadequate. Ang defined multiculturalism as "a government policy to manage cultural diversity within a pluralist nation-state", which implies "an acknowledgement of the co-existence of multiple cultures and peoples within one space, generally the space of the nation-state" (2001, p. 14). Ang compared multiculturalism to the notion of diaspora, which imparts a sense of shared identity with historical roots and destinies *outside* the physical territory of the host nation (2001, p. 12). In contrast to diaspora, multiculturalism involves a multiplicity of cultural and social groups sharing common space. For Ang, however, it is the assumed *mode* of sharing in multiculturalism which is problematic (2001, p. 14). These problems have been inherent within Australia's own multiculturalism and are also reflected in Asia literacy and broader LOTE education in Australia.

Multiculturalism's "mode of sharing" preserves diversity of cultures, but within certain, well-demarcated limits, so as not to dislodge or disrupt national unity and identity. This is what Bhabha described as the ironic simultaneous encouragement and containment of cultural diversity (1990, pp. 207–8). In Australia, which is a self-declared multicultural nation, differences are carefully classified into neat, distinct "ethnic communities", each with their own corresponding "culture".[15] In relation to languages education in Australia, this is evident in "community language schools", which provide LOTE education, particularly to immigrant families, outside conventional education systems and out of school hours. This view of multiculturalism, however, does not respond to the dynamism and interconnections that occur when different groups of people live together and interact, let alone intermarry and start families. And it does not respond to the fact that multilingual home environments in Australia are increasing (Hughes 2012).

For Ang, this ordered view of multiculturalism is a "convenient image from a bureaucratic-managerial point of view" but is problematic because it does not account for forces that subvert the preferred multicultural order (2001, p. 14). "In other words, multiculturalism is based on the fantasy that the social challenge of togetherness-in-difference can be addressed by reducing it to an image of living-apart-together" (Ang 2001, p. 14). This "fixing of mutually exclusive identities" also acts to reproduce dominant and subordinate others; categories such as "Australia" and "Asia" are reproduced and reinforced and the areas of crossover, in-between-ness and marginalities remain unacknowledged.

It is for these reasons that "hybridity" is a more useful concept than "multiculturalism", with the dynamism of the former unsettling the inertness of the latter. Ang defined hybridity as a "cultural force that unsettles the dominant perception that [the] two categories are mutually exclusive", such as the infusion of "Asian-ness" into Australian national identity (2010, p. 137). This challenges the careful classification of national difference within Asia literacy in Australia. Elsewhere, Ang has emphasized the importance of hybridity as a means of bridging and blurring the multiple boundaries which describe "Asian" and "Western" identities as mutually exclusive and incommensurable (2001, p. 193). Felski argued that hybridity recognizes "differences *within* the subject, fracturing and complicating holistic notions of identity" and also addresses "connections *between* subjects by recognising affiliations, cross-pollinations, echoes and repetitions" (1997, p. 12). Hybridity unsettles the mutually exclusive categories of "Asia" and "Australia" within Asia literacy, in which "Australia" is shorthand for "the West", and, as Ang made explicit, "white people cannot be Asian" (2010, p. 131). Hybridity accounts for "social entanglement caused by cross-regional mobility", and it is to this social entanglement that Asia literacy has not responded. This includes the need to include and reward students who have acquired Asia literacy outside formal education systems and to recognize teachers' existing foreign language proficiency and develop their pedagogical skills to teach these languages. In addition to this is the need to acknowledge that Asia literacy can be "learned" or acquired outside schools and universities, such as in home environments, through travel and via other types of exposure and connection.

Hybridity can be viewed as a response to Lewis and Wigen's calls for "new spaces":

> We can shed a different light on these issues by going beyond the official world of regional institutions and international relations. Just as significant for the emergence of "Asia" as a regional entity are the more informal processes of transnational flow that actualise social interactions and cultural interconnections across the region. Whether or not Australia is part of Asia, and how, is not a question of governmental decree, nor will it be realised solely by economic exchange and trade relations. In a more comprehensive way, it would grow out of the complex web of actual interconnections between Australia and different parts of Asia through the myriad human interactions which make societies work: from trade to education, from tourism to research collaborations, from artistic exchanges to social activism. (Ang 2010, p. 135)

The notion of hybridity, and the non-mutual exclusiveness of Asia and Australia, is a practical alternative to "multicultural" in creating "new spaces" between and outside of "Asia" and "Australia". Breaking the categories of "Asia" and "Australia", which pervade both the rationale and content of Asia literacy, opens up other spaces which are in-between or outside of these binary terms.

In this way, hybridity is a third space between and outside the categories of "Asia" and "Australia" that permeate conceptualizations of Asia literacy. Third space is "usually approached from the perspectives of those deemed out of place in an environment", who are often ignored, forgotten about or marginalized, such as the impoverished, the homeless or the elderly (Bustin 2011, p. 55). This resonates for Asia literacy, which is most often *not* viewed from the perspectives of "background speakers", "migrants" and others who have become Asia-literate outside formal places of learning. Within Asia literacy, "Australia" and "Asia" are framed as separate categories, but hybridity exposes other possibilities, including the perspectives of first- and background-language learners of Asian languages, emerging from processes such as labour mobility, cross-cultural marriages, travel and other flows between "Australia" and "Asia".

Conclusion

Asia literacy is a product of how Australians see their place in the world and is inevitably, and necessarily, connected to geopolitics. Other rationales for Asia literacy, however, including sociocultural perspectives, are increasingly important. These posit Asia literacy not just as an exercise in understanding Australia's "neighbourhood" but also in understanding Australia-from-within. In both endeavours, however, there is limited recognition of those places that Asia literacy seeks to prioritize. Asian governments and Asian educators outside Australia are normally not included in Asia literacy programmes in Australia, and Australian teachers and students who have acquired Asia literacy outside schools and universities have also largely been excluded from conceptualizations of Asia literacy in Australia. Recognizing these biases and exploring these dominant categories highlights the importance of hybridity, which provides a more participatory platform through which future framings of Asia literacy can be improved. In this way, the sites of Asian languages and Asian Studies education are not just restricted to schools and universities and include the broader Australian community. In doing so, Asian languages education and Asian Studies education are no longer framed as studies of that which is *foreign* to Australians, but instead of that which is also *familiar*.

Notes

1. This chapter is drawn from the author's doctoral research, which focused on conceptualizations of rationale, objectives and agency within Australia's Asia literacy, in the College of Asia and the Pacific at the Australian National University.
2. Writing in 1995, Kevin Rudd, author of the Rudd Report, commented: "In fact, over the last 25 years the preparation of reports on this particular issue [Asia literacy] has almost generated its own industry with a new report appearing every eighteen months on average and with each report invariably producing the same sorts of recommendations as it predecessors. In short, this subject has been reported to death" (Rudd 1995, p. 22).
3. Their book addressed the premise that "most college-aged Americans have never explicitly studied geography" (Lewis and Wigen 1997, p. xii).

4. In announcing the Australian government's intention to form the committee that later wrote the Auchmuty Report, then minister for education and science, Malcolm Fraser, "pointed to the steady growth in the economic, cultural, political and military links between *Australia* and *Asia* during the last two decades" (Auchmuty 1971, p. 7; emphasis added).

5. In presenting an alternative map of "Asia" which included "Australia", former Australian foreign minister Gareth Evans attempted to disrupt this power/knowledge relationship so as to insert "Australia" into "Asia".

6. The word "engagement" was also a key term used by former Australian prime minister Paul Keating in describing Australia's place in the world in relation to Asia. He wrote, "The twenty-first century ... offers this great opportunity to Australia: to redefine ourselves and our place in the world. Each generation finds its own challenges. The challenge of engagement is ours" (2000, p. 300). John Ingleson authored the Ingleson Report, which was published in 1989, and was interviewed for the author's doctoral research in 2010.

7. This is evident when minority groups within bounded nation states demand their own space and power for self-determination.

8. According to Farish (2005, p. 671), Lewis and Wigen provide "one of the few historical discussions of the Ethnographic Board".

9. This became a "Faculty of Oriental Studies" in 1962 and later a "Faculty of Asian Studies".

10. On 6 November 1970, the Department of External Affairs changed its name to the Department of Foreign Affairs. In July 1987, this department merged with the Department of Trade to become the Department of Foreign Affairs and Trade.

11. The Department of Indonesian and Malaysian Studies at the University of Sydney was also initiated and funded by the Australian federal government, through the Department of External Affairs, the Department of Defence, and the Office of the Prime Minister.

12. It is also important to note here that prior to World War II these "emerging nation states" were European colonies, meaning that before the 1950s and 1960s, Australia's "neighbourhood" did indeed have a strong Euro-focus.

13. For example, there has been a particular focus on China, Japan, Indonesia and Korea within Asian languages education in Australia, particularly from 1995 to 2012.

14. See s3(1) States Grants (Schools Assistance) Act 1978.

15. Hence "Chinese" in Asia literacy and LOTE education in Australia is referred to by an umbrella term and is *not* specified as Mandarin, Cantonese or other Chinese languages.

References

Agnew, John A. "Global Political Geography beyond Geopolitics". *International Studies Review* 2, no. 1 (2000): 91–99.

Ang, Ien. *On Not Speaking Chinese*. London: Routledge, 2001.

———. "Australia, China, and Asian Regionalism: Navigating Distant Proximity". *Amerasia Journal* 36, no. 2 (2010): 127–40.

Auchmuty, J.J. (chair). *Teaching of Asian Languages and Cultures in Australia: Report of the Commonwealth Advisory Committee* [Auchmuty Report]. Canberra: Commonwealth Government Printing Office, 1971.

Bhabha, Homi, and Jonathan Rutherford. "The Third Space: Interview with Homi Bhabha". In *Identity: Community, Culture, Difference*, edited by Jonathan Rutherford. London: Lawrence and Wishart, 1990.

Bustin, Richard. "Thirdspace: Exploring the 'Lived Space' of Cultural 'Others'". *Teaching Geography* 36, no. (2011): 55–57.

Dalby, Simon. "Critical Geopolitics: Discourse, Difference and Dissent". *Environment and Planning D: Society and Space* 9, no. 3 (1991): 261–83.

DEEWR (Department of Education, Employment and Workplace Relations). "National Asian Languages and Studies in Schools Program — Overview" <http://www.deewr.gov.au/scgooling/NALSSP/pages/default.aspx> (accessed November 2012).

Department of the Prime Minister and Cabinet, Australia. *Australia in the Asian Century: White Paper*. Canberra: Department of the Prime Minister and Cabinet, 2012.

Farish, Matthew. "Archiving Areas: The Ethnogeographic Board and the Second World War". *Annals of the Association of American Geographers* 95, no. 3 (2005): 663–79.

Felski, Rita. "The Doxa of Difference". *Signs* 23, no. 1 (1997): 1–22.

FitzGerald, Stephen. "National Education Policy and Asian studies". In *Towards an Asia-literate Society*, edited by Elaine McKay, pp. 9–16. Parkville, Victoria: Asian Studies Association of Australia, 1988.

Flint, Colin. "Political Geography: Globalization, Metapolitical Geographies and Everyday Life". *Progress in Human Geography* 26, no. 3 (2002): 391–400.

Garnaut, Ross. *Australia and the Northeast Asian Ascendancy* [Garnaut Report]. Canberra: Australian Government Printing Service, 1989.

Guthe, Carl E. "The Ethnogeographic Board". *Scientific Monthly* 57, no. 2 (1943): 188–91.

Hall, Robert. *Area Studies with Special Reference to Their Application for Research in the Social Sciences*. New York: Social Science Research Council, 1947.

Hughes, Kirrilee. "Australia's Latent Asia Literacy". *The Interpreter*, 2002 <https://www.lowryinstitute.org/the-interpreter/australias-latent-asia-literacy>.

Ingleson, John. *Asia in Australian Higher Education: Report of the Inquiry into the Teaching of Asian Studies and Languages in Higher Education* [Ingleson Report], vols. 1–2. Canberra: Asian Studies Council, 1989.

Ingram, David. "Languages and the Export Economy". In *Accentuating the Positive*, 6th Biennial Languages Congress of the Australian Federation of Modern Language Teachers Association, Adelaide, 6–9 September 1986, pp. 6–38.

Keating, Paul. *Engagement: Australia Faces the Asia–Pacific*. Sydney: Pan Macmillan Australia, 2000.

Lewis, Martin W., and Kären E. Wigen. *The Myth of Continents*. Berkeley: University of California Press, 1997.

Milner, Anthony. "Approaching Asia, and Asian Studies, in Australia". *Asian Studies Review* 23, no. 2 (1999): 193–203.

Ó Tuathail, Gearóid. *Critical Geopolitics*. Minneapolis: University of Minnesota Press, 1996.

Rudd, Kevin. "Creating an Asia-Literate Australia". In *Living with Dragons: Australia Confronts its Asian Destiny*, edited by Greg Sheridan, pp. 21–44. St Leonards, Sydney: Allen & Unwin, 1995.

Rudd, K.M. (chair). *Asian Languages and Australia's Economic Future: A Report Prepared for the Council of Australian Governments on a Proposed National Asian Languages/Studies Strategy for Australian Schools* [Rudd Report]. Brisbane: Queensland Government Printer, 1994.

Valverde, Estela. *Language for Export: A Study of the Use of Language and Language Related Skills in Australian Export Companies* [Valverde Report]. Canberra: Office of Multicultural Affairs, Department of the Prime Minister and Cabinet, 1990.

Interviews

FitzGerald, Stephen. Sydney, Australia, 18 October 2010.

Garnaut, Ross. Melbourne, Australia, 9 August 2012.

Ingleson, John. Sydney, Australia, 1 November 2010.

Valverde, Estela. Sydney, Australia, 1 November 2010.

4

Maps as Illustrations and Logos: Geopolitical Construction of Asia and South Asia

William L. Richter

"What constitutes Asia?" is a question central to the field of Asian Studies. A geographical term that is attached to a seemingly stable, objectively defined, landmass, "Asia" is in reality a socially constructed concept that has constantly been reshaped or appropriated with changing emphasis. This study considers the question of how Asia and South Asia are portrayed (represented, framed, constructed) by the maps on the covers of books and scholarly journals and by map logos of professional associations. It asks how each region (South Asia and Asia generally) is defined, which features are emphasized or marginalized, and what sorts of distortions are evident. An old adage admonishes us not to judge a book by its cover, but the covers of books and journals are designed to attract readers, to allude to content and to connect with existing perceptions. It is worthwhile to explore what these map illustrations reveal.

Examples of such portrayal may be seen in the two scholarly books that initially prompted this inquiry. Both showed South Asia, but the maps were truncated, distorted or otherwise modified. The cover of C. Raja Mohan's *Crossing the Rubicon: The Shaping of India's New Foreign Policy* (2003) shows a map of India in vivid orange. Border areas are sufficiently blurred so that one cannot read the names of any other countries except India and Nepal. The map on the cover of Baldev Raj Nayar and T.V. Paul's *India in the World Order: Searching for Major-Power Status* (2003) appears to be looking eastward at India on a globe. India, Nepal, Bhutan, and Myanmar (Burma) are labelled, as are the visible Indian states, but the map is truncated at top and bottom so that three northern states (Punjab, Himachal Pradesh, Jammu and Kashmir) and three southern states (Karnataka, Kerala, Tamil Nadu) are not visible or labelled. Pakistani territory is shown but not labelled as such.

There may be various reasons for such distortions, including having an "eye-catching" book cover, but there also appear to be geopolitical considerations. The former princely state of Jammu and Kashmir has been a source of conflict between India and Pakistan since the two countries became independent in 1947. India regards all as an integral part of the Indian Union. Pakistan regards the entire state to be disputed territory.[1] Both countries have outlawed the publication of maps that disagree with their respective positions. Given these political sensitivities, cartographic illustrators sometimes show Kashmir in India and sometimes divided at the current line of control between India-controlled Jammu and Kashmir and Pakistani-controlled Azad Kashmir.[2] Often, however, they finesse the issue by using silhouettes, truncation, blurring or faintness,[3] or topological rather than political maps.

The study required identification of a fairly large sample of books and journals that (a) treat Asia or South Asia (e.g., as indicated by their titles) and (b) use maps as cover illustrations. Since many journals are published by professional associations, such as the Association for Asian Studies, such organizations were also surveyed to see whether they might use maps as illustrations in their logos or on their websites, even if not on their journal covers. Those publications which used national flags as symbols to identify or "map" the areas of their interest were also included.

Online searches were utilized to identify books, journals and organizations. Several websites list Asian and/or South Asian journals and other resources.[4] The Amazon Books website was used to identify books, in part because the site displays covers as well as other book information. A review of the first six hundred titles in a search for "Asia" and the first six hundred for "South Asia" (both numbers arbitrarily determined) approximately doubled the number of books under consideration. The study has some obvious biases, including the fact that all of the publications are in English and most but not all were published in the United States or Europe. As table 4.1 indicates, the resultant sample includes several dozen books, about a dozen journals and a handful of professional associations. These numbers are not large enough for meaningful statistical analyses, but nonetheless yield interesting observations.

TABLE 4.1
Books, Journals and Organizations Reviewed

	Books	Journals	Organizations
Asia	32	8	2
South Asia	30	4	3

Some preliminary observations concerning the books and journals are worth noting. Well over half of the books are in the general field of political science, with many focused on international politics, security, and/or strategic studies. Some of the cartographic illustrations utilize game or puzzle images to allude to the strategic or challenging aspects of the books' subject matter (Dorronsoro 2010; Cohen 2011; Wesley-Smith and Goss 2010; fig. 4.1). Several publishers are specifically concerned with strategic studies, for example, the Strategic Studies Institute (SSI) and the National Defense University (NDU). Even at a preliminary level there is an evident relation between maps as cover illustrations and strategic or geopolitical concerns.

FIGURE 4.1

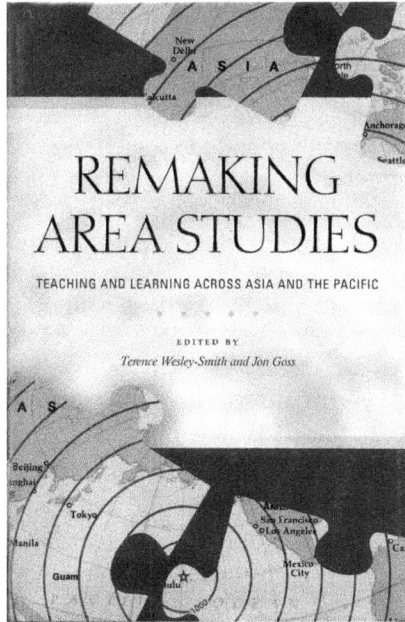

Framing, Social Construction, Cartography and Cover Illustration

The notion of framing in social analysis originated with the sociologist Erving Goffman (1974), who argued that the situations within which people operate and perceive the world are shaped, or "framed", in various ways. We understand the world in terms of our *perception* of reality. Goffman drew upon William James and Alfred Schutz for the development of Frame Analysis, and through them upon Edmund Husserl and phenomenology.

Maps, clearly, frame our understanding of geographic spaces. Geographer Arthur Klinghoffer compares the framing of maps with both movies and journalism. A movie, he writes, is "really an assemblage of discrete frames employed by the director. He, or she, determines what is included or intentionally left out. Frames have fixed borders and are therefore similar to maps, which display only a section of the globe. An atlas may accordingly be compared to a movie — a compilation of frames."

> Taking the movie analogy further, it is instructive to examine the growing symbiosis of cartography and journalism in terms of their framing. In essence, practitioners look through lenses to create frames expressing their psychological and ideological visions. They prioritize, arrange, and interpret in an effort to condition the consciousness of the viewer. Facts are selected based on their furtherance of the story's line. Biases come into play regarding content and pertinence and in controlling the discourse or language.... Maps are thus essential to the portrayal of international history and politics, yet they are just reflections. (Klinghoffer 2006)

Postmodern social theories (many of which also trace their roots to phenomenology) argue that it is not only "situations" that are framed or shaped by our assumptions. Most if not all social phenomena that are assumed to be "natural" or "given" are "socially constructed", including gender, ethnicity, nationality, regions, even continents.[5]

Our understanding of *cartography* — the art and science of map-making — has undergone much the same postmodern revolution in recent decades as other fields of scholarship. The notion that cartography is purely a scientific enterprise dedicated to accurate representation of specific territories on maps has been challenged by J.B. Harley, Denis Wood and numerous other scholars.[6]

As J.B. Harley has noted, "Maps are a way of conceiving, articulating, and structuring the human world" (Harley 1988, p. 278, cited in O'Shea 2004, p. 9). Such constructions of political and geographic reality are typically complex and interactive. Harley laid out many of the arguments against taking the "objectivity" of maps at face value (Harley 1989, 2001). However well-intentioned and objective map-makers may be, their maps carry biases, including what is represented, how the map is illustrated and which projections are used. Maps, as texts, are subject to multiple interpretations, not limited to the intent of the author (Ricoeur 1971, pp. 529–62, reprinted in Richter 2009, pp. 236–47). Moreover, maps represent power. "Maps are never value-free images.... Both in the selectivity of their content and in their signs and styles of representation maps are a way of conceiving, articulating, and structuring the human world which is biased towards, promoted by, and exerts influence upon particular sets of social relations" (Harley 2001, p. 53).[7]

Social construction is a two-way process. People operate within socially defined realities, but they in turn reinforce or modify those realities, intentionally or not. We shape our maps, and then they shape us. Seen from another perspective, the social construction of geographic entities like Asia entails an interplay of physical maps and the "mental maps" of individuals, larger groups and whole cultures. People of different cultures see the world differently. It should not be surprising when their maps reflect their different perspectives and interests (Gould and White 1986; Downs and Stea 1977; Hall 1959, 1990).

One of the best-known examples of bias in map-making is the Mercator projection, probably the most familiar image of the world, but one which magnifies the size of lands nearer the poles and reduces those nearer the equator. Thus, Greenland appears to be more than a third the size of Africa. The Mercator projection that many Americans grew up with was made even more problematic by placing the Western hemisphere in the middle of the map. This allowed Americans to see their own country as the centre of the world, but split Asia into two parts — one on the western edge of the map and one on the eastern. In his classic work on American perceptions of China and India (1962, p. 42), Harold Isaacs noted:

> In the last ten years or so, American map makers have begun to take a somewhat more patriotic view of the world; instead of Europe, they place North America in the world's center. The effect — besides moving the center of the world from Greenwich to the longitude of Peoria, Illinois — is to leave Japan and a chunk of eastern Asia visible on the west, with the remainder of a truncated Asia reappearing far, again, in the east.

As a corrective to the size distortion of the Mercator projection, Arno Peters created an alternate projection (fig. 4.2, from Brandt 1980). The Peters projection has been welcomed by some and strongly opposed by others (Monmonier 1995, pp. 9–44; Black 1997, pp. 33–37; Wood 1992, pp. 58–60). The Brandt Commission Report on International

FIGURE 4.2

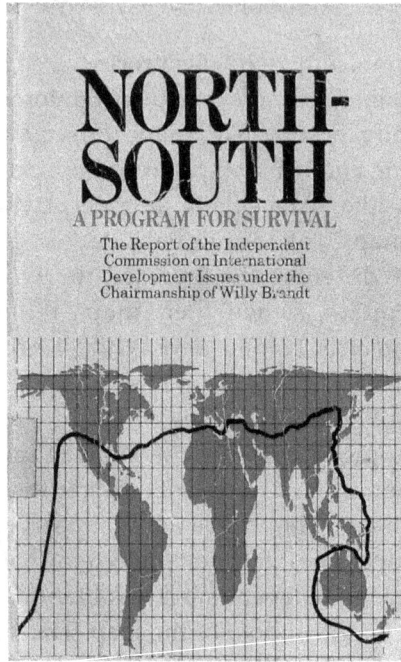

Development explained its reasons for using the Peters projection on its cover:

> The Peters Projection introduces several innovative characteristics: an accurate rendition of the proportion of the land surface area; graphical representation of the entire world surface, including the polar regions; the Equator is placed at the centre of the map; the usual grid of 180 meridians (East and West) and 90 meridians each (North and South) is replaced by a decimal degree network dividing the earth both East and West and North and South into 100 fields each; angle accuracy in the main North–South, East–West projections.

The map description concluded with the declaration that "This projection represents an important step away from the prevailing Eurocentric geographical and cultural concept of the world" (Brandt 1980, p. 2).

Orientation is also a source of bias that is often not recognized by the average map-viewer. Most modern maps have north at the top, west at the left, and so on, though this was not always the case. In earlier times, as the term "orientation" implies, east was at the top and north to the left. The impact of orientation on perception is best demonstrated with McArthur's Universal Corrective Map of the World (fig 4.3; Black 1997), which places south at the top. The intent, as its Australian author proclaimed, was "the first step in the long overdue crusade to elevate our glorious but neglected nation from the gloomy depths of anonymity in the world power struggle to its rightful position — towering over its Northern neighbors, reigning splendidly at the helm of the universe" (Black 1997, pp. 38–39).

FIGURE 4.3

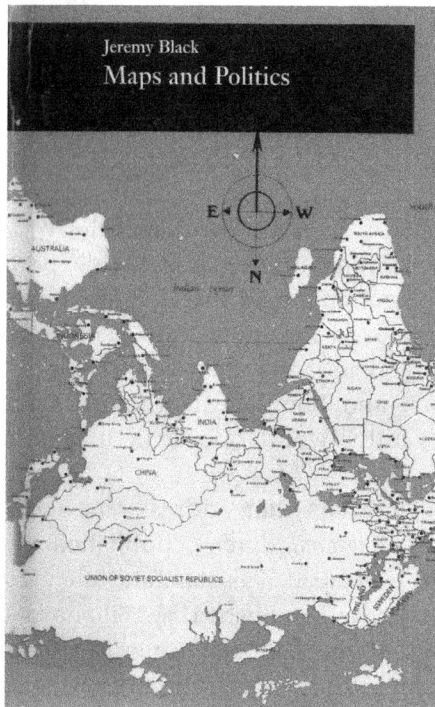

FIGURE 4.4

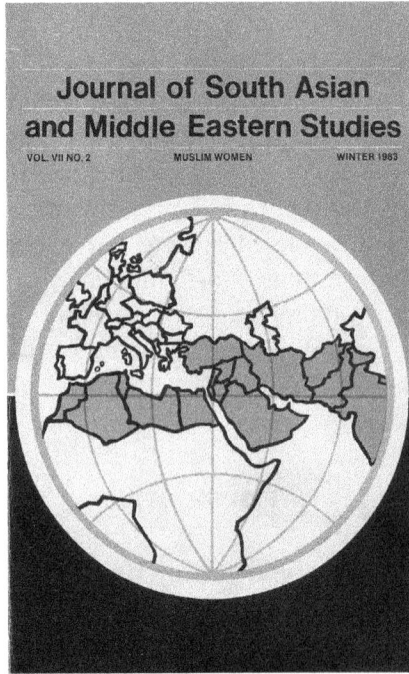

Map-makers often place their own countries at the centre of their maps, thereby consigning other lands to the periphery. Although India may be peripheral on a map that is centred on the United States, most maps of South Asia are quite India-centric. India occupies the centre of the map and is larger than all its South Asian neighbours combined. Pakistan and Bangladesh, though among the ten most populous countries in the world, appear peripheral in an India-centric South Asia.

Two quarterly journals that address this issue with the maps on their covers are *Regional Studies*, published by the Institute of Regional Studies in Islamabad, Pakistan, and the *Journal of South Asian and Middle Eastern Studies*, published by Villanova University (USA) under the auspices of the Pakistan American Foundation. *Regional Studies* displays a map, from East Africa to Bangladesh, in a circle, with Pakistan centred and highlighted in green and all the rest of the countries shown in white.[8] *The Journal of South Asian and Middle Eastern Studies* shows a map of northern Africa and southwestern Asia, with delineated countries from Morocco to the western half of India (fig. 4.4).[9] It may seem strange that a journal with "South Asia" in its title would exclude from the map on its cover more than half of the countries of South Asia (Bangladesh, Bhutan, Sri Lanka, Republic of Maldives, all but a sliver of Nepal and half of India). Both these journals attempt to reframe "region" to make Pakistan central rather than peripheral.

Maps often reflect geopolitical biases. Neighbouring countries with disputed boundaries or territories between them are likely to have different maps, each showing the disputed lands as their own. Such "cartographic aggression" was a significant background factor in the 1962 border war between India and China (Garver 2001, pp. 79–109; Maxwell 1972).

If even objective cartography (that is, maps intended to be scientific and objective) can be seen to have biases, what about maps used as cover illustrations? There are several reasons for using maps on book and journal covers. Maps are attractive and, some argue, inherently interesting (Jennings 2011; Garfield 2013). When the book or journal is focused on a specific geographic area, the map on its cover may delineate the region and let potential readers know what they might find inside. The map may carry subtle or not-so-subtle messages concerning the content of the book or journal.

Most magazine and book covers are one-time creations, although they often utilize common elements to maintain identity and signal continuity. Each issue of *Time*, for instance, is unique, but the red border and familiar font maintains continuity from issue to issue. Most (but not all) professional journals use the same cover design issue after issue. This may reflect the fact that few journals are sold as individual issues, and subscriptions are less likely to need to draw attention to the contents.

In the world of cover illustration, scholarly books and journals have received considerably less attention than paperback novels and popular magazines. Each genre has its own distinctive characteristics, but all share, in varying degrees, connections with cultural values. "The cover", according to cultural theorist Ellen McCracken, "serves not to label only the magazine but the consumer who possesses it" (Crowley 2003, p. 7).

The people who prepare magazine, book and journal covers are predominantly designers and artists rather than professional cartographers. Their intentions are to draw attention to the publication, to give some indication of its contents and to connect with the potential reader. Sometimes a book will provide the name of its cover designer, but most books and journals do not. Even when the designer is identified, that does not necessarily mean that the idea or features of the map were solely or even primarily at the initiative of the designer.[10]

Constructing Asia

Asia is a geographic concept that has evolved over more than 2500 years. Originally, Asia was the term the Greeks applied to the lands that lay to their east — the present Asia Minor — just as they called the lands to their north Europe and to their south Libya (later Africa). Asia eventually came to represent to Europeans generally all that lay to the east.

Asia has traditionally been defined as those parts of the Eurasian landmass that lie east of the Ural Mountains in Russia. A traditional atlas boundary between Europe and Asia is a line running from north to south along the Urals, then to the Caspian and Black Seas, and through the Bosporus to the Aegean and Mediterranean Seas.[11]

The specific boundaries of Asia, however, have fluctuated over time. The nineteenth-century French scholar Elisée Reclus, in his monumental nineteen-volume work, *The Earth and Its Inhabitants*, had four volumes on Asia: India and Indo-China, East Asia, Southwest Asia, and Russian Asia. Reclus's Asia included Malaya and Indochina, but did not include what today is considered insular Southeast Asia. The islands of Indonesia and the Philippines were included in a separate volume on "Oceanica", along with Australia, New Zealand, Melanesia, Fiji, Hawaii, and other island territories (Reclus 1890).[12]

Two geographic works from the mid-twentieth century illustrate the ongoing reframing of Asia and its sub-regions. *The Changing Map of Asia* (1950) divided Asia into six regions. *The Pattern of Asia* (1958), published eight years later, identified only five regions, and the names of two of the regions had changed.[13]

Both books refer to Southwest Asia and Southeast Asia, although that terminology was still new enough in 1950 for the editors of *The Changing Map of Asia* to note that they were abandoning "the old names Further India and the Indo-Chinese Peninsula" for mainland Southeast Asia. They also commented on "The more recent widespread agreement in employing the term Southeast Asia to cover both the Indo-Pacific peninsula (Burma, Siam, Indo-China and Malaya) and the Indonesian and Philippine archipelagos", and questioned whether this "changed emphasis is more than wishful thinking" (East and Spate 1950, pp. 7, 179).

The 1950 book still referred to China and Japan as "The Far East" and former British India as "India and Pakistan", arguing that "'India' is still the most convenient geographical expression for the sub-continent between the Himalayas and the Indian Ocean" (East and Spate 1950, p. 7). By 1958 these two terms had been replaced by "East Asia" and "South Asia", respectively.

Both works draw a distinction between "Euro-Asia" and "Asiatic Asia". The 1958 work devotes its second chapter to "Asian Asia", which it defines "as that part of the Asiatic continent not fundamentally European in civilization" (East and Spate 1950, p. 8; Ginsburg 1958, p. 21).

Even today, what constitutes Asia, and even whether Asia is a meaningful geographic entity, are contested issues. Martin W. Lewis and Kären E. Wigen argue that the traditional division of Europe and Asia into separate "continents" is a myth, that Asian geographic and cultural diversity is too great for Asia to be considered a world region, and that some of the current "boundaries" of Asia are absurd.

> If Asia's internal cohesion has been difficult to ascertain, specifying its geographical limits has proven problematic as well. The conventional southeastern boundary of this so-called continent, while perhaps more obscure than that separating it from Europe, is no less contrived. Extending east-southeast from the Malay Peninsula is a continuous

chain of islands, large and small, which eventually attenuates in eastern Melanesia. The western portion of this island group, contemporary Indonesia, is conventionally included as part of Asia (although in former times this was not always the case), while the eastern portion, Melanesia, is excluded. On cultural and historical grounds such a division might be supportable, but in practice the boundary between the two zones is not consistently dictated by cultural criteria. Rather, New Guinea is typically sliced cleanly down the middle, along the political boundary between Indonesia and Papua New Guinea, and the western half of this unambiguously Melanesian island is ceded to Asia. (Lewis and Wigen 1997, pp. 37–38)

Such appeals to logic and consistency have not kept organizations like the Association for Asian Studies (AAS) and the International Convention of Asian Scholars (ICAS) from developing a thriving Asian Studies enterprise. Even if Asia is a "metageographic myth", that does not keep Asians and others from predicting that the current era will be the "Asian Century". Even if Asia is a socially constructed reality with questionable boundaries, it is nonetheless a meaningful and useful entity for millions of people, Asian and non-Asian alike.

It is possible to identify several historical phases, or layers, of the social construction of Asia. The ancient Greek tradition of regarding Asia as foreign lands to the east was augmented by European colonialism and the academic practice of Orientalism (Said 1971; see also Iyer 1983; Ferguson 2002).

Then came Pan-Asianism and the involvement of Asians themselves in identifying with and defining Asia. The term "Asia" was brought by the Portuguese in the sixteenth century, but it was not until the nineteenth century that the people who lived there came to see themselves as Asians. Prior to that time, those subjected to European colonial expansion tended to regard "Asian" — like "Oriental" — as symbolic of European domination. Had the situation remained so, then the dissolution of European empires in Asia in the twentieth century might also have seen the rejection of "Asia" as a coherent entity by the new nations.

Instead, anti-colonial Indians and Chinese and Turks came to see themselves as having a shared identity and shared interests as Asians. Pan-Asianism became a way of using this shared identity to fight against

European intrusion and colonial domination (Saaler and Szpilman 2011; Mishra 2012; Aydin 2007). Such a shared identity was later used by imperial Japan to support its "Greater East Asia Co-Prosperity Sphere" concept in the 1940s.

Still other layers of social construction were added after World War II, with the breakup of European colonial empires in Asia, the "emergence" of "new" Asian countries, and the Cold War. Asia as a regional entity was manifested in the 1947 Asian Relations Conference in New Delhi and the Asian-African Conference in Bandung in 1955. The establishment of regional associations in Asian subregions, such as the Association of Southeast Asian Nations (ASEAN) and the South Asian Association for Regional Cooperation (SAARC) has further reinforced the notion of Asianness. What constitutes Asia, whether it should be considered a coherent region, and other conceptual questions remain matters of ongoing debate. "Asia, despite its fuzziness and incoherence, has remained a durable, if essentially contested, notion" (Acharya 2012, p. 1001).

How is Asia represented on the covers of books and journals? There appear to be two quite different answers to this question. One, as might be expected, conforms to the standard atlas definition of Asia: from Turkish Anatolia to Japan and from Siberia to Indonesia. In the books reviewed in this study, this is how Asia is represented on the covers of nearly all of the geography or social studies textbooks for children or teenagers (see Chin-Lee and Heo 1997; Donaldson 2005; Drevitch 2009; House and House 1993, 2007; Schaefer 2006).

Scholarly books present a somewhat different picture. The maps on the covers of at least half of the professional works that by their titles purport to cover all of Asia show a much smaller geographic area than the "Atlas Asia" of the children's textbooks (Baik 2012; Beeson and Stubbs 2012; Cotterell 2011; James and Merchant 2013; Ma and Van Zanden 2011; Miller and Wich 2011; Wong and Kaiyu 2013; for a notable exception, see Duara 2013). What is shown on these maps (e.g., fig. 4.5) is an Asia that always includes China, usually includes Southeast Asia, normally includes part or all of South Asia, and typically excludes Southwest Asia, Central Asia, and the Asian parts of Russia. This somewhat corresponds to what the geographies of the 1950s called "Asiatic Asia", but with the further exclusion of the lands to the west of Pakistan.

FIGURE 4.5

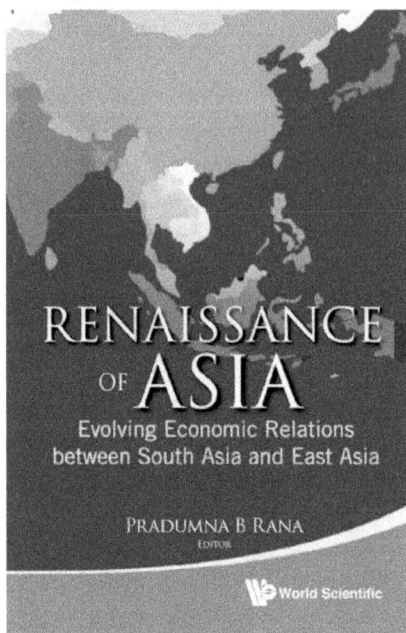

This narrower cartographic definition of Asia is reinforced by the maps on journal covers. Of Asian-content journals with map covers, four delimited Asia in much the same way as the scholarly books. *The Asian Journal of Political Science*, published by the Department of Political Science of the University of Singapore, shows a silhouette of Asia from Pakistan to Japan and Siberia to Northern Australia. *Asian Security* shows outlines of countries from Kazakhstan and Mongolia to Indonesia, excluding Southwest Asia and Russian Asia. *Asian Survey*, a bi-monthly (formerly monthly) published by the University of California Press, no longer displays a map on its cover, but did so for many years. It was also a silhouette of an Asia that included East, Southeast, South, Central, and Russian Asia, but excluded Afghanistan as well as Southwest Asia (fig. 4.6). On its website the journal states, "*Asian Survey* provides a comprehensive retrospective of contemporary international relations within South, Southeast, and East Asian nations" (*Asian Survey* 2013).[14]

FIGURE 4.6

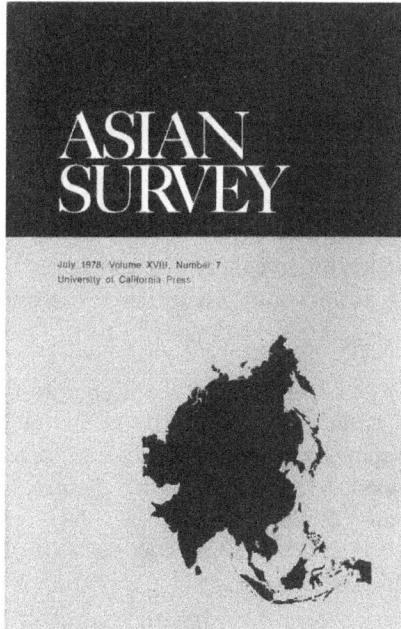

Cover image from *Asian Survey* vol. 18, no. 7, July 1978. © 1978 by the Regents of the University of California. Published by The University of California Press.

The American quarterly journal *Asian Affairs: An American Review* until recently displayed on its cover twenty-two national flags. Not included were the flags of Mongolia, Russia, the five Central Asian republics (Kazakhstan, Kyrgyzstan, Tajikistan, Turkmenistan, Uzbekistan), Afghanistan, and the countries of Southwest Asia. The Maldive Republic's flag was also missing, but probably more because of the country's diminutive population than its geographic location.[15]

The Journal of Asian Studies does not display a map on its cover, but its parent organization, the Association for Asian Studies, displays a map of Asia as part of its logo (fig. 4.7). Like the old *Asian Survey* cover map, the AAS logo shows a black silhouette of Asia that excludes Southwest Asia and Afghanistan, but the AAS also excludes the five Central Asian republics and most of Russian Asia from its cartographic definition of Asia (Association for Asian Studies 2013).[16]

FIGURE 4.7

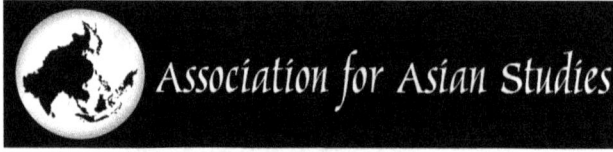

The International Institute for Asian Studies (IIAS), based in Leiden, is in many respects the European counterpart to the AAS. It does not use a map logo but defines Asia in much the same way as AAS and Asian Survey:

> "Asia" as covered by the IIAS includes South, Southeast, East and Central Asia. South Asia, as defined by IIAS, covers the Indian subcontinent, including Afghanistan. Iran and the Middle East are excluded from the area covered by the IIAS. The reasons for the exclusion of Iran and the Middle East are perhaps rather prosaic. Together with the IIAS, established in 1993, another Institute was started in The Netherlands that focused on Iran/Middle East.[17]

To summarize what has been observed so far, the Asia that is represented on the covers of Asia-content scholarly books and journals is much smaller than the Asia described in atlases or the Asia we teach to our school children. It corresponds somewhat to what earlier geographers called "Asian Asia" or "Asiatic Asia", but is limited even more narrowly, primarily to East, Southeast, South, and sometimes Central Asia. Professional associations, journals and other scholarly institutions (such as Asian Studies centres at universities) have framed an Asia that excludes Southwest Asia and for the most part those components of "Atlas Asia" that were formerly in the Soviet Union.

Alice Miller and Richard Wich provide a strategic characterization of this view of Asia:

> Our discussion of Asia is to be understood in a geopolitical sense, not including the Middle East. One of our objectives has been to integrate developments in South and Central Asia along with East Asia into the story of how the region developed from extensive colonial dependence into the vibrant, assertive Asia that it had become by the turn of the new millennium. (Miller and Wich 2011, p. xiii)

Miller and Wich argue that "Asia was not much more than a Western geographical expression at the end of World War II" and that the "geopolitical" Asia on which they focus was largely shaped by the political dynamics of the dissolution of European Asian empires following World War II and the East–West Cold War that occupied the following decades. "Even after the Cold War", they write, "the effects of broader influences continued to shape the geopolitical landscape of Asia as a new century unfolded" (Miller and Wich 2011, p. 44).

Echoing this geopolitical interpretation of post-war Asian cartography, AAS president David Ludden observed in his presidential address (2003):

> Each national state maps the world for itself, but invisible elements in national world maps indicate more complex spatial histories of knowledge lurking inside.... For example, the United States drew its map of Asia by lumping countries that officially define East, Southeast, Central and South Asia; these became areas in area studies. Although many maps depict Asia as including most of Russia and touching the Mediterranean, the U.S. government mapped Asia as to separate the Middle East from Central and South Asia. Scholars, educators, publishers, schools, tourist agencies, news agencies, and countless others in many countries did the same. Attachments to maps of Asia did the same.

Ludden goes on to note an even more specific concentration of American geopolitical interest:

> Invisibly, however, America's Asia mostly means China and Japan. This appears in the fact that roughly 75 percent of the members of the AAS study China, Japan or Korea. This knowledge map is invisible in the AAS logo and reflects a special attachment to East Asia dating back to the days of the Opium Wars and Admiral Perry's adventures. By the 1950s, when area studies took shape in America, a century of mobility across the Pacific had formed a distinctly American geography of attachments to Asia, interests in Asia, and knowledge about Asia. By contrast, European knowledge about Asia evolved over centuries of mobility across the Indian Ocean, and as a result, European Asian studies pay disproportionately more attention to South and Southeast Asia. (Ludden 2003, pp. 1058–59)

This American emphasis on East Asia is reflected also in the history of the Association for Asian Studies, its *Journal of Asian Studies*, and the separate journal *Asian Survey*. The Association for Asian Studies was founded in 1941, "originally as publisher of the *Far Eastern Quarterly* (now the *Journal of Asian Studies*)". Originally called "The Far Eastern Association", it "has gone through a series of reorganizations to serve better the broadening disciplinary and geographical interests of its membership" (Association for Asian Studies).[18] The reorganizations and name change were largely a result of pressure from Indianists and other scholars interested in the countries emerging from European Asian empires. Similarly, *Asian Survey* was originally called *Memorandum* and was published by the Institute of Pacific Relations. Its institutional home is presently the Institute of East Asian Studies at the University of California, Berkeley (IEAS 2013).

Interestingly, only a few of the books under review display this apparent preponderance of American interest in East Asia over South and Southeast Asia. *International Relations of Asia* has a map on its cover that is a silhouette of Asia and excludes everything west of a vertical line drawn through the centre of India (fig. 4.8, from Shambaugh and Yahuda 2008).

The Routledge Handbook of Asian Regionalism claims (in the blurb on its back cover) to be "a definitive introduction to, and analysis of, the development of regionalism in Asia, including coverage of East Asia, Southeast Asia and South Asia". However, the topographical map on its front cover includes only East Asia, Southeast Asia, some of Bangladesh and perhaps a sliver of Northeast India. In all fairness, the map is indicative of the contents: of the thirty-three chapters in the book, only the final one focuses on South Asian regionalism (Dash 2012, pp. 406–19).

Most of the books on Asia may shave off Pakistan and Afghanistan but pretty consistently include India's triangular subcontinental shape. During the past two decades, India and South Asia have become more prominent geopolitically, both because of increased American and European involvement in the subcontinent following 11 September 2001 and because of India's increased economic and strategic strength. Several books investigated in this study deal specifically with aspects of these changes in India's geopolitical role and its

FIGURE 4.8

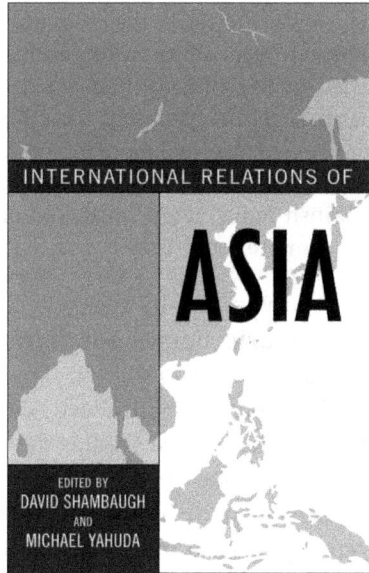

relations with the United States (Blank 2005; Burns, Price, Nye and Scowcroft 2011; Chambers 2002; Kemp 2010; Mohan 2003; Nayar and Paul 2003; Patil and Spittel 2013; Rana 2012; Rana and Dowling 2009; Sokolski 2007).

Constructing South Asia

If the social construction of Asia is ongoing, the same is even more the case with South Asia. Prior to World War II there was no South Asia. The area known today by that name was generally referred to as India, the Indian subcontinent or the Indian Peninsula (Davies 1949, 1959). The partition of the subcontinent in August 1947 into the independent countries of India and Pakistan (then including the present country of Bangladesh) necessitated development of a term for the region that would distinguish it from independent India. Spate's chapter on "India and Pakistan" (East and Spate 1950, p. 119) demonstrated the difficulties of terminology:

> The partition of the Indian Empire is so recent, the old concept of "India" so familiar, the two new dominions have still so much in common, that it is convenient to retain the old name as a geographical expression in general and historical contexts where no ambiguity can arise. It is unfortunate and confusing that a part of the old India should retain the name of the whole, but it would be discourteous as well as inaccurate to use perhaps [the] more logical and certainly more convenient term "Hindustan" for the Indian Union.... In economic and statistical contexts "British India" refers to the old provincial territory, "all India" to the old Empire, both British and States' territory.[19]

Expanded American involvement in the world also helped shift terminology from Eurocentric names for parts of Asia to terms independent of the location of the observer. The "Far East" became East Asia, "Hither India" became Southeast Asia, and "the Indian subcontinent" became South Asia. Area studies developed around these "world areas" in the United States in the 1950s within the context of Cold War geopolitics. "Government promotion of international studies began in a period when, along with the Cold War–driven globalization of U.S. strategic interests, the United States began investing heavily overseas" (Carlile 2010, p. 80). Area studies centres and students at American universities received NDEA (National Defense Education Act) and NDFL (National Defense Foreign Language) funding from the U.S. government. The justification for spending defence funds on education stressed the importance of preparing Americans to be more knowledgeable about Asia, Africa and Latin America in order to compete effectively with the Soviets. In the 1990s, after the end of the Cold War, area studies suffered a decline in national and academic support.[20]

Earlier discussion identified a distinction between "Atlas Asia" and "Geopolitical Asia". A similar but more complex distinction can be seen in the social construction of South Asia. Part of the complexity lies in the fact that "Atlas South Asia" has been considerably more ambiguous than "Atlas Asia".

Norton Ginsburg's *The Pattern of Asia* (1958) identified South Asia as including five independent countries: "The new South Asian nations of India, Pakistan, and Ceylon, which have recently gained their independence, and the old nations of Afghanistan and Nepal, which now are emerging from isolation, provide the political framework through which the people of the subcontinent seek to express their national aspirations" (Ginsburg 1958, p. 523). In the next few years the political map of South Asia changed considerably. Goa and other Portuguese enclaves were secured by India by force in 1961. War between India and China in 1962 over disputed territories still left territories in dispute. The Pakistani civil war in 1971 led to the independence of East Pakistan as the new Republic of Bangladesh. Ceylon changed its name to Sri Lanka in 1972. India took over Sikkim in 1975. The Maldives, formerly a British protectorate, became independent as a sultanate in 1965 and a republic in 1968. In *The Historical Atlas of South Asia*, Schwartzberg (1978, 1992) defines South Asia as including India, Pakistan, Bangladesh, Afghanistan, Nepal, Sri Lanka, Bhutan, and the Republic of Maldives.[21]

Table 4.2 indicates the countries included in South Asia by selected books (as indicated by their content and/or the maps on their covers) and organizations. All are in agreement that five countries (India, Pakistan, Bangladesh, Nepal, Sri Lanka; referred to hereafter as the "five standard countries") are part of South Asia. Some maps or logos fail to include Bhutan or the Maldives, in part because of their relatively small size. A couple of organizations include countries generally regarded as outside the region.

TABLE 4.2
Which Countries Constitute South Asia?

	Ind	Pak	Ban	Nep	SrL	Afg	Bhu	Mal	Bur	Tib
Kingsbury, 2nd ed.	■	■	■	■	■		■			
Schmidt	■	■	■	■	■					
Ginsburg	■	■	■	■	■	■				
Schwartzburg	■	■	■	■	■	■	■	■		
SAARC 1985–2007	■	■	■	■	■		■	■		
SAARC Post 2007	■	■	■	■	■	■	■	■		
AAS	■	■	■	■	■		■			
SASA	■	■	■	■	■	■	■	■		
EASAS	■	■	■	■	■		■			
Wisconsin	■	■	■	■	■	■	■	■		■

The greatest ambiguity has concerned the question of whether to include Afghanistan in South Asia. Regionally, Afghanistan has been variously treated as belonging to the Middle East (Southwest Asia), Central Asia, or South Asia. The ambiguity is illustrated by the covers of two South Asia atlases. Robert Kingsbury's *South Asia in Maps* (2nd ed., 1974) displays a silhouette map on its cover that includes the five standard countries plus Sikkim and Bhutan. Afghanistan and the Maldives are not included in the map, but both are treated briefly inside the book.[22] Karl Schmidt's *Atlas and Survey of South Asian History* (1995) displays a map on its cover that similarly includes (and labels) the standard five plus Bhutan, but not Afghanistan or the Maldives.

This ambiguity concerning Afghanistan's inclusion in South Asia has been reflected in the history of the South Asian Association for Regional Cooperation (SAARC). When SAARC was created in 1985 it did not include Afghanistan. Afghanistan was admitted to SAARC in 2007, bringing the total membership to eight.

It has already been noted that the Association for Asian Studies logo map of Asia excludes Afghanistan, presumably considering it to be part of the Middle East. The European Association for South Asian Studies similarly displays a silhouette map of South Asia that includes the standard five countries and Bhutan, but excludes Afghanistan and the Maldives (fig. 4.9, by courtesy of EASAS).

FIGURE 4.9

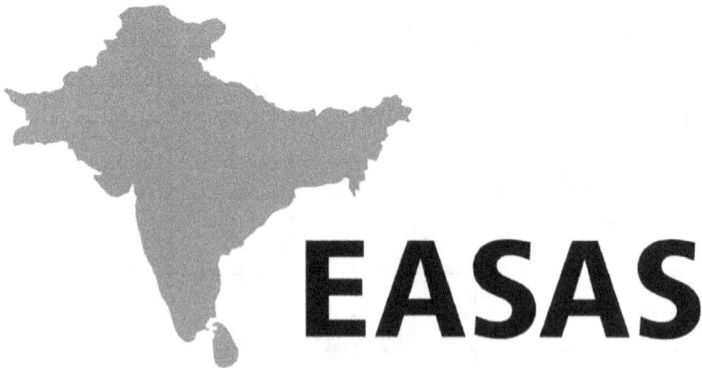

The two organizations with more idiosyncratic definitions of which countries to include in the region are the South Asian Studies Association (SASA) and the University of Wisconsin Conference on South Asia. SASA displays a stylized logo showing India, Sri Lanka and a bit of Bangladesh. Pakistan, Afghanistan and Bhutan are absent from the logo, but the association's website defines South Asia as consisting of nine countries, including all of these plus Nepal, the Maldives and Myanmar (Burma). This may reflect the fact that Burma was part of British India from 1885 to 1935. The Burma flag that is displayed is the one that was in use until 2010. Burma's new flag and new name are controversial symbols of the military regime that still controls the country, despite recent elections and the appearance of some movement towards democratization.

In what is perhaps the most exceptional definition of South Asia, the University of Wisconsin's Annual Conference on South Asia displays on its website a map which shows the standard five plus Afghanistan, Bhutan — and Tibet! There are long-term cultural ties between Tibet and South Asia, and many Tibetans, including the Dalai Lama, have been resident in India for decades.[23] Inclusion of Tibet in a South Asia dominated by India could easily be interpreted by the People's Republic of China as an unwelcome geopolitical statement. There is an active Tibetan independence movement, and Tibetans continue to protest, in Tibet and abroad, against Han Chinese domination.

As with Asia generally, it is possible to identify several maps on book covers that portray a "Geopolitical South Asia". Geopolitical Asia, it will be recalled, includes East, Southeast and South Asia and excludes Southwest, Central, and Russian Asia. Geopolitical South Asia includes India, Pakistan and Afghanistan and largely ignores the rest of the region.

Several books in our study display cover maps that emphasize such a geopolitical representation of the region. *The Security of South Asia: American and Asian Perspectives* (fig. 4.10, from Cohen 1987), for instance, shows a silhouette map that excludes Bangladesh and Bhutan as well as the Maldives. The cover is accurately descriptive of the contents of the book — all of the contributors were Indians, Pakistanis or Americans.

FIGURE 4.10   FIGURE 4.11

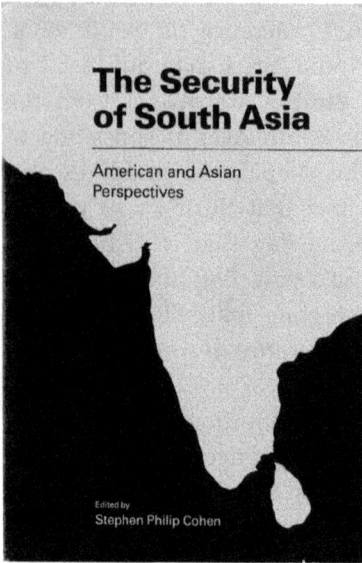

The Security
of South Asia

American and Asian
Perspectives

Edited by
Stephen Philip Cohen

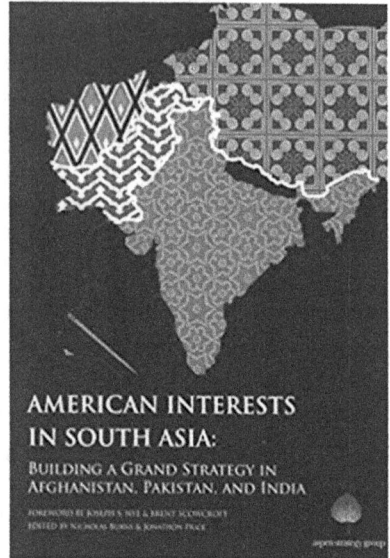

AMERICAN INTERESTS
IN SOUTH ASIA:
BUILDING A GRAND STRATEGY IN
AFGHANISTAN, PAKISTAN, AND INDIA

FOREWORD BY JOSEPH S. NYE & BRENT SCOWCROFT
EDITED BY NICHOLAS BURNS & JONATHON PRICE

aspen strategy group

Two other books on strategic issues are even more explicit in highlighting an emphasis on the geopolitical core of South Asia. *South Asia in 2020: Future Strategic Balances and Alliances* (Chambers 2002) displays a map of Asia with a magnified section that shows India, Pakistan and Afghanistan but excludes Bangladesh and Sri Lanka. *American Interests in South Asia: Building a Grand Strategy in Afghanistan, Pakistan, and India* (fig. 4.11, from Burns, Price, Nye and Scowcroft 2011) represents India, Pakistan, Afghanistan and China as pieces of fabric, with a needle and thread indicating the challenge of "stitching" these diverse interests together. Everything else, including the Indian Ocean, Bangladesh and Nepal, is simply black background. The book's title and map deliver the same message: American interests in South Asia are centred on the three geopolitical priorities. The other countries of the region, regardless of their size (e.g., Bangladesh) or civil wars and other internal security issues (e.g., Sri Lanka, Nepal), are essentially irrelevant to American interests. The co-editors of this volume have all been officials in the American foreign policy establishment.

Summary and Conclusions

World regions may seem like natural divisions of the earth, but — like nations — are socially constructed entities. Some of these constructions, like the notion that Europe and Asia are continents, may last for millennia. Others, like South Asia as a world region, are only decades old but rest on deeper roots in the cultural unity of historical India.

This study of Asian and South Asian book and journal covers has demonstrated at least two broad cartographic constructions for each region — an atlas or official definition and a geopolitical or strategic definition. The atlas definition predominates in school texts but the narrower geopolitical region frames most discussions of international affairs. People may simply carry both mental maps in their heads and draw on whichever one seems appropriate in context. For example, Saudi Arabia is technically in Asia (according to the atlas) but Saudis are generally not considered Asians.

Social construction is an ongoing process. The French philosopher Ernest Renan referred to nationalism as a daily plebiscite (Renan 1882). "Asia" and "South Asia" may seem like natural "givens", but they have changed within our lifetimes and may continue to change. For instance, there has been the increased inclusion of Afghanistan in South Asia. To speak of "the Asian century" is not only to recognize the growing economic, political and strategic roles of China, India, and other Asian countries, but also to recognize that Asia as an organizing concept is probably more popular now than at any time in the past.

The maps on the covers of books and journals, and in the logos of professional associations, are part of this ongoing cartographic reframing of Asia and South Asia. By connecting with our mental maps of the region, they seek to draw us to their publications' contents, or to identify the scope of their association. At the same time, they frame expectations of what will be found — and not found — inside the publication or organization.

It is not mere coincidence that most of the books and journals that illustrate their covers with maps focus on international security, politics or related subjects. Cartographic illustration adds another, often political, layer to traditional cartography.

Geopolitical, strategic and security considerations relate to these maps in several ways. Contemporary constructions of Asia and its various subregions have been shaped by the geopolitics of decolonization and the Cold War, especially by American global involvement and by the globalization of higher education.

Other world regions might be expected to show similar patterns of cartographic construction to what has been observed with respect to Asia and South Asia (see, for instance, Culcasi 2006). The patterns observed here could also be compared to how the U.S. government, the United Nations and other organizations have spatially organized their understanding of the world. The numerous South Asian and Asian Studies centres and other regional educational programmes at universities around the world provide additional representations of the social construction of these world regions. All these institutions, and more, help to frame our understanding of Asia and South Asia.

Notes

1. See Milam (2009). The cover map reproduces a Pakistani stamp from the period before 1971, when Bangladesh became independent. Besides showing Kashmir, the map also shows in white some other disputed territory on the Kathiawar Peninsula of what is today the Indian state of Gujarat. This was the princely state of Junagadh, which initially acceded to Pakistan, an action which India reversed by force of arms. Pakistan maps continued to show Junagadh as either Pakistani or disputed territory at least until 1971.

2. One text (Mekenkamp 2002) uses multiple maps to try to placate all interests. This book does not have a map on its cover, but has a map at the beginning of each of its regional and country sections. The map on South Asia (p. 209) uses the Line of Control as the boundary between India and Pakistan. The map on India (p. 325) treats all of Jammu and Kashmir as Indian. The map on Pakistan (p. 447) treats all of Jammu and Kashmir as Pakistani. All three maps, however, are unlikely to have been well received in India, however, since they show the Aksai Chin region (occupied by China but claimed by India) as Chinese.

3. For two additional examples of blurred or faint maps on book covers, see Haggerty (2005) and Paul (2010).

4. These include SASNET (www.sasnet.lu.se), New York University Library (nyu.libguides.com) and Duke University Library (http://library.duke.edu).

5. On ethnicity, see Tilley (2002). On nations, see Anderson (1983). On regions and continents, see later citations in this chapter.

6. These "New Cartography" scholars have in turn been influenced by Michel Foucault, Jacques Derrida, Roland Barthes, and other postmodern social theorists. See Soja (1989); Peet (1998); and Harley (2001).

7. Nearly a century ago, another British geographer noted the dependence of geographical understanding upon perception and how reality has been framed by experience: "[O]ur view of the geographical realities is colored for practical purposes by our pre-conceptions of the past. In other words, human society is still related to the facts of geography, not as they are, but in no small measure as they have been approached in the course of history" (Mackinder 1919, p. 30).

8. The Institute for Regional Studies and its journal were founded in 1982 by Lt. Gen. (Ret.) A.I. Akram. The current acting president is Brig. (Ret.) Bashir Ahmed. The IRS website indicates that the institute's "mission [is] to provide in-depth understanding and objective analysis of regional and global issues". It further states: "IRS is uniquely placed to facilitate the exchange of knowledge among academia, governments, NGOs, agencies and institutions carrying out studies and analysis of non-traditional and traditional issues. As a think tank, our goal is to enlighten public opinion and other institutes in Pakistan by disseminating knowledge which can bring a better appreciation and understanding of neighboring countries." (http://www.irs.org.pk/message.htm; accessed 7 August 2013). In some of the maps in its publications, the Institute for Regional Studies labels the large body of water that lies south of Pakistan and India the "Afro-Asian Ocean" rather than the Indian Ocean.

9. The website for this journal states that its "major objective is to provide a forum for scholars engaged in study of the modern Islamic and non-Islamic societies and leaders in public affairs in a wide range of areas and disciplines" (http://www1.villanova.edu/villanova/artsci/about/journals_publications.html#asian; accessed 7 August 2013). The journal is edited by Dr Hafeez Malik.

10. One designer disclosed in a personal email that he thought maps were used too frequently for book-cover illustration. He said that in one instance he had been instructed by his publisher to use a map on the cover of a specific book. The publisher's editor of that book explained that the cover, on a South Asia book, had used a map design that was similar to one on an East Asian book by the same publisher. Personal discussion with editor, Association for Asian Studies annual meeting, Honolulu, 1 April 2011.

11. The National Geographic Geopolitical Map of Asia is large enough to show East Africa and all of Europe, but delineates Asia along these traditional

"continental" lines (http://maps.nationalgeographic.com/maps/atlas/asia-geopolitical.html).

12. There is a nice brief biography of Reclus on Wikipedia.

13. The difference in the number of regions is explained by the earlier work's category of "High Asia", including Tibet, Sinkiang and Mongolia. In *The Pattern of Asia* these are all included in China. One of the important geopolitical developments that occurred between 1950 and 1958 was the Chinese assertion of control over Tibet and the flight of the Dalai Lama and many other Tibetans to India.

14. It should be noted, however, that the journal has included articles on Central Asia.

15. The twenty-two flags represent Bangladesh, Bhutan, China (PRC), Japan, North Korea, India, South Korea, Thailand, Laos, Cambodia, Sri Lanka, Vietnam, Nepal, East Timor, Singapore, Pakistan, Brunei, Burma (Myanmar), Malaysia, Indonesia, Republic of China (Taiwan) and the Philippines. Interestingly, the Burmese flag that is shown is the one used until 2010, but not currently. After this study was completed, *Asian Affairs* dropped the cover display of flags and began using a map that shows all of Asia and much of East Africa.

16. The map appears to include Mongolia and, strangely, just a small portion of far eastern Russia, the coastal areas and Kamchatka Peninsula surrounding the Sea of Okhotsk.

17. Email communication from IIAS Director via Martina C. van den Haak, 9 July 2013. In the United States, also, the Middle East Studies Association (MESA) covers the countries of Southwest Asia.

18. The same webpage mentions the area councils by which the AAS governs itself: "In 1970 four elective Area Councils — China and Inner Asia (CIAC), Northeast Asia (NEAC), South Asia (SAC), and Southeast Asia (SEAC) — were established to guarantee each area constituency its own representation and a proportionate voice on the Board of Directors." One might have expected the four regional divisions to be East, Southeast, South, and Central, but that would have left seventy-five per cent of AAS members, who are East Asianists (according to Ludden's figures), with only one-fourth of the representation.

19. Spate regarded "Hindustan" as potentially "discourteous" because that was a term used for India primarily by Hindu nationalists and Pakistanis. Another option Spate could have mentioned is *Bharat*, the name recognized in the Indian Constitution but much less commonly used than *India*.

20. In a 1997 paper, David Ludden raised the question, "[W]hy did area specific knowledge become a national priority in the 1950s and lose its priority status in the 1990s?" (Ludden 1997). For discussion of links between

United States' intelligence agencies and academic area studies centres, see Cumings (2002).

21. As we shall see later, not all South Asia atlases include all of these countries, with Afghanistan and the Maldives being the two most likely to be excluded, but Schwartzberg's is considered the definitive atlas on the region.

22. There is a three-page chapter on Afghanistan (pp. 93–95), including four maps. The Maldives are mentioned in a chapter on "Sri Lanka and Other Indian Ocean Islands" (pp. 84–87), including one map of the Maldive archipelago. These two chapters, plus one on Sikkim and Bhutan and another on Nepal, are in the final section, entitled "The Peripheral States" (pp. 84–95). Sikkim is included as an independent unit because it was not taken over by India until 1975.

23. As a leading Wisconsin South Asianist explained the situation: "I THINK the way to explain why Wisconsin's Center for South Asia includes Tibet as part of South Asia would be to 'follow the money'. Wisconsin's East Asian Language and Literature Department has had no interest in teaching Tibetan. Wisconsin's Center for South Asia has needed to teach Tibetan for many years. The language is important for students studying South Asian Buddhism. Other South Asia students (e.g., anthropologists) have also needed to study Tibetan. The northern sections of Nepal (clearly within South Asia) speak Tibetan, as do sections of Ladakh (also clearly within South Asia). Two of the documentary films I have made have used Tibetan. So our South Asia Center has been helping finance the teaching and study of Tibetan on the Madison campus for many years.... I'm quite sure there never was a committee meeting at which Wisconsin academics and administrators voted on whether or not Tibet is part of South Asia. I guess the lesson is: If South Asia pays for Tibetan, then Tibet belongs to South Asia" (email from Joe Elder, 31 August 2013).

References

Acharya, Amitav. "Asia is Not One". *Journal of Asian Studies* 69, no. 4 (November 2010): 1001.

Anderson, Benedict. *Imagined Communities: Reflections on the Origin and Spread of Nationalism*. London: Verso, 1983.

Asian Survey. 2013 <http://ucpressjournals.com/journal.php?j=as> (accessed 4 August 2013).

Association for Asian Studies. 2013 <http://www.asian-studies.org/> (accessed 4 August 2013).

Aydin, Cemil. *The Politics of Anti-Westernism in Asia: Visions of World Order in Pan-Islamic and Pan-Asian Thought*. New York: Columbia University Press, 2007.

Baik, Tae-Ung. *Emerging Human Rights Systems in Asia*. Cambridge: Cambridge University Press, 2012.

Beeson, Mark, and Richard Stubbs, eds. *Routledge Handbook of Asian Regionalism*. London: Routledge, 2012.

Black, Jeremy. *Maps and Politics*. Chicago: University of Chicago Press, 1997.

Blank, Stephen J. *Natural Allies: Regional Security in Asia and Prospects for Indo-American Strategic Cooperation*. Carlisle Barracks, PA: Strategic Studies Institute, U.S. Army War College, 2005.

Brandt, Willy. *North–South: A Program for Survival*. Cambridge, MA: MIT Press, 1980.

Burns, Nicholas, Jonathan Price, Joseph S. Nye, Jr., and Brent Scowcroft, eds. *American Interests in South Asia: Building a Grand Strategy in Afghanistan, Pakistan, and India*. Washington, DC: The Aspen Institute, 2011.

Carlile, Lonny E. "The Evolution of 'Area Studies' in Japan". In *Remaking Area Studies: Teaching and Learning across Asia and the Pacific*, edited by Terence Wesley-Smith and John Goss. Honolulu: University of Hawai'i Press, 2010.

Chambers, Michael R. *South Asia in 2020: Future Strategic Balances and Alliances*. Carlisle, PA: Strategic Studies Institute, U.S. Army War College, 2002.

Chandra, Kanchan, ed., *Constructivist Theories of Ethnic Politics*. New York: Oxford University Press, 2012.

Chin-Lee, Cynthia, and Yumi Heo. *A is for Asia*. New York: Orchard Books, 1997.

Cohen, Stephen P., ed. *The Future of Pakistan*. Washington, DC: The Brookings Institution, 2011.

Cohen, Stephen Philip, ed. *The Security of South Asia: American and Asian Perspectives*. Urbana: University of Illinois Press, 1987.

Cotterell, Arthur. *Asia: A Concise History*. Singapore: Wiley, 2011.

Crowley, David. *Magazine Covers*. London: Beazley, 2003.

Culcasi, Karen. "Cartographically Constructing Kurdistan within Geopolitical and Orientalist Discourses". *Political Geography* (2006): 680–706 <http://www.geo.wvu.edu/~kculcasi/final%20article%20in%20print.pdf>.

———. "Cartographic Constructions of the Middle East". PhD dissertation, Syracuse University, 2008 <http://surface.syr.edu/geo_etd/1/>.

Cumings, Bruce. "Boundary Displacement: The State, the Foundations, and Area Studies during and after the Cold War". In *Learning Places: The Afterlives of Area Studies*, edited by Masao Miyoshi and H.D. Haroutunian. Durham, NC: Duke University Press, 2002.

Dash, Kishore C. "Dynamics of South Asian Regionalism". In *Routledge Handbook of Asian Regionalism*, edited by Mark Beeson and Richard Stubbs, pp. 406–19. London: Routledge, 2012.

Davies, C. Collin. *An Historical Atlas of the Indian Peninsula*, 2nd ed. Oxford: Oxford University Press, 1959.

Donaldson, Madeline. *Asia*. Minneapolis: Lerner, 2005.

Dorronsoro, Gilles. *Afghanistan: Searching for Political Agreement*. Washington, DC: Carnegie Endowment for International Peace, 2010.

Downs, Roger M., and David Stea. *Maps in Minds: Reflections on Cognitive Mapping*. New York: Harper & Row, 1977.

Drevitch, Gary. *Asia*. New York: Scholastic, 2009.

Duara, Prasenjit, ed. *Asia Redux: Conceptualising a Region for Our Times*. Singapore: Institute of Southeast Asian Studies, 2013.

East, W. Gordon, and O.H.K. Spate, eds. *The Changing Map of Asia: A Political Geography*. New York: Dutton, 1950.

Embree, Ainslie T., and Carol Gluck. *Asia in Western and World History*. Armonk, NY: Sharpe, 1997.

Ferguson, Niall. *Empire: How Britain Made the Modern World*. London: Allan Lane, 2002.

Garfield, Simon. *On the Map: A Mind-Expanding Exploration of the Way the World Looks*. New York: Gotham Books, 2013.

Garver, John W. *Protracted Contest: Sino–Indian Rivalry in the Twentieth Century*. Seattle: University of Washington Press, 2001.

Ginsburg, Norton, ed. *The Pattern of Asia*. Englewood Cliffs, 1958.

Goffman, Erving. *Frame Analysis: An Essay on the Organization of Experience*. Cambridge: Harvard University Press, 1974.

Gould, Peter, and Rodney White. *Mental Maps*, 2nd ed. Boston: Allen & Unwin, 1986.

Haggerty, Devin. *South Asia in World Politics*. Lanham, MD: Rowman & Littlefield, 2005.

Hall, Edward T. *The Silent Language*. Garden City, NY: Doubleday, 1959.

———. *The Hidden Dimension*. New York: Anchor Books, 1990.

Harley, J.B. "Maps, Knowledge and Power". In *The Iconography of Landscape: Essays on the Symbolic Representation, Design, and Use of Past Environments*, edited by Dennis Cosgrove and Stephen Daniels. Cambridge: Cambridge University Press, 1988.

———. "Deconstructing the Map". *Cartographica* 26, no. 2 (Summer 1989) 1–20.

———. *The New Nature of Maps: Essays in the History of Cartography*, edited by Paul Laxton. Baltimore: Johns Hopkins University Press, 2001.

House, R. Scott, and Patti M. House. *Map Skills–Asia*. Dayton, OH: Milliken, [1993] 2007.

IEAS. "*Asian Survey*". 2013 <http://ieas.berkeley.edu/publications/asian_survey. html> (accessed 4 August 2013).

Isaacs, Harold R. *Images of Asia: American Views of China and India*. New York: Capricorn Books, 1962. Originally published in 1958 as *Scratches on Our Minds*.

Iyer, Raghavan N. *Utilitarianism and All That*. New York: Grove Press, 1983.

Kemp, Geoffrey. *The East Moves West: India, China, and Asia's Growing Presence in the Middle East*. Washington, DC: Brookings Institution Press, 2010.

Kingsbury, Robert C. *South Asia in Maps*. Chicago: Denoyer-Geppert, 1974.

Klinghoffer, Arthur J. *The Power of Projections: How Maps Reflect Politics and History*. Westport, CT: Praeger, 2006.

Lewis, Martin W., and Kären W. Wigen. *The Myth of Continents: A Critique of Metageography*. Berkeley: University of California Press, 1997.

Ludden, David. "The Territoriality of Knowledge and the History of Area Studies". University of Pennsylvania, 6 December 1997 <http://www.sas. upenn.edu/~dludden/areast1.htm> (accessed 7 August 2013).

———. "Presidential Address: Maps in the Mind and the Mobility of Asia". *Journal of Asian Studies* 62, no 4 (November 2003): 1058–59.

Ma, Debin, and Jan Luiten Van Zanden. *Law and Long-Term Economic Change: A Eurasian Perspective*. Stanford: Stanford University Press, 2011.

Mackinder, Halford J. *Democratic Ideals and Reality*. New York: Holt, 1919.

Maxwell, Neville. *India's China War*. Garden City, NJ: Anchor Books, 1972.

Mekenkamp, Monique, Paul van Tongeren, and Hans van de Veen, eds. *Searching for Peace in Central and South Asia: An Overview of Conflict Prevention and Peacebuilding Activities*. Boulder, CO: Rienner, 2002

Milam, William B. *Bangladesh and Pakistan: Flirting with Failure in South Asia*, ADS-DACOR Diplomats and Diplomacy Series. New York: Columbia University Press, 2009.

Miller, Alice Lyman, and Richard Wich. *Becoming Asia: Change and Continuity in Asian International Relations since World War II*. Stanford: Stanford University Press, 2011.

Mishra, Pankaj. *From the Ruins of Empire: The Intellectuals Who Remade Asia*. New York: Farrar, Straus, Giroux, 2012.

Mohan, C. Raja. *Crossing the Rubicon: The Shaping of India's New Foreign Policy*. New York: Palgrave McMillan, 2003.

Monmonier, Mark. *Drawing the Line: Tales of Maps and Cartocontroversy*. New York: Holt, 1995.

National Geographic. "Geopolitical Map of Asia" <http://maps.nationalgeographic. com/maps/atlas/asia-geopolitical.html>.

Nayar, Baldev Raj, and T.V. Paul. *India in the World Order: Searching for Major-Power Status*. Cambridge: Cambridge University Press, 2003.

O'Shea, Maria T. *Trapped between the Map and Reality: Geography and Perceptions in Kurdistan.* New York: Routledge, 2004.

Patil, Amitendu, and Gloria Spittel. *South Asia in the New Decade: Challenges and Prospects.* Singapore: World Scientific, 2013.

Paul, T.V. *South Asia's Weak States: Understanding the Regional Security Predicament.* Stanford: Stanford University press, 2010.

Peet, Richard. *Modern Geographical Thought.* Oxford: Blackwell, 1998.

Rana, Pradumna B. *Renaissance of Asia: Evolving Economic Relations between South Asia and East Asia.* Hackensack, NJ: World Scientific, 2012.

Rana, Pradumna B., and John Malcolm Dowling. *South Asia: Rising to the Challenge of Globalization.* Hackensack, NJ: World Scientific, 2009.

Reclus, Elisée, with Augustus Henry Keane. *The Earth and its Inhabitants, Oceanica.* New York: Appleton, 1890.

Renan, Ernest. *Qu'est-ce qu'une nation?: conférence faite en Sorbonne, le 11 mars 1882.* Paris: Lévy, 1882. Available at <http://archive.org/details/questcequunenat00renagoog>.

Richter, William L. ed. *Approaches to Political Thought.* Lanham, MD: Rowman & Littlefield, 2009.

Ricoeur, Paul. "The Model of the Text: Meaningful Action Considered as a Text". *Social Research* 38, no. 3 (1971): 529–62. Reprinted in Richter 2009, pp. 236–47.

Saaler, Sven, and Christopher W.A. Szpilman, eds. *Pan-Asianism: A Documentary History.* Lanham, MD: Rowman & Littlefield, 2011.

Said, Edward W. *Orientalism.* New York: Vintage, 1971.

Salter, Christopher L. *South and East Asia and the Pacific.* Houghton Mifflin Harcourt, 2007.

Schaefer, A.R. *Asia.* Mankato, MN: Capstone Press, 2006.

Schmidt, Karl J. *An Atlas and Survey of South Asian History.* Armonk, NY: Sharpe, 1995.

Schwartzberg, Joseph. *Historical Atlas of South Asia.* Chicago: University of Chicago Press, 1978.

Shambaugh, David, and Michael Yahuda. *International Relations of Asia.* Lanham, MD: Rowman & Littlefield, 2008.

Soja, Edward J. *Postmodern Geographies: The Reassertion of Space in Critical Social Theory.* London: Verso, 1989.

Sokolski, Henry. *Gauging US India Strategic Cooperation.* Carlisle Barracks, PA: Strategic Studies Institute, U.S. Army War College, 2007.

Spate, O.H.K. "India and Pakistan". In *The Changing Map of Asia: A Political Geography,* edited by W. Gordon East and O.H.K. Spate. New York: Dutton, 1950.

Tilley, Virginia Q. "The Role of the State in Ethnic Conflict: A Constructivist Reassessment". In *Constructivism and Comparative Politics*, edited by Daniel M. Green, pp. 151–74. Armonk, NY: Sharpe, 2002.

Wesley-Smith, Terence, and John Goss, eds. *Remaking Area Studies: Teaching and Learning across Asia and the Pacific*. Honolulu: University of Hawai'i Press, 2010.

Wong, Jack, and Raymond Tong Kaiyu. *Handbook of Medical Device Regulatory Affairs in Asia*. Boca Raton, FL: CRC, 2013.

Wood, Denis. *The Power of Maps*. New York: Guilford Press, 1992.

Part II

Geopolitical Framing of Western Discourse

5

From Geertz to Ricklefs: The Changing Discourse on Javanese Religion and its Wider Contexts

Riwanto Tirtosudarmo

> It is particularly true that in describing the religion of such a complex civilization as the Javanese any simple unitary view is certain to be inadequate; and so I have tried in the following pages to show how much variation in ritual, contrast in belief, and conflict in values lie concealed behind the simple statement that Java is more than 90 per cent Moslem. (Geertz 1960, p. 7)

> Much is about religion and politics, about the relationship between two forms of authority, knowledge and power and those who wield them. (Ricklefs 2012, p. xviii)

This essay, through reading of books written in English, analyses the changing discourse of the Javanese religion in the last half century. The analysis starts with Clifford Geertz's book *The Religion of Java*[1] that was first published in 1960, seven years after he started his fieldwork in Java. It was only after the publication of *The Religion of Java* that a discussion on the notion of religion in Java among scholars was sustained. The last book in this analysis to comprehensively deal with the topic is *Islamisation and Its Opponents in Java*[2] by Merle C. Ricklefs, published in 2012, seven decades after Geertz began his study. There is a clear discursive genealogy linking these two books, with *Islamisation and Its Opponents in Java* providing a convenient ending to the analysis. In between, several books were analysed, most notably Robert Hefner's *Hindu Javanese: Tengger Tradition and Islam*[3] (1985), Andrew Beatty's *The Variation of Javanese Religion: An Anthropological Account*[4] (1999), Denys Lombard's *Nusa Jawa: Silang Budaya*,[5] especially volume two, published in Indonesia (1996), and Mark Hobart's *Java, Indonesia and Islam*[6] (2011).

The above-mentioned books are viewed as landmarks of Western scholarly discourse concerning Javanese religion, spanning the eras from the Cold War to the War on Terror. Certainly there are many other books and journal articles — as shown in the list of references — that could be quoted to support the arguments in this chapter. The chapter is chronologically structured by locating Indonesia's political development in three periods: during the Cold War (1950–70), during and after the New Order (1970–2000), and during the War on Terror (2001–13). It argues that the geopolitical contexts, namely the Cold War and the War on Terror, have influenced scholars in their research on religion in Java and the way they constructed Islam in particular, in response to the demand for knowledge created by the changing geopolitical contexts.

Java and American scholarship in the Cold War

The island of Java is the home of the Javanese and to a lesser extent the Madurese (in the central and eastern parts) and the Sundanese and the Bantenese (in the western parts). Java has always been the centre of political gravity in the archipelago. Since independence in 1945, Indonesia has been continuously plagued by social and political conflicts where ideologies were mobilized through ethnic and religious identities. In 1948 an armed conflict occurred in Madiun, East Java, where the communists rebelled against the national government. After recovering from this major ideological conflict, party politics flourished in which "the nationalists", "the communists" and "Islam" represented the three major ideologies.

The short occupation by the Japanese (1942–45) constituted a critical period. Under the Japanese military government, Indonesian leaders prepared the Constitution and for the country's independence. The attempt by the Dutch military to return after the Japanese surrender encountered strong resistance. Through diplomatic negotiations mediated mostly by the United States, in 1949 the Dutch accepted Indonesian national sovereignty. So, since the early 1950s Indonesia has embarked on its own national political agendas. Yet, as global political developments after the war were increasingly polarized between the United States and the Soviet Union, such a geopolitical conflict could not be avoided by the young Indonesian Republic.

Sukarno and the nationalist group, together with the nationalist leaders of other newly decolonized countries in Asia and Africa, campaigned for non-Bloc alliances as their response to the growing tensions between the United States and the Soviet Union. In reality, however, domestic rivalry between political ideologies could not be isolated from global political dynamics. It was during this period that a number of research collaborations were conducted between Indonesian and American research institutions and universities. American scholars began to enter Indonesian studies that had previously been dominated by Dutch scholars, as Benjamin White (2005) observes:

> In the years following the Second World War American strategic interest in Indonesia (as in Southeast Asia generally) was reflected in the establishment of active Indonesian studies programs in a number of American universities. Among these were Cornell's Southeast Asia Program and its "Modern Indonesia Project;" Yale's Southeast Asia Program which included various research activities in Indonesia, mainly of a more traditional ethnological kind; the collaboration between University of California at Berkeley and the Department of Economics at the University of Indonesia (the collaboration which later gave us the "Berkeley mafia"); and the Indonesia Project at the Center for International Studies, Massachusetts Institute of Technology.[7] The MIT project, funded by the Ford Foundation and directed by the economist Benjamin Higgins, included among various activities an "Indonesia Field Team."[8]

Among this wave of American scholars was a group of younger social scientists from Harvard University who were just beginning their studies of Javanese society. The influence of the wider geopolitical contexts of the Cold War on the development of scholarship on Indonesia cannot be overestimated, as Antlov and Helman (2005) note:

> Studies of Southeast Asia experienced an upswing in the mid-1950s, led by scholars from the United States. As had been the case with the early Dutch literature, there were geopolitical reasons behind this new development. An increasing American involvement in Indochina made it strategically important to study Southeast Asia. Unable to do fieldwork in Indochina, and bearing the Cold War domino theory in mind, Thailand and Indonesia became central fieldwork areas. Starting with MIT and the Ford Foundation's major multidisciplinary study of Pare, a district in east Java, American studies of Indonesia and Java intensified rapidly.

The demand from the American government for American universities to focus their study on the development of communism in Asia and in new developing countries created a dilemma among American scholars. George Kahin, a pioneer in the study of nationalism and revolution in Indonesia, was among the scholars who received pressure from the American government to focus their studies on the likely growing influence of communism in Asia. In his testament (2003, p. 140) he observed the beginning of U.S.-based research projects that concern social and agrarian change, particularly in densely populated rural Java:

> During the course of 1953 and early 1954 Langer worked out arrangements at Yale with Professor Karl Pelzer to establish a research program on Indonesian agriculture and agrarian problems, and with an MIT economist, Benjamin Higgins, to develop a program focused on the Indonesian economy. It was this research program which developed a close working relationship with Harvard's Douglas Oliver and enlisted several able anthropologist protégés of his interested in Indonesia, including Clifford Geertz.

Clifford Geertz began to publish his research findings in the mid to late 1950s. His thesis turned into a book, *The Religion of Java*, in 1960, followed in 1963 by *Agricultural Involution*. While Geertz is certainly not the first Western scholar to study religion in Java, it was only after him that discourse on religion in Java became more intensified and contentious. *The Religion of Java* successfully attracted other scholars to study religion in the area, many posing different arguments and criticism of what Geertz concluded in his thesis. Harsya Bachtiar (1973) criticized the lack of a definition of religion in *The Religion of Java*. Kees van Dijk (2006) argued that the study of Islam was treated merely as a subsection of *adat* law that led to an underestimation of Islam as only a part of the religion of Java. Woodward (1999, p. vii), despite his different view on Islam in Java, notes the undeniably powerful influence of Geertz on the discourse on religion in Java. Based on his fieldwork in the Sultanate of Yogyakarta in the mid-1990s, Woodward argued that Javanese Islam is an entity in itself and cannot be seen as a continuation of pre-Islamic pasts, particularly Hinduism, as implied by Geertz and his followers. Denys Lombard (1996), while not directly disputing Geertz's argument, notes the cosmopolitanism of Javanese Islam by showing the osmoses between Java and China before the arrival of Europeans.[9]

Despite all the criticism, *The Religion of Java* sustains strong interest even today, more than seventy years after the book was published. In the last paragraph of his introduction, Clifford Geertz (1960, p. 7) writes:

> Java — which has been civilized longer than England; which over a period of more than fifteen hundred years has seen Indians, Arabs, Chinese, Portuguese, and Dutch come and go; and which has today one of the world's densest populations, highest development of the arts, and most intensive agricultures — is not easily characterized under a single label or easily pictured in terms of dominant theme.

On the same page Geertz explains:

> If I have chosen, consequently, to accent the religious diversity in contemporary Java — or more particularly in one given town-village complex in contemporary Java — my intention has not been to deny the underlying religious unity of its people or, beyond them, of the Indonesian people generally, but to bring home the reality of the complexity, depth, and richness of their spiritual life.

Robert Hefner, who began his study of Javanese religion almost two decades after Clifford Geertz's fieldwork in Java, confirms that it was the American postgraduate students from Harvard University studying Java after the war who discovered (and constructed) two different categories of Javanese Muslims (Hefner 1985, p. 3n1). The first, known as *santri*, included those Muslims who carry out the ritual and ethical prescriptions of Islam in a strict manner. The second, known as *abangan*, referred to those in Java's Muslim community who are less rigorous in their performance of orthodox duties and are influenced by the artistic and ritual styles of Java's pre-Islamic past. The strong interest of American scholars in Islam during the 1960s and 1970s also coincided with modernization theories that expected *santri* to be the potential middle-class entrepreneurs needed in the process of modernization (Inglis 2000; Latham 2000; Najib 2013).

Clifford Geertz (1960) noted that Islam was perceived as the dominant religion in Java. The perception of the domination of Islam in Java — as well as in Indonesia — often refers to the very simplistic statement that ninety per cent of people in Java (and in Indonesia) are Muslim. Such a statistic, "ninety per cent are Muslim", indeed glosses over the reality and begs the question about the deeper aspects of religion, such as religiosity and other characteristics. The Javanese are not a homogenous group, socially, culturally or politically. Although the majority are generally perceived as Muslim, the official statistics always state that Javanese religions are varied and diverse. However, this variety of Javanese religions, particularly the dichotomy between *abangan* and *santri*, as discovered by Geertz in the 1950s, cannot be isolated from the wider Cold War–context and the domination of modernization theories among American scholars.

Islam under and after the New Order

Western scholars enchanted by Java, from Geertz to Ricklefs, have provided us with a substantial body of knowledge on religion on the island, particularly of Islam. Java and the Javanese religion, arguably, invoked not only scholarly passion and curiosity but also the underlying ideology used to understand the behaviour of the "other", as argued by Barten (2005):

> Like the Orientalists Said has analyzed, modernization theorists, policy makers, and the nation's media also went about framing an identity for the United States based on "positional superiority". They emphatically characterized their society as uniquely advanced "in comparison with all the non-European peoples and culture". While holding that all societies passed through the same, universal stages of development, theorists and policy makers also drew sharp distinctions between the West they belonged to and the world they classified.

The production of knowledge in the social sciences, besides becoming increasingly difficult and dichotomized between the West and the East, is perhaps most clearly shown during the Cold War in the continued imbalance between foreign and local scholars. In this situation, the religion of the Javanese as subject matter apparently developed from its relatively "neutral" status in the early 1950s into a more "political" status later.

In 1965 Indonesia plunged into a political conflict, later known as the "G 30 S event", in which the communists and their sympathizers were the losers. The aftermath of the 1965 tragedy made way for the military rather than Islam to attain power. *Abangan* and *santri*, two of the three Javanese religious variants discovered by Clifford Geertz in the 1950s, entered a new political episode in which *abangan*, associated by Geertz with the Indonesian Communist Party, was practically demolished. Yet it does not mean that its rival, *santri*, became politically more powerful. The military that was apparently beyond Geertz's close observation ascended to power, as it was the military that was able to orchestrate the *santri* in destroying the *abangan*.[10] *Santri* and *abangan*, as constructed by Geertz, continue to be fundamental concepts in the analysis of political developments in Indonesia.[11]

Robert Hefner and Andrew Beatty are perhaps the two anthropologists to have most closely followed in the footsteps of Geertz in their focus on Javanese religion. Conducting their research after the mass killing event when many *abangan* died, both Hefner and Beatty were able to demonstrate how the Javanese have perceived, endured and adapted themselves to the post-conflict situation, in which being an *abangan* is remarkably difficult, even futile. The process of converting to the new religion for the *abangan* is a painful and complex one. Hefner studied the Hindu-Tengger community on Bromo Mountain and Beatty studied the Osing people near Banyuwangi, both in East Java. These two communities are among the limited Javanese population relatively able to practise Javanese beliefs and rituals, and therefore can be seen as representing the last *abangan* as construed by Geertz.[12]

Compared to Geertz, Hefner is much more engaged socially and politically with Indonesia. In his words:

> The anthropology of the 1980s had taught me to value "reflexive" interaction with the people and society where one works — recognizing that the "other" with whom one interacts in a field setting is a full and dignified human being, with his or her own voice and initiative.

Hefner's conscious decision to work on the anthropology of democracy since the early 1990s is clearly motivated by the expectation that Indonesians, Muslims in particular, are a promising group able to practice democracy.[13] In 2000 Hefner published *Civil Islam: Muslims and Democratization in Indonesia*, a testament to his conviction that Islam is compatible with democracy. Hefner in a sense can be seen as following in the footsteps of Geertz, as he also started his anthropological research on Javanese religion in a place not far from where Geertz conducted his fieldwork in the early 1950s. But Hefner is among those American scholars who grew up after the end of the Cold War.[14]

The collapse of the Soviet Union created a new geopolitical setting in which the United States was left as the sole superpower and forced to reposition itself in world affairs. In this regard, the publication in the early 1990s of Samuel Huntington's writings indicated which direction the United States might go. The core idea in Huntington's *Clash of Civilizations* is the proposition that culture is the most important dimension in determining human affairs. Based on this proposition, Huntington perceived that future war would be determined by differences in cultures, in which religion is the core element. Huntington questioned the compatibility of Islam, Confucianism and other non-Western civilizations with liberal democracy, and predicted that there would be a clash in the future.[15] It is not at all coincidental that Robert Hefner, once a student of Huntington's, decided to focus his anthropological research on Islam in Indonesia.[16] After 1965, as *abangan* became politically insignificant, only *santri* had the potential to ascend to power.[17] Located in the wider geopolitical context, it is the *santri* that represent Islam as a group that merits attention in post–Cold War Indonesia.

In his writings, Hefner did not hide his empathy with the cause of Indonesian Muslim intellectuals' struggle to form a democratic Indonesia amidst the heavy political suppression of Soeharto's authoritarian regime. In his article in the Cornell journal *Indonesia* (October 1993) — "Islam, State and Civil Society: ICMI and the Struggle for the Indonesian Middle Class" — Hefner shows his optimism for a bright future for the Muslim middle class in Indonesia as represented by the ICMI (Ikatan Cendekiawan Muslim Indonesia, or Indonesian Muslim Intellectuals' Association) in reasserting their political bargaining power with Soeharto's military government. Hefner's persuasiveness has gained sympathy among the different groups of Indonesian intellectuals and think tanks, which provide him with immense first-hand information on what is happening in the political development of Islam in Indonesia. He is perhaps the most active scholar in the United States advocating the idea of Islam — more specifically, Indonesian Islam — as representing a potential civil and democratic class that the Western world should give serious attention to.

The Islamization of Java and the War on Terror

In his preface to *Polarizing Javanese Society*, Merle Ricklefs wrote that he was puzzled not to locate any references in his historical research to the contentions in Javanese society that led to the fatal conflict in 1965. Ricklefs feels disappointment with the way scholars simplify religion in Java, especially the absence of any historical explanation concerning *abangan*, *santri* and *priyayi* as major variants of the Javanese religion. As a historian, Ricklefs perceives a lack of historical explanation of the ethnographic study by Geertz of Java,[18] and has exhaustively employed the available historical data to interpret the process of Islamization in Java. Islam, in its orthodox sense, according to Ricklefs, has become the religion that is widely adopted by the Javanese, no matter what their socio-economic class or political and ideological orientation.[19] He argues that while the opposition to Islamization continues to exist, it is too insignificant to resist the massive process of Islamization in Java.

For Ricklefs' latest book, *Islamisation and Its Opponents*, he and his Indonesian research teams collected a significant amount of data through interviews with resource people in several places in Java. In contrast to Clifford Geertz, who plunged into Java without any kind of prior conscious personal plan, Ricklefs, being a student of O.W. Wolters, a Southeast Asian historian at Cornell University, seemed to be fully aware of what he wanted to study in Java in the 1960s. Ricklefs studied the history of the Mataram Kingdom, and has since continued research in Java with Islam as an indispensable part of it. His doctoral thesis was published as "Jogyakarta under Sultan Mangkubumi, 1749–1792" (1974); yet the decision to focus specifically on the historical processes of Islamization in Java — apparently after 2005, when he officially retired as a professor at Melbourne University — warrants an explanation.

In the preface of his most recent book he provides us with a clue to his motivation in writing it, although it sounds rather clichéd:

> It may be worth briefly reminding ourselves of the scale of significance of this Javanese story. The ethnic Javanese total about 100 million people — about 40 per cent of Indonesia's total population approaching 250 million. Indonesia is the fourth largest nation in the world, the world's largest Muslim-majority and its largest democracy.

Furthermore, Ricklefs argued, "the political, social, cultural and religious transformations that we are about to chart here are no small-scale matters". No doubt Merle Ricklefs wanted to make the Javanese historical experience of its Islamization more widely known, particularly in the Western world. The Javanese story, as Ricklefs argues, can significantly contribute to a better understanding of Islam. The timing of the publication of his books (2006, 2007 and 2012) also indicates a kind of urgency among scholars in the Western world to respond to the call for an appropriate answer to problems in dealing with Islam.

The 9/11 event (2001) in which a terrorist group in the name of Islam directly attacked a symbol of Western civilization undoubtedly reinforced the need to comprehend Islam as a politically powerful "other". The striking response of President George W. Bush of declaring a War on Terror only underlined the desperation of the Western world in its relations with the Islamic world. It is perhaps within such a rapid change of geopolitical context that we should properly locate the scholarly contribution of Merle Ricklefs' books on Islam in Java.

It is interesting to note that the term *abangan* first came to be known by Ricklefs (2012, p. 16) through Dutch missionary reports from the 1850s. However, it is really a wonder that Ricklefs could find any references to *abangan* among the local sources. The term *abangan* was actually coined by Westerners, namely in the reports of Dutch missionaries. It is arguable whether the term *abangan* is a socially constructed one by Westerners. Ricklefs (2012, p. 16n14) traces the etymology of the term and suggests that it "has become more regular in its meaning of nominal, non-observing Muslims as the years passed, and to have spread across the Javanese-speaking heartland".

Again, it is interesting to note how Ricklefs (2012, p. 17) describes the antagonistic relationship between *abangan* and *putihan* (a term that is equivalent to Geertz's term *santri*) to support his observation on the likely increasing polarization within Javanese society. The description, however, is too simplistic and a caricature that could be interpreted as being crafted to support what occurred following the G 30 S event.

> The *putihan* were wealthier, active in business, better dressed, had better homes, seemed more refined in manners, avoided opium and gambling, observed the pillars of Islam, gave their children more education and disciplined them more. The *abangan* were poorer, were not involved in trade and did not provide their children with education. *Abangan* still observed some religious activities, but did so in the name of village solidarity. Whereas the *putihan* read Arabic works and discussed the Islamic world's affairs, the *abangan* watched *wayang* performances and other entertainments in which indigenous spiritual forces were at work. The two groups mixed with the like-minded. These were worlds far apart from one another and becoming more so. They were distinguished by religious style, social class, income, occupation, dress, education, manners, cultural life and the mode of raising children. Because many of Java's money-lenders were from the *putihan* and many of their debtors were *abangan*, their interactions carried the seeds of conflicting interests. In the early 20th century, this mix would be made more volatile by the addition of political competition.

Parsudi Suparlan (1995), based on his fieldwork among the Javanese in Surinam, provides a more reasonable explanation with regard to the differences in the Javanese religion. According to Parsudi Suparlan:

> Although Javanese religion has several variants, they overlap to form a continuum. At one extreme are the reformists, and at the other are the traditionalists. In between are moderate reformists and moderate traditionalists. Among the traditionalists are those who syncretise Islam with *Agama Djawa*, taken as a separate doctrine, and those who basically believe only in *Agama Djawa* but pronounce themselves Muslims. (1995, p. 139)

The idea of Javanese religion as a continuum is in fact in line with what Clifford Geertz means when he describes his *Religion of Java*, stating in 1960 that:

> On the basis of a presentation of the content of the three religious variants in Modjokuto alone, one might easily come to the conclusion that *abangan, santri, and priyayi* are encapsulated "pure types", and that Modjokuto community life consists of three sub-communities whose main relationships with one another are geographical and perhaps economic — a "plural society" within a plural society, so to speak. Such a notion would be totally incorrect; for the three groups are all enclosed in the same social structure, share many common values, and are, in any case, not nearly so definable as social entities as a simple descriptive discussion of their religious practices would indicate.

It would be therefore too speculative indeed to say that the polarization of the Javanese as shown by Ricklefs (2007), between *abangan* and *putihan*, was the reason behind the bloody killings after the G 30 S event.[20] Yet, as John Rossa (2008) convincingly argues, the G 30 S event was used by Soeharto and the military apparatus as a pretext for mobilizing *santri* against *abangan* accused as communists or sympathizers. It is in this regard that the publication of Geertz's anthropological study conducted during 1952–54 in a small town in East Java (Pare) became instrumental, as it indicates the close association of *abangan* with the Indonesian Communist Party. It is indeed fascinating to observe how the invention of a term (*abangan*) and its location at an antagonistic position to another term (*putihan* or *santri*) has influenced the discourse and practice of religion and politics in Java. Clifford Geertz, on his visit to a small town in East Java in the 1970s and 1980s, wrote that the residents in that small town recalled the killings after the G 30 S event as "an episode in history that sometimes is remembered as the result of politics". Referring to Geertz's famous essay on a cock fight in Bali, the killing that occurred in Bali after the G 30 S event, "largely by one another — the worst outburst in the country", Rossa claims (2008, pp. 34–35) that such an argument reflects the disappointing cultural explanation adopted by Geertz and also Ricklefs on the reasons for the mass killings.

The significance of studying Java, as Ricklefs (2012, p. xix) posits, is related to the sheer number of Javanese people, of around a hundred million, around forty per cent of Indonesia's total population approaching 250 million, and the largest Muslim-majority nation in the world. Indeed, it is due to the demographic significance of Java (and Indonesia) that Ricklefs (2012, pp. 467–79) attempts to relate the implications of his study to the problem of the contemporary Islamic world. Referring to the results of studies by Olivier Roy (1994, 2004) and Gilles Kepel (2000, 2002) on the failure of Islam in its attempts to reassert political power in much of the Islamic world, he argues that Java could be the place from which the West could learn.

Ricklefs makes a substantial effort to make the case that his social construction of Javanese Islam could be an alternative to what he sees as the failure of Western scholars to understand political Islam. For example (2012, p. 469), he notes:

> An excursus on this matter may be appropriate, for there is a commonly held myth which seems to me unhelpful. That is, the idea that a separation of the religious and the political is a specifically modern and Western idea, one that is contrary to the traditions of Islam, or the non-Western world more generally. That idea suits Islamists just as well as it suits Western commentators who wish to depict Islam (or the non-Western generally) as fundamentally, culturally and in other ways, so unlike the West that a "clash of civilisations" (to borrow Huntington's dubious term) is likely, even inevitable. But it is not so. It is true that "church" and "state" came to be regarded as separate sources of authority in Europe. But in fact two distinguishable forms of elites and their authority can also be found in non-Western traditions.

In the context of the War on Terror, the place of Indonesia as a major Muslim country is indisputable, both from the perspective of the West as Ricklefs makes the case but also from the perspective of Islamic radicals. In an interview — published in *Open Democracy* on 30 August 2013 — Gil Loscher, an Oxford professor and the survivor of a bomb attack on the UN Headquarters Office in Baghdad on 19 August 2003, explains that Sergio Vieira de Mello, a Brazilian diplomat who was killed, was the target of an Islamist group led by Abu Muzab Al-Zarkawi, mainly because Sergio was working for the United Nations Transitional Administration in East Timor. The Islamic radicals perceived that Sergio separated East Timor from Indonesia. "By helping East Timor become independent of Indonesia — the largest Muslim country in the world — he had, apparently, committed a crime."

Concluding Remarks

The Cold War context set the frame for Clifford Geertz to construct the *Religion of Java* in which he invented the terminology of *abangan* and *santri* as the major religio-cultural groupings. The invention of *abangan* as representing the nominal Muslims closely associated with the Indonesian Communist Party was particularly relevant to the Cold War, as the Indonesian Communist Party was regarded as the largest communist party outside the Soviet Union and China. As a scholar, Geertz played an important role in describing not only the religious behaviour of the Javanese but also their economic and political tendencies. Although Geertz himself never clearly identified with scholars that belong among the modernization theorists, his description of the economic behaviour of the *santri* implied what modernization theories called for; namely, middleclass entrepreneurs. It was the *santri* that fit the expectations of the modernization theorists that they should be supported in an alliance in order to counter the increasing communism of developing countries. The detailed ethnographic study by Clifford Geertz and his American colleagues on Java was indeed instrumental for the American Cold War strategists.

While the Cold War context set the frame in the 1950s for Clifford Geertz to explore Javanese religion, the increasing demand from the West, particularly the United States, to comprehend Islam, constitutes the new geopolitical context that further drives the study of Islam in Java. The total demolition of the Indonesian Communist Party following the failed coup of 30 September 1965, that implicated the Javanese *abangan*, demands further understanding of *santri* as the entrepreneurial middle class in Indonesia. For the United States, the downfall of the Shah of Iran in 1979 and the triumph of the Islamic revolution under Ayatollah Khomeini were obviously shocking. The economic developments that the Americans supported proved to have failed in safeguarding the Shah from the Islamic revolution.

Although the process of "santrinization" in Indonesia has deepened, political Islam was marginalized under the military government of Soeharto. In the mid-1990s, Hefner began to observe the increasing politically disguised role of Indonesia's Muslim intellectuals under Soeharto's authoritarian government. Soeharto's stepping down from power in 1998 opened a new political space for Muslims. In Java, according to Ricklefs, Islamization has been an unstoppable process, especially since the 1970s, despite the resistance of its opponents. While the 9/11 attacks that prompted George W. Bush to declare the War on Terror were seen by some observers as proof of Huntington's *Clash of Civilizations* thesis, Hefner and Ricklefs argue that Islam should be perceived differently. While Hefner demonstrates that Islam in Indonesia is strongly characterized as civil and compatible with democracy, Ricklefs — through his latest book, *Islamisation and Its Opponents in Java*, especially the final part — makes the case for Islam in Java as his scholarly contribution to the Westerners' long desperate quest to comprehend Islam.

Notes

1. *The Religion of Java* was originally a doctoral thesis submitted in 1956 to the Department of Social Relations, Harvard University. Geertz's publications in the 1960s also included, among others, *Agricultural Involution* (1963) and *Islam Observed: Religion and Development in Morocco and Indonesia* (1968).
2. This book is the final part of a trilogy on Islamization in Java. The first part is *Mystic Synthesis in Java: A History of Islamisation from the Fourteenth to the Early Nineteenth Centuries* (2006); the second part is *Polarising Javanese Society: Islamic and Other Visions c. 1830–1930* (2007).

3. This book was originally a doctoral thesis at the University of Michigan, prepared in 1981–82 during his stay at the Institute of Advanced Study, where Clifford Geertz was the director. Robert Hefner is a prolific writer and perhaps the most productive author on contemporary Islam in Indonesia. Among his many books, *Civil Islam: Muslims and Democratization in Indonesia* (2000) is the most relevant to this chapter.

4. Andrew Beatty, a British anthropologist, wrote a doctoral dissertation at Oxford University on Nias, published as a book, *Society and Exchange in Nias* (1992), before he moved to Java to study the religion of the Javanese in Banyuwangi, East Java. After the publication of *The Variation of Javanese Religion: An Anthropological Account* (1999), he published *A Shadow Falls in the Heart of Java* (2009), also based on his fieldwork in Banyuwangi, East Java.

5. Denys Lombard, a French historian, began his studies on the Acehnese Sultanate before embarking on his study of Java that resulted in the three-volume *Le Carrefour Javanais* (1990).

6. India was his first study area before moving to Java and writing his doctoral dissertation at the University of Illinois, *Islam in Java: Normative Piety and Mysticism in the Sultanate of Yogyakarta* (1989).

7. According to Ben White, those who like "conspiracy" theories of American social sciences in the Cold War–period will be happy to know that the centre's director at the time, Max Millikan, had moved there from the CIA, where he had been assistant director of the Office of Research and Reports.

8. The team consisted of six young Harvard doctoral candidates — five anthropologists and one sociologist, students of Douglas Oliver (Alice Dewey, Donald Fagg, Clifford Geertz, Hildred Geertz, Robert Jay and Edward Ryan) — together with their field team leader, Rufus Hendon (of Yale University), and some of their spouses; a total of eleven Americans.

9. According to Woodward (1999), many of Geertz's critics ironically are also developing their criticisms based on Geertz's basic arguments.

10. John Rossa's *Pretext for Murder: The September 30th Movement and Suharto's Coup d'Etat in Indonesia* (2006) is the most elaborate explanation of the role of the military in the deadly conflict between *abangan* and *santri* after 1965.

11. The association between Geertz's three religious variants (*abangan, santri, priyayi*) and the political parties of the 1950s — elaborated further in his two other books, *Peddlers and Princes: Social Change and Economic Modernization in Two Indonesian Towns* (1963) and *The Social History of an Indonesian Town* (1965) — was shown in the result of the 1955 general election, in which the Indonesian Communist Party (PKI), the Indonesian Nationalist Party (PNI) and the Islamic parties (Masyumi and NU) closely identified with the

three. The influential discourse set out by Geertz in his book, particularly his description of the antagonistic tendencies between the three Javanese religious variants, have had long lasting effects, as shown by the references cited in the burgeoning publications of political analysis by foreign and Indonesian scholars alike.

12. Andrew Beatty is far less assertive than Robert Hefner in propagating the Javanese religion in his publications. His latest book, *A Shadow Falls in the Heart of Java* (2009), eloquently describes the subtle process of how orthodox Muslims slowly gained control over life in the neighbourhood of the village that he had studied.

13. The surge in Islamic studies in the United States began after the events of 9/11 (2001), although it had been developing since 1980, a year after the Islamic revolution and the fall of the Shah of Iran in 1979 (Ernst and Martin 2010).

14. See Najib Burhani (2012) on the shift in American scholars' research on Islam in Indonesia in the early 1980s from Muhamadiyah to NU.

15. In 1993 Samuel P. Huntington wrote "The Clash of Civilization?" in *Foreign Affairs* and in 1996 turned it into a book, *The Clash of Civilizations and the Remaking of World Order*.

16. In 1997–98, Hefner participated in the seminar on cultural globalization at the Harvard Center for International Affairs chaired by Samuel Huntington, a senior professor of government at Harvard University (Hefner 2000, p. xii).

17. See the chapter by Hefner, "Where Have All the *Abangan* Gone? Religionisation and the Decline of Non-standard Islam in Contemporary Indonesia", in Picard and Madinier (2011).

18. In the same vein as Ricklefs, Latham (2000, p. 14), in his book *Modernization as Ideology*, also criticizes Geertz's lack of historical narratives: "defining modernization simply as culture, in Geertz's terms alone, risks ignoring vitally important historical questions about how, why, under what conditions, and to what effect the ideological 'web' has been spun over time".

19. The work of Ricklefs has been appreciated by other scholars as providing a more comprehensive development of Islam in Java. Picard and Madinier (2011), for instance, note that "It has long been customary in the academic milieu to view Islam in Java as a superficial veneer, underneath which endured a syncretic indigenous and Hindu-Buddhist heritage. This prejudice has been denounced from different quarters, and a more balanced vision emerged recently with the historiographical work of Merle Ricklefs."

20. Ricklefs certainly does not make any speculations on the bloodshed that ensued. Picard (2011) notes that Ricklefs has subtly construed the Islamization of Java as an alternation of conflict and accommodation between competing identities, Javanese and Islamic, leading to a "mystic

synthesis" which by the turn of the nineteenth century combined a commitment to Islamic identity, observation of the five pillars of the faith, and acceptance of local spiritual powers, all within the context of Sufism.

References

Antlov, Hans, and Jorgen Hellman. "Introduction: Images of Java in Academic Discourses". In *The Java That Never Was: Academic Theories and Political Practice*, edited by Antlov and Hellman. Münster: LIT Verlag, 2005.

Bachtiar, Harsya W. "The Religion of Java: Sebuah Komentar" [The religion of Java: A commentary]. *Majalah Ilmu-Ilmu Sastra Indonesia*, no. 1 (January 1973).

Barten, Edgar. "Resurrecting 'Java': A Call for 'Javanese Anthropology'". In *The Java That Never Was: Academic Theories and Political Practice*, edited by Antlov and Hellman. Münster: LIT Verlag, 2005.

Beatty, Andrew. *Varieties of Javanese Religion: An Anthropological Account*. Cambridge: Cambridge University Press, 1999.

——. *A Shadow Falls: In the Heart of Java*. Faber and Faber, 2011.

Ernst, Carl W., and Richard C. Martin. *Rethinking Islamic Studies: From Orientalism to Cosmopolitanismi*. Columbia: University of South Carolina Press, 2010.

Geertz, Clifford. *The Religion of Java*. Chicago: University of Chicago Press, 1960.

——. *Agricultural Involution: The Processes of Ecological Change in Indonesia*. Berkeley: University of California Press, 1963.

——. *Islam Observed: Religious Development in Morocco and Indonesia*. New Haven, CT: Yale University Press, 1968.

——. *The Interpretations of Culture*. Glencoe: Basic Books, 1973.

Gil, Loscher. "An Interview with Gil Loscher". *Open Democracy*, 30 August 2013.

Hefner, Robert. *Hindu Javanese: Tengger Tradition and Islam*. Princeton, NJ: Princeton University Press, 1985.

——. *Political Economy of Highland Java: An Interpretive History*. Berkeley: University of California Press, 1990.

——. *Civil Islam: Muslims and Democratization in Indonesia*. Princeton, NJ: Princeton University Press, 2000.

——. "Where Have All the *Abangan* Gone? Religionization and the Decline of Nonstandard Islam in Contemporary Indonesia". In *The Politics of Religion in Indonesia: Syncretism, Orthodoxy, and Religious Contention in Java and Bali*, edited by Picard and Madinier. London: Routledge, 2011.

——. *Peddlers and Princes: Social Development and Economic Change in Two Indonesian Towns*. Chicago: University of Chicago Press, 1963.

——. *The Social History of an Indonesian Town*. Cambrige, MA: MIT Press, 1965.

Huntington, Samuel P. *The Clash of Civilizations and the Remaking of World Order*. New York: Touchstone, 1996.

Inglis, Fred. *Culture, Custom and Ethics*. Oxford: Polity Press, 2000.

Kahin, George. *Southeast Asia: A Testament*. London: RoutledgeCurzon, 2003.

Kepel, Giles. *Jihadi: The Trail of Political Islam*, translated by Anthony F. Roberts. Cambridge, MA: The Belknap Press of Harvard University Press, 2002.

Latham, Michael. *Modernization as Ideology: American Social Science and "Nation Building" in the Kennedy Era*. Chapel Hill, University of North California Press, 2000.

Lombard, Denys. *Nusa Jawa: Silang Budaya*. Jakarta: PT Gramedia, 1996.

Najib, Burhani. "North American Scholarship on Indonesian Islam: The Shift from Muhammadiyah Studies to Nahdlatul Ulama Studies". Paper presented at the International Research Conference on Muhammadiyah, Malang, Indonesia, 29 November – 2 December 2012.

Picard, Michael, and Remy Madinier. *The Politics of Religion in Indonesia: Syncretism, Orthodoxy, and Religious Contention in Java and Bali*. London: Routledge, 2011.

Ricklefs, Merle. *Jogjakarta under Sultan Mangkubumi, 1749–1792: A History of the Division of Java*. London: Oxford University Press, 1974.

———. *Mystic Synthesis in Java: A History of Islamization from the Fourteenth to the Early Nineteenth Centuries*. White Plains, NY: EastBridge, 2006.

———. *Polarising Javanese Society: Islamic and Other Visions, 1830–1930*. Singapore: NUS Press; Leiden: Koninklijk Instituut voor Taal-, Land- en Volkenkunde, 2007.

———. *Islamisation and Its Opponents in Java: A Political, Social, Cultural and Religious History, c. 1930 to the Present*. Singapore: NUS Press; Hawaii: University of Hawai'i Press, 2012.

Rossa, John. *Pretext for Mass Murder: The September 30th Movement and Suharto's Coup d'État in Indonesia*. Madison: University of Wisconsin Press, 2005.

Roy, Olivier. *The Failure of Political Islam*, translated by Carol Volk. Cambridge, MA: Harvard University Press, 1994.

Suparlan, Parsudi. *The Javanese Suriname: Ethnicity in an Ethnically Plural Society*. Phoenix: Arizona State University, 1995.

Van Dijk, Kees. "The Study of Islam and Adat in Java". In *The Java That Never Was: Academic Theories and Political Practice*, edited by Antov and Hellman, pp 133–56. Münster: LIT Verlag, 2005.

White, Ben. "Java and Social Theory: Agrarian Debate, Past and Present". In *The Java That Never Was: Academic Theories and Political Practice*, edited by Antov and Hellman. Münster: LIT Verlag, 2005.

Woodward, Mark. *Islam in Java: Normative Piety and Mysticism in the Sultanate of Yogyakarta*. Tucson: University of Arizona Press, 1989.

———. *Islam, Java, Indonesia*. London: Springer, 2011.

6

Framing Cambodian Affairs: French and American Scholarship, Media and Geopolitics

Gea D.M. Wijers

The turbulence of internal conflicts, the takeover by the Khmer Rouge (1975–79) and the Vietnamese intervention (1979–89) attracted international media attention to the Kingdom of Cambodia. The United States and France stand out among the nations that became entangled in the geopolitics surrounding Cambodian affairs in these years. Their political perspectives also dominated media debates, referred to here as "mediatizations" because of the non-fact-based nature of these discourses that express a partisan view. The dynamics of the media's "agenda-setting" and "framing" of Cambodian issues have distinct qualities, which will be examined in this chapter (Lippman 1922). These dynamics are understood as the selective influencing of perceptions in the representation of Cambodian issues in the French and American press, thus the mediatization of practices outside of the country.[1] Descriptions, examples and case studies will show how the social construction and evolution of these media frames are related to geopolitical relations and scholarly traditions. The findings contribute to the understanding of how and why the period of the Khmer Rouge is labelled as "genocide" while not actually fitting the conditions that define this category. The labelling as genocide, nevertheless, evolved into a discourse adopted by, among others, the Cambodian Genocide Program at Yale University and has been attached to the international perception of Cambodian society ever since.[2]

A study of the geopolitical dimension of the mediatization of Cambodian affairs is relevant, as few analyses have been conducted on the distinct character of the framing of issues in the decades following the traumatic events of the Khmer Rouge. The dynamics and their relation to geopolitical as well as national trends and traditions have not been studied as an integrated Cambodian history. While both France and the United States have produced their fair share of "leftist", socialist-inspired, and "rightist", conservative-inspired, reporting, they have their basis in different traditions. As documented in, among others, Clymer (2007), Edwards (2007), Gunn and Lee (1991) and Wijers (2013), France's relations can be characterized as founded in a paternalist discourse on Cambodia as a former colony with a rich cultural heritage and a "sweet-natured and innocent" population. In contrast, the United States rather seemed to perceive Cambodia as a pawn in Cold War politics and a supportive neighbour to a former U.S. foe, Vietnam. As this study proposes, these perceptions coloured their scholarly traditions and the formation of public opinion, and, eventually, also contributed to the differences between the friendly reception of Cambodian refugees in France and the cautious refugee resettlement process they entered into in the United States (Masse 1996; Wijers 2013).

The discussion presented here proposes to fill a gap in research on Cambodia as well as acknowledge the awareness that media reporting is not a politically, socially or culturally neutral activity (see, for instance, Luyendijk 2006). Next to Gunn and Lee's *Cambodia Watching Down Under: A Critical View of Western Scholarship and Journalism on Cambodia since 1975* (1991), that directly addresses this subject, most academic publications only bear indirect reference to the ideological convictions that influenced reporting on Cambodian affairs. Since the condemning account in the first written report on the violence accompanying the Khmer Rouge regime in Francois Ponchaud's *Cambodge: Année Zéro* (1977), controversies on events in Cambodia and their interpretation have grown.

Generally, English language media tended to concur with Ponchaud and featured the dramatic anti-communist observations registered by Pilger in his documentary, *Year Zero: The Silent Death of Cambodia* (1979), compared to the more nuanced analysis of Anglophone Cambodia scholars in Australia such as Kiernan (see 1993 and 1996) and Vickery (see 1984). In contrast, and initially declining a public showing of Pilger's documentary, French media chose to represent the pro-communist views of opinion makers like Jean-Paul Sartre, Jacques Attali and Bernard-Henri Lévy (1979). Years later, to the world, it was the movie *The Killing Fields* (Joffe 1985) that brought home the undeniable reality of death and destruction in 1975–79, that was later to be labelled a "genocide".

During the 1970s and 1980s, while geopolitical positions and foci changed, ideologically infused local and international reporting on Cambodian issues continued to force the general audience into ideological stances instead of offering mere fact-based analysis (see, for instance, Brinkley 2011; Mysliwiec 1988). The framing of the Cambodian situation has contributed to the Khmer Rouge takeover being interpreted by an international audience as "exceptional" and "unique". It became a crime without precedent, orchestrated by the "madman" Pol Pot.

The lack of attention to the ways in which distinct elements of Khmer Rouge ideology, such as debates on being a "pure Khmer" (*Khmai daem*; see, for example, Delvert 1961 and Forest 1980), are embedded in Cambodian history have overly simplified the situation. From the singular label of "genocide" and "exceptional circumstances", a negative imago has become associated with Cambodia and Cambodians. For instance, simplifying the situation into cause and consequence, the period of the Khmer Rouge regime is generally perceived to be a genocide that was determined by one "evil" leader, a unique "phenomenon" named Pol Pot (Kiernan 1993). As Cambodia observers have argued, and in contrast to mainstream media reporting, a more appropriate label for the events in these years would be to refer to an "auto-genocide", because rural Cambodians fought the more metropolitan Cambodians, or refer to it as a "civil war", because the Khmer Rouge victims were not distinguishable as ethnic, racial or religious groups (Kiernan 1996; Rechtman 2000). Psychologists treating traumatized Cambodian victims have proposed that, to the Cambodians then and now, the frame we use makes a big difference. As (auto)genocide is considered one of the gravest crimes against humanity, this label inadvertently branded

Cambodians, nationals and refugees, as "criminals" (Rechtman 2000; Van Schaack et al. 2011).

The arguments in this chapter are based on data collected from interviews; relevant academic and non-academic literature; the study of newspapers, journals and other media; as well as archival research in France, the United States and Cambodia. The data represent findings of multisited comparative research conducted in Lyon (France) and Long Beach (California, USA) in 2010 and 2011. This doctoral research inquired into the social adaptation of first-generation Cambodian-French and Cambodian-American refugees.

During fieldwork, 129 semi-structured interviews were conducted with members and leaders of overseas Cambodian associations on topics related to their reception and social adaptation as well as their socialization within migrant communities. The analysis of the information thus collected shows that, in their experience, the geopolitical situation and its framing had profoundly affected the respondents' resettlement. Manifest factors in these dynamics have been explored by the additional study of academic written sources.[3]

The exploration proceeds in the following steps. After an introduction of Cambodian history and society, the French and American scholarly traditions in Asian Studies are discussed. Next, the three phases that can be discerned in the media framing of the Cambodian situation are described and analysed. Finally, bringing these dynamics back to their real-life consequences, the scholarly and media frames adopted in France and the United States are illustrated by the experiences of resettled Cambodians in Lyon and Long Beach.

A History of the Cambodian Conflict

The Khmer Rouge and Post-colonial Cambodia

On 17 April 1975, the Khmer Rouge soldiers completed their civil war by conquering the capital city of Phnom Penh, and with it the whole of Cambodia.[4] This is "Year Zero" of democratic Kampuchea (Ponchaud 1978; Pilger 1979). The Khmer Rouge was a communist movement inspired by Maoism. The aim of the movement was to establish an independent and self-sufficient Cambodia built on agricultural achievements, and they were proud of the country's Khmer identity.

Their nationalist ideology thus followed the Chinese example (Samphan 1959). By social engineering, they wanted to reinstate rice cultivation as the foundation of the economy. The return to an agricultural state was intended to erase the "decadence" of the "Westernized" well-educated and "capitalist" urban elites. Ironically, the rice produced was meant for export and trade with just these Western nations.

Under chairman Pol Pot, "Angkar", the leadership of the Khmer Rouge movement forced those that did not fit their image of the "pure" and humble Cambodian farmer into "re-education". Millions of urbanites were moved into rural labour camps, with little food or comfort. Effectively, for the four years that followed, Cambodia was locked off from the outside world and ruled by a totalitarian regime (Kiernan 2002; Vickery 1984). First-hand information about the nature of the regime and the lives of the Cambodian people was not available to the outside world, except for some arranged visits by sympathizers of the regime and the experiences shared by those who managed to escape. No news came out. Between 1975 and 1979, Cambodia was a black spot on the media monitor. It took years before these "missing years" were retrieved and reinterpreted in the public eye.

Distinctive elements of Khmer Rouge ideology, such as resistance to Western influences, can be traced in Cambodian history. In order to embed the arguments in historical continuity, as opposed to "unique" events, two trends are presented here:

1. In 1953, a seminal moment in Cambodian history, after nine decades of French colonization (1863–1953), the French colonizers gave in to Cambodian public demand and left the country. A number of distinct conditions, however, had to be fulfilled. The most notable of the demands was for the king to no longer be an absolute ruler and for the country to have a democratically elected government, following the French example (Chandler 1993). In post-colonial fashion, however, Prince Norodom Sihanouk distanced himself from the cultural legacy of the French. After the 1955 Bandung Conference, he led Cambodia to become one of the founding members of the Non-Aligned Movement, which was advocating a middle course between the Western and Eastern blocs in the Cold War. In speeches and articles he explained that the Western-

based economic and social models for Cambodia should be exchanged for modern Asian examples (Daravuth and Muan 2001). This can be identified as the first step in the events that would lead to Khmer Rouge ambitions for complete autonomy.

2. Post-colonial independence brought Cambodia into a difficult position in relation to French and American interests in the region. While the Americans were wielding their political influence in the region, France condemned the Vietnam War, did not support military solutions to threats in Southeast Asia, and professed its commitment to national sovereignty. In the turmoil, Cambodia was trying not to become a pawn in the game of American–French rivalry. In general, building on their long historical relationship, contacts and exchanges with France remained intense, with a continued interlacing of institutional frameworks, and Cambodian actions can be characterized as supporting French international relations.[5] These can be considered "preliminary movements" that would find formalization during the Cold War.

It also merits mentioning that post-colonial history describes Cambodian debates on who may be considered a "pure Khmer" and deserves to participate in Cambodian society. These issues can be considered part of an ongoing historical discourse. While the aggression against "Westernized" civilians is often considered a revolutionary component in Khmer Rouge ideology, it could just as well be interpreted as a cultural norm that developed largely under French influence. As researchers have demonstrated, the ways in which the French inspired a portrayal of the Khmer as a superior race added to the cultivation of the picture of Cambodia as the cultural heir to the mythical Angkor empire (Edwards 2007; Straus 2010). Under Sihanouk and in the Khmer Republic (1970–75), this nationalist ideology had already instigated fierce "pogroms" that hurt the Vietnamese and Cham communities. Later, this ideology of being a "pure Khmer" would also affect other social groups living in Cambodia.

Thus, in the post-colonial era, Cambodia was by no means an ethnically homogeneous, tranquil Buddhist nation inhabited solely by the "pure and original Khmer". The ideas of "purity" and the need to return to agricultural traditions would reach their climax under the Khmer Rouge regime. The continuity in this discourse of being a "pure Khmer" is still apparent, as the current Cambodian government professes that the inhabitants of Cambodia are ninety-nine per cent ethnic Khmer, while it is known that a significant number of the country's inhabitants are of Chinese descent (Willmott 1967; for current research on the ethnic Chinese, see Verver 2012).

After the Khmer Rouge

When Khmer Rouge rule ended in 1979, years of communist-inspired Vietnamese rule were to follow. This is a part of Cambodian history that is not widely acknowledged in the Western world. This decade, however, did have a major impact on nationalist perceptions and the Khmer identity (Becker 1998). In 1979 the Vietnamese army invaded Cambodia and took over power from the weakened Khmer Rouge regime. In the years to follow, the Vietnamese regime was not able to eradicate the influence of the Khmer Rouge leaders: neither domestically, in all of the regions of Cambodia, nor in the international community.

The Vietnamese-controlled government of the People's Republic of Kampuchea that was established upon this intervention is often considered a client regime that brought a new brand of communist rule to the country (Gottesman 2003). While the "genocide" under the Khmer Rouge is often perceived as a unique event, the "purity" ideology it is founded on remains a part of Cambodian society.[6]

Meanwhile, on the other side of the planet, perceptions of Maoist Khmer Rouge ideology and the Vietnamese regime seem to have been positively affected by the new wave of political consciousness that ruled the 1970s (Masse 1996). It may be said that the Chinese revolution had inspired communist idealists all over the world, as did the Cuban revolution. While demonstrations against "American imperialism" in Vietnam were held all over Europe and the Americas, uprising was in the air (Bourseiller 1996; Dreyfus-Armand et al. 2000). In the zeitgeist, a carte blanche seemed to be accorded to revolutionary movements that were supported by the media and civil society and that did not want to "play the imperialists' game" (Luken-Roze 2005, p. 99). In parallel to these societal tendencies, by filtering the news on Cambodia, the media were actively setting the agenda for political action (Chan 2004; Gunn and Lee 1991, p. xi).

Cambodian Studies and Cambodian Refugees' Reception in the United States and France

Media reporting in France and the United States may be best interpreted within the framework of each countries' academic contexts as a blueprint for its societal stance. For instance, when it comes to some of the historical perceptions on Cambodia, the mono-ethnic, and fundamentally nationalist, governmental perception of Cambodia as a "pure" Khmer nation was not seriously contested in many post-conflict Anglophone publications on Cambodia (Becker 1998; Freeman 2004; for an exception, see Wilmott 1967). In the Francophone tradition of "Cambodian studies", however, Cambodia is traditionally treated as a distinctly multi-ethnic nation (Forest 1980; Tan 2008). As observed by Edwards in her seminal work *Cambodge* (2007), French Cambodia watchers seem to have accepted that the national debate on being "pure" Khmer and in perfect relation to the Khmer motherland can be considered a political "tool" used by subsequent rulers of Cambodia to legitimize choices in awarding some ethnic groups access to economic opportunities while denying others (Edwards 2007, p. 242).

These distinct differences in perspectives on Cambodian affairs are most easily understood within the framework of French and American historical relations with Cambodia.

As of 1860, the protectorate Cambodge was subject to intense study and ambitions to fulfil the *Mission Civilisatrice* of the French government. Effectively, French archaeologists, art historians, linguists and anthropologists contributed to the dynamics that created a benign patrimonial image of an innocent friendly people with a "Khmer smile" that lived among the remnants of the mythical Angkor kingdom (Edwards 2007). This is a view of Cambodia that is hard to reconcile with the standardized view that Vickery would describe much later.

French interest in Cambodian culture resulted in intense academic exchanges between France and Cambodia (Peycam 2010). In 1908, the first courses in Khmer, the Cambodian language, were organized in the school of foreign languages in Paris. Long before this, however, the Ecole Française d' Extreme-Orient (EFEO) had undertaken extensive studies of Cambodian religion, language, arts and culture. Their *Bulletin* was a main resource for information on the country, as it reported on the latest findings in Khmer studies. The work of early French scholars such as Aymonier, Cœdès, Maspero and Groslier can hardly be overestimated for their contributions to "producing" Cambodian culture and to creating an awareness of its heritage. These researchers mostly focused on culture and customs and religion and the arts (Lamant 1995, p. 15).

In contrast, the majority of scholars in America who became interested in Cambodia only started to focus seriously on the country some forty years ago, after it had become independent and accessible by air. Except for a first account of a visit to the temples of Angkor in 1870 (Vincent 1872), American scholars seemed to have had very little interest in the region (Clymer 2007). The University of Michigan in 1870, followed by Berkeley in the early 1900s, thus remained the only research centres for Cambodian studies for many decades.

However, this situation changed after World War II, with federal funding of area studies centres beginning in the 1950s and the Peace Corps programme started by John F. Kennedy in the 1960s. Currently, centres for the study of Southeast Asia at Cornell (established 1950), the universities of Hawaii and Ohio (1960s), Northern Illinois (1963), Wisconsin (1973) and Washington (1986) are still offering course programmes with Cambodian expertise. Explicitly, these centres were instated with governmental aid to support American military involvement in the region. The 1965 creation of a programme providing national resources to be claimed by the centres for Southeast Asian Studies played an important role in this.[7]

Cambodia was mostly studied by anthropologists and historians in the decades after its decolonization in 1953 (for instance, see Ebihara 1966 and Wilmott 1967). After 1975, the events of the Khmer Rouge drew many newcomers into the study of political issues. In the United States, the Genocide Archives at Yale University in New Haven became a main resource for research on the subject, and thus attracted Cambodia students from around the world.

Even at this time, however, academic reports on Cambodia did not explicitly address the "good" or "bad" of the communist takeovers by the Khmer Rouge and the Vietnamese forces. As David Chandler, an Australian expert still acclaimed to be Cambodia's main historian, reflected upon his own position during these years:

> Why did I, and so many American and Australian scholars take this *attentiste* position? Why were we so slow to condemn the Khmer Rouge? I think the reason we did so is that most of us were bitterly opposed to US and Australian intervention in the region, and in particular to the destruction wrought in Cambodia by the United States. (Chandler, cited in Lamant 1995, p. 219)

Cold War Press Politics and the "Cambodian Genocide"

The First Wave of Reporting on Cambodia (1975–78)

The reception of the work of François Ponchaud may be considered exemplary of some of the differences between France and the United States during the first wave of reporting on Cambodia. In France, Ponchaud published the first widely accepted account of the Khmer Rouge regime, entitled *Cambodge, année zero* (1977). As a French Roman Catholic priest who had lived and worked in Cambodia for many years, Ponchaud based his reports mostly on his own observations and convictions. Building on the testimonials of Cambodian refugees, the book strongly condemns the Khmer Rouge regime and its treatment of distinct groups in Cambodian society. In France, however, within the relatively pro-communist sociocultural context, the publication made little impact. News on Cambodia slowly trickled down to those who were interested, and the events did not lead to a wide outcry among the lay audience or the Cambodian community. Many did not feel convinced of its veracity, and within intellectual circles Ponchaud's reports were even met with some scepticism. For instance, as Thion, a researcher at the French National Centre for Scientific Research, wrote:

> Missionaries in Indochina had been a particular brand of ultra-conservative, rabid anti-communists anyway. Propaganda, as a concept and a word, had been invented by the Church. The ones I had met in the field had given me no reason to trust them. (Serge Thion 1993)

In later years, reports on the Cambodian situation in France seemed not to refer to an international situation, but were presented as a "local" problem. As its former colony, Cambodia and its issues were familiar to the French public. The director of a refugee centre who studied in Lyon at the time mentioned: "For us, we all knew about the camp, Khao I Dang [a Cambodian refugee camp on the Thai border], it was like the village next door" (interview, Lyon, March 2010).

As the region was considered a "stepchild" of the French Empire, it was hard for the French media to articulate their position on the Vietnamese–Cambodian animosities. Illustrative of this national framing of the Cambodian situation was the group of critical left intellectuals surrounding Jean-Paul Sartre and Bernard Henri-Lévy. Starting out as supporters of Vietnam, their changing positions from *pro* to *contra* the Vietnamese invasion of Cambodia produced mixed reactions in public opinion. Even in 1979, Sartre addressed the government on the issue of the "boat people" (referring to all Southeast Asian refugees) but refused to denounce the Vietnam-based communist regime in Cambodia (Meslin 2006).

In 1978 an English translation of *Cambodia Year Zero* (1977) reached an Anglophone audience and prompted debates in American media. In general, lay audiences were still so caught up in the Vietnam War and local communist suspicions that they did not question Ponchaud's harsh stance on the situation. Intellectually, however, Ponchaud was challenged from the United States by, among others, Daniel Burstein of the American Communist Party, as well as by the well-known commentator Noam Chomsky. This is illustrative of the divide in the intellectual debates in the United States. Both authors may be considered marginalized by their position on the political left, yet, individually, they argued their doubts about the veracity of Ponchaud's work quite differently. Chomsky expressed his doubts about the account but did not question that crimes against humanity were actually taking place in Cambodia. His main issue was the lack of factual reporting (Chomsky and Herman 1979). Alternatively, Burstein was prone to deny the accusations against the regime altogether:

> Everyone knows about the war waged by the US in Cambodia from 1970–1975. But very few people know about or understand the war that is waging today against that country.... It is mainly a propaganda war, a consciously organized, well-financed campaign to spread lies and misinformation about Kampuchea since the victory of its revolution in 1975. (Burstein 1978, A21)

As a communist sympathizer, Burstein had been invited to visit Cambodia. He joined what turned out to be a staged tour by the Khmer Rouge regime in order for him to "report" on the "success" of the Cambodian communists. To his advantage in the debate, his arguments were thus based on real-life observations that contested Cambodian refugees' stories and seemed to prove Ponchaud wrong (Burstein 1978). In reality, as became clear much later, he had been witnessing a staged performance by the Khmer Rouge regime aimed at getting some positive press.

Strong ideological polemics between "left" and "right" distinguish the discussion on the Khmer Rouge regime in the United States from that in France. The contestations were most mainstream until 1978, when, as more news came out of Cambodia, gradually, ideological proponents became aware of being manipulated by the Khmer Rouge regime. People in the public eye started to change their perspective. Even after the opening of Cambodia in 1979, however, there was disagreement in the press — on all sides — over the intentions and "success" of the Khmer Rouge regime, on communism as such, and on the true nature of the "genocide" and devastation on the ground (Gunn and Lee 1991).

The Second Wave of Reporting on Cambodia (1979–81)

The Australian scholar Michael Vickery suggests that the Khmer Rouge regime's opponents seem to agree to — as he labels it — a "Standard Total View" (STV) of its actions. He describes the STV as based on the magnification of reports on "atrocities", human suffering and Pol Pot's crimes. As he demonstrates by presenting his own eyewitness accounting, however, in many cases these reports are based on hearsay collected by reporters who do not speak Khmer. In the STV, communist ideology is to blame for the events in Cambodia, and the Khmer Rouge regime is considered an "anomaly of nature" without precedent or links to Cambodian history or society. Cambodian citizens, moreover, are portrayed as hapless political victims who need "rescuing" by the West. Of course, this vicitimization of the "good" against the "bad" communists found warm reception in the United States, especially in the midst of Cold War antagonism. Vickery proposed that the STV put forward by the press should therefore be interpreted as a call to charity and action (Vickery 1984).

Vickery's perception concerning the bias of reporting in these years builds on his own insights and experience in Cambodia and the region since 1960. Another Cambodia expert, Ben Kiernan, joined him in proposing that the "politically correct" seem united in condemning the Khmer Rouge's acts and in simplifying the background to its actions. Together, Vickery and Kiernan agree that reporting on Cambodia affairs turned into a political cliché and propaganda was carelessly mixed with facts (Kiernan 1993).

In the East and West, in practice, the situation in Cambodia raised some difficult questions of solidarity. Questions that demanded answers in France, but also in the United States, included the following:

- How can we come to terms with the Cambodian accusations of aggression and takeover by Vietnam? This was problematic, as Vietnam's position was defended by many left-wing activists that campaigned against the "imperialist tendencies" of the United States.
- How do we come to terms with groups of people (not the whole nation) who claim to be seriously harmed and oppressed by a communist regime? This was problematic, as communism at the time was still perceived as the path to "liberation of the poor".

The entanglement of ideological theory, the Cold War discourse, and the sparse images and eyewitness accounts that appeared in the press resulted in a lot of debate on the veracity and the "right" and "wrong" of a situation about which relatively little was known. It does not require much imagination to conclude that it must have seemed more opportune to focus on the uniqueness of a Cambodian "genocide" than to untangle the webs of history, tradition and cultural continuity that may have led to these events.

The Third Wave of Cambodia Reporting (1981–89)

The Vietnamese again locked Cambodia off from the international community. A short period of openness in 1979 and 1980, however, contributed to renewed speculation and controversies in the foreign press. Still, few people were aware of what actually happened in the People's Republic of Kampuchea, as reporters were rarely allowed into the country by the Vietnamese regime. In hindsight we can see that this limited number of eyewitness reports, moreover, was not "heard" by the mainstream in many countries. Keeping things simple, opinion leaders and the general media aligned along Cold War divisions, and would not hear of dissenting opinions from the STV.

Based on their research on the Australian media, Gunn and Lee propose that talking about the "Cambodia problem" evolved from the Vietnamese Intervention in 1979 (Gunn and Lee 1991, p. 176). At the time, the "Cambodia problem" started to refer to the question of which party could bring post-conflict stability to Cambodian society. Most of the informants in my research in France and the United States confirm, indeed, that the "Cambodia problem" forced the media into more nuanced positions. This represented a change of attitude that also affected the treatment of the Cambodian refugees in resettlement. This was a short-lived openness, after which information on Cambodia became scarce again. With a renewed closing of the country, ambiguities based on ideological orientations continued.

The effects of isolation from the mainstream are confirmed in an overview of those who published the most widespread and well-read reports on Cambodia.

John Pilger already opened the world's eyes with his filmed documentary *Year Zero* (1979). It was a direct report from Phnom Penh that showed the city's devastation. Notably, the reason Pilger was allowed into the country by the Vietnamese regime at the time was his known sympathy for the communist cause. Building on their ideological sympathies, in this way, aid workers, documentary journalists and media personalities with a pro-poor political agenda all contributed to the perception of current affairs in Cambodia and their relation to international politics. Among others, from the refugee camps in Thailand, Eva Myscliewic, director of an aid organization, published *Punishing the Poor: The International Isolation of Kampuchea* (1988), which left no doubt as to her thoughts on American interference and contains a sharp condemnation of the West's policies (Lamant 1995).

Experiences of Resettling Cambodians

The indirect effects of the bias in media reporting during these three waves were most felt by Cambodian refugees in resettlement.

The media's engagement and solidarity with the Vietnamese as victims of American imperialism clearly affected the attitudes the Cambodians encountered in their resettlement in France (Wijers 2011). Pierre Bayard even speaks of "a collective denial" when it comes to the way the French press wrote about the Khmer Rouge regime (Bayard and Phay-Vakalis 2013). Even after the "liberation" of Cambodia by the Vietnamese, many of Vietnam's defenders refused to acknowledge the unlawful takeover of Cambodia. These pro-Vietnamese convictions were not without consequences, and sometimes resulted in negative actions. For instance, as one of my respondents shared, in cities governed by more "leftist" city councils it would be harder to find housing. This was no coincidence, and reflected the idea that "People who flee the Vietnamese Communists cannot be good people" (interview, community leader, Lyon, April 2010).

Ida Simon-Barouh writes in Solier and Fenet (1984, p. 166) about the French government not wanting to "expose" the Southeast Asian refugees and, instead, practising a "politics of indifference" aimed at their complete assimilation into French society. As there are no French statistics on the education levels, labour markets and social progress achieved by the Cambodian resettlers, unfortunately, proof of the effectiveness of this approach will remain anecdotal.

Also, in line with this "strategy of neglect", Cambodian cultural associations are not funded and healthcare for traumatized Cambodians is not readily made available. In public perception, thus, the Cambodians who had come to France after 1975 were living a life "in the shadows" of French society (Prak 1992). Media-reporting, colonial institutions and government policies thus affected their lives in resettlement.

A different integration process awaited the Cambodians in resettlement in the United States. The United States is often perceived as an "immigrant nation"; its foundation is the diversity of immigrants, religions and cultures that have taken up the challenge to leave their home countries behind and realize their "American Dream". For refugees, however, entering and resettling in the United States is a different matter. Refugees escaping conflict and violence have not chosen to leave their home country and, often, do not mean to spend the rest of their lives in the United States. In this way, the Cambodian refugees have depended on the support structures accompanying their refugee status to help them find their way in a new life. In contrast to the situation in France, however, very few strong Cambodian communities existed in the United States prior to 1980 that could help the newly arrived Cambodians in resettlement (Wijers 2013). To illustrate the atmosphere, here is the reception that a Cambodian widow who arrived in Chicago in 1981 described:

> In the culture class, we were taught that American people didn't like the smell of most Asian food. So we had to be careful not to cook food that had a stinky smell, like pickled fish.... Being aware that our culture was so different from American culture, it made us fear what we would confront when we came to live in America. (Seng 2005, p. 243)

While the new American Cambodians were made aware that their presence may be a "burden" to the locals at a very early stage, they were also warned not to try to behave just like "home" in the longer term. A sense of exclusion and seclusion of individual Cambodians and even those gathered in Cambodian communities evolved. This sense of exclusion is still affecting the Cambodian community. In Long Beach's Cambodia Town, known as the largest Cambodian community outside of Cambodia, Sothy, a teacher (51) tells me:

Often people say that Cambodians are dumb. A lot of Cambodian
people when you ask them where they are from, they say they are
Chinese. They are ashamed. The Cambodians themselves! They don't
want to be Cambodian. The kids also, they say: "All things about
Cambodia are bad". (Interview, Long Beach, February 2011)

In line with the treatment they received, some resettled Cambodians
developed the same "strategy of ignorance and abandon" towards
American society. Still, many of them do not speak the language and/or
have not acquired citizenship. These Cambodians lead a marginalized
existence in the United States (Chau-Pech Ollier 2006). The stigma
created by media representations such as *The Killing Fields* has had an
enduring effect on their American existence. Indirectly, the perception
of Cambodians as victims of genocide was founded in the 1950s,
when the academic climate that brought forth Asian (and Cambodian)
Studies evolved. A discourse on the Cambodian genocide was instigated
by the United States' political ambitions and the need to mobilize
knowledge in order to better "divide-and-rule" in the region. In later
years, the "genocide" provided fuel to Cold War propaganda that
also suited Western forces, yet left its marks on Cambodians all over
the world.

Conclusion

Exploring the ways in which the dynamics of geopolitics helped frame
media reporting on the Cambodian situation in the 1970s and 1980s
and interacted with historical relations and scholarship traditions
in France and the United States, this chapter has illustrated how
these social constructions contributed to perceptions of the Cambodian
"genocide" as well as influenced the resettlement of Cambodian
refugees.

In line with Tirtosudarmo's arguments in chapter 5 of this volume,
this chapter on geopolitics, media influence and scholarly traditions
in France and the United States has provided additional evidence that
the subjects that are compiled into Asian Studies are not established
in a neutral process, but are affected by temporal variations in
internal and external political constellations and public opinion. This is
illustrated by the descriptions of the ways in which the simplified

frames on "genocide" have affected the reception of Cambodian refugees in both countries. Within each zeitgeist, media reporting and scholarly traditions contributed to the population expressing a relative sympathy with the fate of the refugees in Lyon, but could not help lift the Cambodians above being the "minority among minorities" in Long Beach. Also, the negative association with the Killing Fields and the "genocide" that seems ingrained in the STV on the Khmer Rouge takeover has marked mainstream reporting by American media. It is at the root of most academic attention initiated by the United States on Cambodia, and thus may have contributed to the "inferiority complexes" of resettling Cambodians.

Thus, to this day, Cambodia's image abroad tends to revolve around the tragic events that occurred between 1975 and 1979. That is why it is important to create awareness of the true complexity of the events and their relation to geopolitical dynamics. The stereotyped nature of current debates on genocide suggests that the simplified portrayal of Cambodian genocide continues to affect more recent perceptions of conflict, such as the massacres in Rwanda (1994) and the war in Bosnia (1992–96), by offering material of one-dimensional comparison. I want to propose that, following Arendt (1958), more accurate interpretations should acknowledge the banality of the evil that we refer to as "genocide". Among others, she argues that ideological, ethnic or racially inspired killings should be interpreted as recurring events that build on existing institutions and societal tendencies, far less "unique" than mainstream interpretations would have us believe (Kissi 2006; Newbury 1998; Straus 2010). Moreover, acknowledging the complexity of the events leading to a genocidal situation could play a role in facilitating processes of reconciliation among societal groups, which is so needed in post-conflict situations.

These issues related to media and perceptions have long gone under-researched, especially in the Cambodian context. They clearly merit further research to gain insight into a more complete list of consequences of geopolitics as related to frames used in academic and media reporting. For instance, the ongoing Khmer Rouge tribunal, instigated by the international community, aims to bring justice to Cambodia. As Kiernan (2007) and Sellars (2015) describe, these trials should also certainly be assessed in the light of geopolitical power relations. By steering clear of government rhetoric and the interests of donors and Western NGOs and, instead, embedding events within Cambodian history and tradition, the tribunal might provide both justice and public perceptions more reflective of real events.

Acknowledgements

The author gratefully acknowledges the support of the NWO-WOTRO Science for Development organization through the Cambodia Research Group, as well as the support of the Graduate School of the Faculty of Social Sciences at the VU University Amsterdam in preparing this chapter.

Notes

1. The press is here understood to include unique as well as daily, weekly and monthly reports in written and broadcast news media, for both lay and specialized audiences.
2. Parallel to World War II in Europe, labeling the Cambodian events a "genocide" — meaning the "intent to destroy, in whole or in part, a national, ethnical, racial or religious group" (United Nations 1948) — has determined the way the Khmer Rouge takeover and its aftermath have gone down in public history.
3. The comparison in this chapter, however, is not meant to bring forward an exhaustive enumeration of the structural and ideological differences between French and American press reporting, their institutional structures or scholastic traditions. It does not have the ambition to categorize opinions or developments as determined by geographic, cultural and/or historic characteristics. The basic assumption is that the comparison of information may provide important insights into the impact of geopolitical dynamics, scholastic traditions and historical relations on what are often considered "neutral" media reports, and thus on the general audiences' perceptions of Cambodia.
4. The Khmer Rouge was established in 1968 as an offshoot of the Vietnam People's Army from North Vietnam. Cambodian nationals consider Khmer to refer to both their ethnicity and their language. Much of Khmer identity is derived from the Khmer Empire and the monumental grounds of Angkor Wat that laid the foundations for current Cambodia. In this chapter, "Khmer" and "Cambodian" are used interchangeably and alternately to describe the people and the language.

5 Until 1970 and the coup that "dethroned" Sihanouk and started the U.S.-oriented Khmer Republic (1970–75) under Lon Nol.

6. This study has chosen to limit its time-period to the moment that the Vietnamese left the country in 1989. It is important to note, however, that, establishing a formal peace, in October 1991, the Paris Peace Accords were signed by all Cambodian factions. In 1992 the United Nations Transitional Authority in Cambodia (UNTAC) forces arrived to assist the provisional government in the implementation of these accords and to make sure that democratic elections took place. Cambodia was now officially a "country in transition" (Becker 1998; Gottesman 2003).

7. See also the discussion on Geertz in Indonesia in chapter 5 of this volume.

References

Arendt, Hannah. *The Human Condition*. Chicago: University of Chicago Press, 1958.

Attali, Jacques, and Bernard-Henri Lévy. "Réponse a Noam Chomsky. Et Timor, et le Cambodge". *Le Matin de Paris*, 17 December 1979.

Bayard, Pierre, and Soko Phay-Vakalis, eds. *Cambodge, le génocide effacée*. Paris: Cecile Defaut, 2013.

Becker, Elizabeth. *When the War Was Over: Cambodia and the Khmer Rouge Revolution*. New York: Simon and Schuster, 1998.

Brinkley, Joel. *Cambodia's Curse: The Modern History of a Troubled Land*. New York: Public Affairs, 2011.

Burstein, Daniel. "On Cambodia: But, Yet". *New York Times*, 21 November 1978, A21.

Chan, Sucheng. *Survivors. Cambodian Refugees in the United States*. Illinois: University of Illinois Press, 2004.

Chau-Pech Ollier, Leakthina, and Timothy Winter, eds. *Expressions of Cambodia*. London: Routledge, 2012.

Chomsky, Noam, and Edward S. Herman. *After the Cataclysm: Postwar Indochina and the Reconstruction of Imperial Ideology: The Political Economy of Human Rights*, vol. 2. Boston: Southend Press, 1979.

Clymer, Kenton. *Troubled Relations: The United States and Cambodia since 1870*. Chicago: Northern Illinois University Press, 2007.

Daravuth, Ly, and Ingrid Muan. *Cultures of Independence: An Introduction to Cambodian Arts and Culture in the 1950s*. Phnom Penh: The Prince Claus Fund and Reyum Publishing, 2001.

Delvert, Jean. *Le paysan cambodgien*. Paris: Mouton, 1961.

Ebihara, May. "Interrelations between Buddhism and Social Systems in Cambodian Peasant Culture". In *Anthropological Studies in Theravada Buddhism*, edited by Nash Manning. New Haven: Yale University, 1966.

Edwards, Penny. *Cambodge: The Cultivation of a Nation, 1860–1945*. Honolulu: University of Hawai'i Press, 2007.

Forest, Alain. *Le Cambodge et la colonisation Française. Histoire d "une colonisation sans heurts (1896–1920)*. Paris: L'Harmattan, 1980.

Freeman, Michael. *Cambodia*. London: Reaktion Books, 2004.

Gottesman, Evan. *Cambodia after the Khmer Rouge: Inside the Politics of Nation Building*. New Haven: Yale University Press, 2003.

Gunn, Geoffrey C., and Jefferson Lee. *Cambodia Watching Down Under: A Critical View of Western Scholarship and Journalism on Cambodia since 1975*. Bangkok: Institute of Asian Studies, Chulalongkorn University, 1991.

Joffe, Roland. *The Killing Fields*. Movie. Los Angeles: Warner Brothers, 1985.

Kiernan, Ben. *The Pol Pot Regime: Race, Power and Genocide in Cambodia under the Khmer Rouge 1975–1979*, 2nd ed. New Haven: Yale University Press, 2002.

———. *Genocide and Resistance in Southeast Asia: Documentation, Denial and Justice in Cambodia and East Timor*. New Brunswick: Transaction, 2007.

———. *Genocide and Democracy in Cambodia: The Khmer Rouge, the United Nations and the International Community*. New Haven: Yale University Press, 1993.

Kissi, Edward. "Rwanda, Ethiopia and Cambodia: Links, Faultlines and Complexities in a Comparative Study of Genocide". *Journal of Genocide Research* 6, no. 1 (2006): 115–33.

Lamant, Pierre L., ed. *Bilan et Perspectives des Etudes Khmères (Langue et Culture)*. Paris: L'Harmattan, 1995.

Lippmann, Walter. *Public Opinion*. New York: Harcourt, Brace, 1922.

Luken-Roze, Dominique. *Cambodge: Vers de nouvelles tragédies? Actualité du génocide*. Paris: L'Harmattan, 2005.

Luyendijk, Joris. *Het zijn net mensen*. Amsterdam: Podium, 2006.

Masse, Jean-Pierre. "L'exception indochinoise: Le dispositif d'accueil des refugies politiques en France 1973–1991". Phd dissertation, EHESS, Paris, 1996.

Meslin, Karine. "Accueil des boat people: une mobilization atypique". *Plein Droit* 70 (2006): 36–39.

Mysliwiec, Eva. *Punishing the Poor: The International Isolation of Kampuchea*. Oxford: Oxfam, 1988.

Newbury, David. "Understanding Genocide". *African Studies Review* 41, no. 1 (1998): 73–97.

Peang-Meth, Abdulgaffar. *Cambodia and the United Nations: Comparative Foreign Policies under Four Regimes*. PhD dissertation, University of Michigan, 1980.

Peycam, Philippe M.F. "Sketching an Institutional History of Academic Knowledge Production in Cambodia (1863–2009). *SOJOURN: Journal of Social Issues in Southeast Asia* 25, no. 2 (2010): 153–77.

Pilger, John. *Year Zero: The Silent Death of Cambodia*. 1979 <http://johnpilger.com/videos/year-zero-the-silent-death-of-cambodia> (accessed 8 July 2012).

Ponchaud, Francois. *Cambodia: Year Zero/Cambodge: Annee Zero.* Harmondsworth: Penguin Books, 1977.

Prak, Vath. "La Communauté Khmère dans l "ombre. Les difficultés rencontrées par les Refugiés Cambodgiens pour leur installation en France". Thesis, Université Lyon: Institut de Formation aux Pratiques Psychologiques, Sociologiques et Educatives, 1992.

Rechtman, Richard. "Altérité suspecte et identité coupable dans la diaspora Cambodgienne". In *La Haine de Soi. Difficiles identités*, edited by Eduard Benbassa and Jean C. Attias. Brussels: Complexe, 2000.

Samphan, Khieu. *The Economy of Cambodia and its Problems with Industrialization.* Phd dissertation, University of Paris, 1959.

Sellars, Kirsten, ed. *Trials for International Crimes in Asia.* Cambridge: Cambridge University Press, 2015.

Seng, Vatey. *The Price We Paid: A Life Experience in the Khmer Rouge Regime.* London: IUniverse Books, 2005.

Sihanouk, Norodom. *Chroniques de guerre et d'espoir.* Paris: Hachette, 1979.

Solier, Gerard, and Alain Fenet, eds. *La France au Pluriel?* Paris: L'Harmattan, 1984.

Straus, Scott. "Organic Purity and the Role of Anthropology in Cambodia and Rwanda". *Patterns of Prejudice* 35, no. 2 (2010): 47–62.

Tan, Danielle. *La diaspora chinoise du Cambodge. Histoire d'une identité recomposé.* Paris: Institut d'Etudes Politiques de Paris, 2006.

Thion, Serge. *Watching Cambodia.* Bangkok: White Lotus, 1993.

United Nations. "Convention on the Prevention and Punishment of Genocide". 1948 <http://untreaty.un.org/cod/avl/ha/cppcg/cppcg.html> (accessed 17 September 2013).

Van Schaack, Beth, Daryn Reicherter, and Youk Chhang, eds. *Cambodia's Hidden Scars: Trauma Psychology in the Wake of the Khmer Rouge.* Phnom Penh: Documentation Center of Cambodia, 2011.

Verver, Michiel. "Templates of 'Chineseness' and Trajectories of Cambodian Chinese Entrepreneurship in Phnom Penh". *Cross Currents: East Asian History and Culture Review*, no. 4 (2012) <http://cross-currents.berkeley.edu/e-journal/issue-4> (accessed 19 December 2012).

Vickery, Michael. *Cambodia, 1975–1982.* Sydney: Allen & Unwin, 1984.

Vincent, Frank. *The Land of the White Elephant.* London: Kessinger, [1872] 2004.

Wijers, Gea. "Reception of Cambodian Refugees in France". *Journal of Refugee Studies* 24, no. 2 (2011): 239–55.

———. *Navigating a River by its Bends: A Comparison of Cambodian Returnees' Contributions to the Transformation of Cambodia.* Amsterdam: VU University Press, 2013.

Willmott, William E. *The Chinese in Cambodia.* Vancouver: University of British Columbia, 1967.

7

Studying Taiwan: The Politics of Area Studies in the United States and Europe

Hardina Ohlendorf

Taiwan Studies is a relatively new field of research which challenges the conventional model of area studies. Taiwan Studies started off as an emancipatory project in Taiwan itself and has since spread to the regional and global sphere. The notion of Taiwan that is constructed through academic discourse remains a contested subject and is influenced by power configurations.

Taiwan Studies as a new field of academic research has evolved at a time when area studies in general have experienced a serious crisis of legitimacy. They have been challenged due to their roots in the colonialist tradition, their frequent political complicity with U.S. policy during the Cold War and a growing awareness of the contingency of boundary drawing and calls for more universalist knowledge in the age of globalization (Palat 2000).

Contrary to this trend, Taiwan Studies has emerged as a new academic field in the United States and Europe very recently, since the late 1980s, and has expanded since then. It differs from traditional area studies, which were often set up by hegemonic powers seeking to gain knowledge and control over their colonial territories or partitioning the world into regions according to the geopolitical settings of the Cold War. It could be argued that the debate on area studies has had limited impact. The revival of area studies in the United States with regard to the Middle East, the Arab region and Central Asia demonstrates how acute security concerns make specialized regional expertise appear immediately relevant again. The contested claim of sovereignty over Taiwan creates a potential security risk in East Asia, which could spread to the United States as Taiwan's key ally. While the status quo is already built on weak foundations — essentially the fiction that the Chinese Civil War has never ended — recent developments in Taiwan have complicated the situation even more. A growing sense of Taiwan identity on the island has gradually undermined the one-China principle upon which the alleged stability of the status quo rests. It is therefore not surprising that Taiwan's domestic developments have received particular attention from outside it.

This, however, does not explain why Taiwan has been taken out of the larger context of China Studies and developed as a distinct field. Converging perspectives on Taiwan as a distinct region cannot easily be explained by hegemonic power interests. Internationally, Taiwan's status is highly contested, and few countries are willing to acknowledge political autonomy for the island as a separate entity. Its relatively strong economy and liberal democracy notwithstanding, the country has become increasingly marginalized in terms of diplomatic recognition.

In contrast to other area studies, the institutionalized academic study of Taiwan as a distinct region has primarily been locally driven, in a bottom-up fashion, with academics challenging the prevalent perspective on Taiwan as being part of and congruent with China. The motivation to study Taiwan separately from China can be linked to a shifting national identity and rising Taiwanese nationalism on the island, in which the study of the local and the consciousness of being Taiwanese rather than Chinese have been mutually reinforced. From the very start, Taiwan Studies has been a contested subject, since any study of Taiwan implies to various extents certain recognition of autonomy for that region (Harrison 2006). The study of local cultures, languages or histories can be found in other nationalizing contexts; for instance, in the Gaelic Revival movement in the late nineteenth century in Ireland

and the establishment of Celtic Studies. However, whereas most of these studies of local culture have been confined to the local sphere or the diasporas, the field of Taiwan Studies has quickly expanded over various geographical scales.

There are numerous works tracing the development of area studies and analysing its crisis. Criticism of area studies based scholarship has come from various parties. Firstly, the changed geopolitical settings in the 1990s triggered a critical re-evaluation of research during the Cold War and the complicity with government interest of academia in general (Diamond 1992; Winks 1996) and of area studies in particular (Wallerstein 1997). While some authors have considered the fact that area studies have also produced some of the most outspoken critics of their governments, referring, for example, to the Committee of Concerned Asian Scholars' challenge to the U.S. government over its policy in Asia (Madsen 1995, pp. 53–55), critics have charged that the project of area studies had primarily been constructed to further the strategic interests of the United States, making it intellectually as well as morally suspect (Cumings 1999).

A second line of criticism concerns the epistemological foundations of area studies. The resort to sovereign states as the basic building blocks of area studies has been linked to the particular historical circumstances of decolonization which witnessed increasing numbers of new nation-states. The role of those nation-states as basic units of analysis has been questioned on the grounds that those states were often the relatively recent product of European imperialism and contained within their boundaries starkly differing social, economic and cultural forms (Kelly and Kaplan 2001).

The recognition of globalization as a central historical process after the end of the Cold War (Appadurai 1996) and its utilization as a theoretical basis for efforts to reorganize knowledge (Resnik 2008) has invoked a debate on whether the imagined convergence of social, political and cultural formations of places has reduced the importance of trying to understand regional particularities, and in that sense made traditional area study scholarship appear parochial and outdated (Kratoska, Nordholt and Raben 2005; Burgess 2004). As a result, suggestions have been made to reconfigure area studies into studies with more cross-regional (Kurzman 2007), cross-cultural elements (Dirlik 2010).

The opposition of disciplinary studies towards area study scholarship on the basis that such research is not sufficiently grounded in universal theory has again been challenged as an implicitly hegemonic model of knowledge production. Scholars have pointed out that theoretical concepts taught in Western universities are by and large produced in the West, and that there is not much problematizing of their historical basis and core (Szanton 2004). The critical assessment of the epistemological foundations of Western scholarship reaches further back and situates the origins of area studies in a colonial setting in which hegemonic powers constructed knowledge on dominated spaces and embedded research on areas in Eurocentric concepts of a "universal human history", with its master narratives of capitalism, industrialization, nationalism and modernization. As Pheng Cheah has argued, the areas under scrutiny, the objects of area studies, were exactly "that which is not universal.... Or, an area is precisely that which is not capable of universality" (Cheah 2008, p. 58).

At the same time, there is a different perspective, which sees the production of knowledge on localities not necessarily as a process marked by hegemonic power politics but which suggests local knowledge as one of the bases from which to challenge single overarching theories. Theories of post-colonialism, postmodernism and subalternity have emphasized the study of local particularity as a way both to critically assess mainstream ideas in the social sciences that are generally regarded as unproblematic and to generate alternative concepts and theories (Alatas 2006).

Among the different perspectives on the production of local knowledge, there seem to be two major tendencies. The first regards knowledge production as a means of domination, imposed by a hegemonic power, often exogenous to the place investigated. This entails a view of area studies in the long tradition of orientalism, and, more recently, hegemonic power interests during the Cold War. Characteristically, this approach concentrates on the external production of knowledge and perspectives on the place from outside. The second perspective perceives emancipatory potential in the production of local knowledge, where indigenous knowledge can jeopardize dominant concepts and discourses and create a sense of identity and autonomy from below vis-à-vis either an external hegemon or a ruling domestic elite. This view focuses very much on the domestic arena or the diaspora and internal identity politics.

Taiwan Studies is difficult to locate in such a framework. Taiwan Studies has quickly expanded over various geographical scales. It has thus started to resemble a classical area study, with different research institutions in Taiwan, China, Japan, Europe, Australia and the United States all producing knowledge on an area: "Taiwan". However, the prevalent dynamics at work are not those usually effective in classical area studies. To make this point clearer it will be helpful to distinguish between impulse and effect. Effectively, academic discourse on Taiwan does indeed "produce" or reify a region, Taiwan. In that sense, exogenous "hegemonic" powers construct Taiwan as a coherent region through knowledge production in their various Taiwan Studies institutions. However, the impulse and motivation for this process stem from the local. The construction of Taiwan through academic discourse is essentially an emancipatory project that departs from the One-China principle dominating political discourse outside as well as partly inside Taiwan. There are certainly different motivations underlying the field of Taiwan studies, and emancipatory politics and hegemonic interests interlink, depending on the position of the actors involved.

In this chapter, I discuss Taiwan Studies in the United States and Europe as case studies to demonstrate that the development and construction of Taiwan Studies has not been monolithic and dependent on political, social and historical contexts. I then offer some suggestions on how to position Taiwan Studies in the general discussion of area studies and knowledge production.

My own interest in this subject started when I witnessed the expansion of a small Taiwan Studies programme in London into a full Centre of Taiwan Studies. I write from my perspective as a former student and later staff member of the centre.

Taiwan Studies in the United States

The United States has been in a very close and complex relationship with Taiwan, which has had an impact on the way Taiwan Studies evolved as a field. Systematic knowledge production on Taiwan has a long tradition in the United States. However, the model under which the island has been studied has changed with the political circumstances. The outbreak of the Korean War and fear of expanding communism in Asia made the United States a key ally of the exile Republic of China (ROC) government in Taiwan. Subsequently, the Kuomintang (KMT) government of the ROC received vast U.S. aid and support in its standoff with the communist rival regime on the mainland.

The KMT on Taiwan had a vital interest in portraying the Republic of China as the legitimate China where traditional Chinese culture was continued and preserved. Archives played a key symbolic role in this regard. Most famously, this has been exemplified by the National Palace Museum, which was built to house the most important collection of Chinese artefacts worldwide, a collection that was moved from mainland China to the island by the KMT in 1948 and 1949. Scholars responded to such material incentives to study traditional China on Taiwan, thus fostering the implicit link between the Chinese past and the island through their scholarship (see, for instance, Susan Naquin's [1976] work on millenarian movements in China). In the 1960s, changes in the international setting significantly influenced Taiwan's appeal as a site for research. During the Cultural Revolution, the People's Republic of China closed its doors to the West, thus leaving scholars without access to the mainland for their field research. Anthropologists especially turned to Taiwan as a surrogate, which was seen as a rich and open site of Chinese culture and society. One example is Emily Ahern, who published her book *The Cult of the Dead in a Chinese Village* in 1973 with Stanford University Press. Under the bipolar setting of the Cold War, the academic field was also shaped by an ideological interest in the existence of a non-communist and prosperous Chinese polity. Depicted as the "Free China" versus "Red China", Taiwan fulfilled an important role in this aspect. Early social science studies of Taiwan focussed on the island's economic development without further elaborating on the political context (see, for instance, E. Stuart Kirby's *Rural Progress on Taiwan* [1960] and Neil H. Jacoby's *US Aid to Taiwan* [1966]). The political circumstances of the White Terror under Chiang Kai-shek's regime were largely ignored in scholarly writings on Taiwan (George H. Kerr's book,

Formosa Betrayed [1965], gives a detailed account of the so-called 2-28 Incident, an anti-government protest which resulted in the killings of numerous civilians by the KMT regime, but his work is an exceptional case).

While the Cold War environment influenced conceptual models for the study of Taiwan, such as a perspective on Taiwan as a site of archives, as a surrogate for China, and as a development model, it also created institutional mechanisms for the systematic production of knowledge on Taiwan. The Stanford Center for Chinese language acquisition and the Fulbright Foundation's exchange programme between the United States and Taiwan allowed young American scholars to spend time on the island for Mandarin studies or research projects. The Inter-University Program for Chinese Language Studies, better known as the Stanford Center, was set up in 1963 in Taipei to provide students, mainly from the United States, with Mandarin training. It became the most important overseas language institute for students of Chinese. Its students predominantly came from the ten sponsoring schools: Columbia, Cornell, Harvard, Princeton, Yale, Stanford, the University of California–Berkeley, the University of Chicago, the University of Michigan, and the University of Washington (Taipei CCAS 1975). Thus, virtually every student of Chinese language from a prestigious university in the United States went through the Stanford Program, which created a pool of promising students who could potentially become interested in Taiwan in their research.

On the research level, the Fulbright Program started in 1946 as an initiative to promote international exchange and understanding in the aftermath of World War II. Its Chinese branch in Nanjing was temporarily suspended during the Chinese Civil War and later reopened on Taiwan in 1957, reflecting the new alliance between the United States and the Republic of China. In Taiwan, the programme operated under the name, "US Educational Foundation in the Republic of China" (Fulbright Taiwan n.d.).

The Sino–American rapprochement in the 1970s radically changed the situation for Taiwan. As the PRC started to open up to the West, the island lost its exclusivity as a site for field research in Chinese Studies. The new U.S. foreign policy also put Taiwan's political status into a new context. The recognition of China as a great power meant that Henry Kissinger and Richard Nixon had to treat seriously Beijing's claims of sovereignty and territorial integrity regarding Taiwan. The strengthening ties between the PRC and the United States had immediate effects on the academic field. The prestige associated with the pioneer visits to China strengthened the contemporary China Studies field in the public perception. Apart from the media attention, the renewal of political contact between China and the United States gave scholars in the academic field of China Studies a rare chance to convert their cultural capital into economic and political capital as consultants to the government and major corporations (Madsen 1987, p. 200). The opening of the PRC to foreign students and scholars for study and research visits led to a wave of academics going to China. Resumed and newly opened funding and exchange programmes further strengthened the position of the mainland as a destination for field research. Institutions such as the National Program of the Committee on Scholarly Communication with the People's Republic of China and the Fulbright Program provided institutional frameworks for regular academic exchange with the PRC (Lampton, Madancy and Williams 1986, p. 54).

As the general trend in Chinese Studies shifted to research on the PRC, and as the choice of Taiwan became controversial politically, Taiwan scholars were confronted with the necessity to develop legitimizing strategies for their particular research interest in the island. Academics researching Taiwan started to reflect on the relationship between the island and the mainland in their research. Through the process of considering the relationship between the two sides of the Taiwan Strait epistemologically, rather than just taking the island as a miniature version of the mainland, small Taiwan Studies circles emerged that elaborated on Taiwan as a distinct subject of research (see, for instance, Ronald G. Knapp's article, "The Geographer and Taiwan", which was published in 1978 in the *China Quarterly*). At the same time, more critical perspectives on the KMT regime were published. For instance, Thomas Gold's seminal book, *State and Society in the Taiwan Miracle*, stressed the importance of the 2–28 Incident for the development of Taiwanese society at a time when the event was still treated as taboo by the KMT government (Gold 1986). The 2–28 Incident refers to an uprising by the local Taiwanese population on 28 February 1947 which was crushed in a massacre by the KMT troops.

However, there is another dimension to the formation of academic Taiwan Studies, and this is related to American post-war strategic thinking. While the United States officially abandoned the KMT as the official representative government of China, it stayed committed to Taiwan's security as expressed in the Taiwan-Relations Act of 1979. Taiwan's strategic importance for U.S. security interests in the Asia-Pacific guaranteed continued interest in developments on the island. Yet, at the same time, Taiwan also mattered as a case study to support U.S. hegemony. Taiwan demonstrated the benefits of U.S. leadership after World War II. The island had benefited enormously from U.S. aid and the openness of the U.S. market for Taiwanese exports. The country's comparatively smooth transition to a democracy seemed to complete the success of the American model and provided a strong counter-example to the theory of "Asian Values" and the alleged incompatibility of democracy and East Asian societies (Wong 2010).

Yet, it was not only U.S. interest in Taiwan as a showcase model that fuelled the expansion of Taiwan-related research. It was also the financial support for such projects by the Taiwanese government. The isolated ROC government tried to bolster its legitimacy by drawing attention to its domestic achievements. The democratic transition played a key role in this regard, as it contrasted starkly with the developments in the People's Republic of China. In 1989, the year of the Tiananmen Massacre in Beijing, the government in Taiwan invited numerous U.S. political scientists as observers to the Taiwanese election.[1]

However, Taiwan's political transformation has had ambiguous implications for the KMT government, as well as for observers in the United States. On the one hand, democratization could complete the perspective on Taiwan as a model of success and an alternative to the communist version of China. In this context it seems not surprising that one of the first programmes of Taiwan Studies supported by the KMT government was set up at the Walker Institute at the University of South Carolina. It is named after Richard L. Walker, a former U.S. ambassador and scholar known for his anti-communist stance and support for the Republic of China (see, for instance, Richard L Walker, "Taiwan's Development as Free China", 1959).

On the other hand, Taiwan's political change confronted observers with the problems linked to Taiwan's representation as the Republic of China. As Taiwan's democratic reforms were tied up with the increasing visibility of Taiwanese nationalism on the island, they constituted a challenge to the one-China principle and, thus, the status quo in the Taiwan Strait. Consequently, Taiwan featured prominently in studies of international relations and politics in the United States, with national identity becoming a major issue of scholarly concern. The emphasis on Taiwanese nationalism as a security issue hints at the ambiguity of Taiwan Studies, not only in the way it potentially challenged U.S. policy on the island but also in its implications for the KMT regime, which had based its legitimacy on a claim of representing the Chinese nation.

Within Taiwan, the increased demand for Taiwan-centred academic studies as an expression of a growing sense of Taiwanese identity was controversial under authoritarian KMT rule. U.S. academia provided a space where Taiwan Studies could develop when Taiwan research institutions were still controversial on the island itself. An important driving force of Taiwan Studies in the United States consisted of Taiwan Studies "activists" from Taiwan who studied in the United States. They promoted research on Taiwan through establishing and participating in new institutions such as the North American Taiwan Studies Association or the Conference Group on Taiwan Studies of the American Political Science Association.

Political opening in Taiwan changed the situation. Under the KMT's indigenization strategy and the opposition's push for Taiwan Studies, new institutions of Taiwan Studies were created on the island itself, one of the earliest being the Preparatory Institute of Taiwan History at Academia Sinica in 1992, followed later by various institutions at Taiwanese universities. Many of the Taiwanese studying and working in the United States returned to Taiwan to take up positions in the growing field of Taiwan Studies on the island. Migration between the United States and Taiwan has created partly overlapping academic fields.

Some of the old institutions of Taiwan Studies in the United States, such as the influential M.E. Sharpe book series "Taiwan in the Modern World" or the Harvard Taiwan Studies Workshop, have been closed or significantly scaled down. The Stanford Language Program moved from Taipei to Beijing in 1997, which may result in a new generation of Mandarin learners with little exposure to Taiwan. While some of the older institutions of Taiwan Studies have disintegrated, a range of new institutions has been set up in recent years, mostly in the fields of cultural studies and literature. This reconfiguration of the academic field is strongly driven by Taiwan through financial and personal support and marks a divergence from the predominant interest in Taiwan as a factor of U.S.–China relations in public discourse in the United States.

Taiwan Studies in Europe

Just as the older institutions of Taiwan Studies in the United States started to disintegrate, new centres of Taiwan Studies began to emerge in Europe (Ohlendorf 2017). The construction of European Taiwan Studies has followed much more that of traditional area studies. Compared to the United States, Europe is politically less sensitive about Taiwan, since Europe has no military commitments in the East Asian region. At the same time, the lack of a special relationship with Taiwan and the comparatively smaller Taiwanese diaspora means that overall there has been less awareness of Taiwan in Europe. Nevertheless, Europe has become one of the most vibrant sites of Taiwan Studies. New Taiwan Studies institutions have been set up in various countries. Taiwan has become the subject of specialized university courses, a range of book series and journals provide special venues for publications on Taiwan, and the annual conference of the European Association of Taiwan Studies has become one of the largest Taiwan Studies conferences in the world. Characteristic of the development of Taiwan Studies in Europe has been the conscious effort to institutionalize the academic field. Financial overtures from Taiwan for academic studies of Taiwan have found very fertile ground in Europe, which has to do with the distinct tradition of area studies on the continent, the historical moment of Taiwan's transition to a quasi-sovereign democracy, intensified attempts to coordinate academic research on a supranational level, and finally the personal commitment and cooperation among leading Taiwan scholars in Europe.

The historical setting is important when comparing the institutionalization of Taiwan Studies in the United States and in

Europe. The first institutions in the United States evolved at a time when Taiwan had witnessed decades of economic growth but was still under martial law and ruled by an authoritarian regime, which limited the appeal to a Western audience. In contrast, the institutionalization of European Taiwan Studies began later, by the end of the 1990s and early 2000s, after Taiwan had already taken important steps towards successful democratization. Its political liberalization gave Taiwan important symbolic capital. The view of democracy as something inherently good becomes clear in the way the Taiwanese government has tried to use Taiwan's democracy as a key argument to mobilize support for the island (Rawnsley 2003).

Also, in this context, it is important to remember that European Taiwan Studies evolved when Taiwan had already firmly endorsed the principle of pragmatic diplomacy in its foreign policy. In this regard, the emerging field of Taiwan Studies in Europe experienced circumstances slightly different from those earlier in the United States, when Taiwan still presented itself as the sole legitimate representation of China. The promotion of scholarly activities formed an important component of this new overall effort by Taiwan to widen de facto, semi-official ties with other countries through flexible diplomacy.

Academic sponsorships have become an important part of Taiwan's public diplomacy in Europe, where interest in Asia has grown since the collapse of the Soviet Union but where Asian Studies has been affected by the wider trend of shrinking government funding for universities in general and for research and training in the humanities in particular (Osander 2001). Somewhat ironically, the cuts in government financial support have provided an important opportunity for Taiwan Studies. Foundations in Asia have stepped in to assist the development of Asian Studies and museum collections in Europe. The importance of external support becomes especially clear in the case of Taiwan Studies. In the case of Korean Studies, Japanese Studies or Chinese Studies, external funding helped strengthen or expand existing fields of study. Even the youngest discipline, Korean Studies, already had a tradition of several decades in Europe. Furthermore, each of the three subject areas was structured around a specific language expertise in each case, and thus was clearly identifiable as a distinct field of study. Taiwan Studies, on the other hand, did not have any institutional predecessors in Europe before the 1990s and shared its linguistic foundations with Chinese Studies. Financial incentives from Taiwan were instrumental in constructing the new field of Taiwan Studies. Taiwanese government agencies like the Taiwan Ministry of Foreign Affairs and the Taiwan Ministry of Education as well as the Chiang Ching-kuo Foundation (CCKF) have played key roles in this regard.

Support by the CCKF for European research projects began in 1991. In 1997, the foundation set up the International Sinological Center at Charles University in Prague. As the name suggests, the activities of the foundation initially mainly targeted the field of Sinology. This has to do with the background of the foundation, which was established to honour the legacy of late ROC president Chiang Ching-kuo. Even though Chiang Ching-kuo had displayed considerably more pragmatism towards Taiwan's relations with the People's Republic of China and other countries, as well as domestic pressure for more democratic procedures, Chiang had never abandoned the One China principle as a political priority (Hughes 2006, p. 50). For his supporters he could therefore be seen as a symbol of political change under the name of Chinese nationalism.

At the same time, the tensions arising from the implications of his political reforms to the one-China principle may explain the importance placed on culture as a means to underline the legacy of Chinese nationalism. Consequently, this may also be the reason for the relative absence of support for European Taiwan Studies by the CCKF initially, compared to funding for U.S.–Taiwan Studies projects starting as early as the late 1980s. Since the early programmes in the United States tended to be social sciences oriented, they conflicted less with the idea of Taiwan as a repository of Chinese culture. In Europe, some of the early projects on Taiwan were linked to cultural studies or literature, either through research themes or institutional bases, which may explain the limited support offered by the CCKF. Systematic institutional enhancement of Taiwan Studies in Europe started only in the late 1990s with a grant for the establishment of a research unit on Taiwanese Culture at Ruhr-University in Bochum in Germany. In recent years the CCKF has become the largest sponsor for Taiwan Studies activities in Europe, most notably through its support for the European Association of Taiwan Studies.

The first institution with the term "Taiwan Studies" in the title was not sponsored by the CCKF, but by the Taiwan Ministry of Foreign

Affairs. In 1999 the School of Oriental and African Studies (SOAS) in London set up a Taiwan Studies Programme based on financial support from the ministry. There was no clear blueprint for the evolving Taiwan Studies Programme at SOAS, but representatives of the school and the Taiwan Ministry of Foreign Affairs agreed upon an emphasis on the social sciences.[2] From the Taiwanese perspective of foreign policy, the focus on the social sciences reflected its new strategy of promoting support for Taiwan through its economic and democratic achievements. At the same time, during the first phase of the funding, 1999–2003, the programme was symbolically still linked to the KMT legacy through the choice of the name "Chiang Ching-kuo Chair of Taiwan Studies". Chiang Ching-kuo was Chiang Kai-shek's son and his successor as the president of the Republic of China on Taiwan. The historical memory of Chiang Ching-kuo is very complex in Taiwan, where he is remembered not only for his economic policies that accelerated Taiwan's modernization under his presidency and for his relaxation of authoritarian rule and lifting of martial law in the second half of the 1980s, but also for his role as the director of the secret police during the period of White Terror. It may testify to Taiwan's generally positive image in the West as a modern democracy that the institutionalization of a Chiang Ching-kuo Chair of Taiwan Studies based on government money from Taiwan did not raise much concern. Part of it may have been the handling of the funding through the school's management and staff. A donation from the Iranian government to SOAS in 1999, the same year that the Taiwan Studies Programme was set up, led to protest letters by academics expressing their concerns about good governance and the school's link to a repressive regime (*Times Higher Education*, 10 December 1999).

While the Taiwan Studies Programme at SOAS served as a hub within the European academic community by creating a focal point of Taiwan Studies for individual researchers within Europe, the concentration and rapid expansion of Taiwan Studies in London also encouraged subsequent fragmentation and diversification of the field. The financial support from Taiwan for activities in London sent a positive signal to individual researchers and institutions that there was a potential source of funding available for projects dealing with the island, which increased the stakes in the game. Since the late 1990s, the number of Taiwan Studies institutions in Europe has continued to grow. There are now institutionalized Taiwan Studies in various countries, including the United Kingdom, France, Germany, Austria, Slovenia, and the Czech Republic. Many of the institutions are very small and linked to the leadership of individuals. This situation could have easily led to the fragmentation of Taiwan Studies in Europe. However, Taiwan Studies in Europe has developed a very effective mechanism to synergize activities through the creation of a Europe-wide network of Taiwan Studies.

The European Association of Taiwan Studies (EATS) was founded in 2004. It drew inspiration from the existing EU–China network as well as the North American Taiwan Studies Association (NATSA). Many of the EATS members had previously gained experiences at North American Taiwan Studies events. EATS was modelled on NATSA, yet modified according to what the founders perceived as necessary improvements. While NATSA until recently was primarily a graduate student conference, EATS tried to balance participation of faculty members, doctoral students and, more recently, master's students, so as to bring different segments of the research community together. During its first decade it followed broad definitions of research areas to increase participation and actively sought to expand geographically by holding conferences in different locations all over Europe. EATS has also allocated resources on a European level, most visibly by the organization of joint book projects and events such as the EATS Graduate Teaching Workshops.

Conclusion

The starting point of this chapter was the question of how to position Taiwan Studies in the general discussion of area studies and knowledge production. I have argued that Taiwan Studies has the potential to suggest a new type of area study, an "area study in reverse" in which the main motivation and impetus for the exogenous study of the field stems from the local. In the United States, which has strong political and security interests in cross-strait affairs, the field of Taiwan Studies has developed partly as a counter-discourse to the predominant interest in the ROC as the "Other China", or in Taiwan as a security factor in U.S.–China relations. More recent institutional constructions of the field have treated Taiwan as a subject of knowledge in its own right, not necessarily subordinated to a larger discourse on China. Taiwan Studies has thus diverged from mainstream political discourse on the island. In Europe, where there has been less awareness of Taiwan and less political sensitivity about the island, Taiwan Studies has quickly grown into a distinct academic field with specialized research and teaching institutions, publications and conference series. Relative to the public awareness of Taiwan in Europe, the academic field of Taiwan Studies seems to have expanded exponentially, with a rapid growth in the overall number of Taiwan Studies institutions, but also in the strength of the institutions themselves.

Funding remains a key issue in Taiwan Studies. Most academics and institutions rely on financial support from Taiwan. For instance, the research for this chapter was partly funded by the Center for Chinese Studies at the National Central Library, Taiwan and the Taiwan Fellowship of the Taiwan Ministry of Foreign Affairs. The dependency on a single source of funding, mainly from Taiwanese government organizations, has ethical implications. On the one hand, the availability of financial support from Taiwan means that some academics are able to pursue studies outside the academic mainstream. In that sense, Taiwan Studies should have the potential to be critical and innovative. However, there is always the risk of Taiwan Studies becoming isolated in the wider academic field and thus becoming very limited in its impact. More serious, however, is the question of how far scholars involved in Taiwan Studies can maintain their academic independence vis-à-vis the Taiwanese government and other funding agencies. The scandal over Libyan funds at the London School of Economics and Political Science (*The Guardian*, 3 March 2011) and the unease over PRC-government-sponsored Confucius Institutes at universities (Hughes 2014) have already opened up some debates, but there is relatively little discussion in academic Taiwan Studies on this issue. It may be argued that Taiwan as a liberal democracy is a different case and that the Taiwanese government does not impose serious restrictions on researchers. However, self-censorship by academics may actually be the bigger problem. It is difficult for researchers not to become instrumentalized. Writing a paper on the field of Taiwan Studies, for instance, is hard to disentangle from the wider project of legitimizing Taiwan Studies (and thus "Taiwan") as a subject. Support for academic Taiwan Studies abroad has been one of the key features of Taiwan's public diplomacy. There is a lot at stake for a country whose international status is contested. On the other hand, self-conscious reflection on this issue as well as on the broader connections of power and knowledge production is one of the potentials of Taiwan Studies.

It is necessary to diversify the sources of funding for Taiwan Studies. One way to do this is to place Taiwan Studies in the wider academic field and thus also to confront the problem of "insularity" or "parochialism". The study of Taiwan in its uniqueness is a very interesting and valuable project in itself that may also generate new research questions or theoretical approaches. However, one of the challenges for Taiwan Studies is how to make Taiwan "relevant" to other fields. Comparative studies have been among the most successful works developed in Taiwan Studies, and the comparative framework still offers a lot of room for expansion, not just within Taiwan Studies but also across regions, times and disciplines.

One fear expressed by some in the field of Taiwan Studies is that Taiwan Studies will eventually be subsumed under "China Studies". This is linked to the concern regarding Taiwan's geopolitical status and identity. China is actively engaging in academic diplomacy through its Confucius Institutes, the establishment of Chinese-sponsored lectureships abroad, and the establishment of "branches" of prominent Western universities in the PRC. While it is possible that Taiwan Studies will eventually be subsumed under "China Studies", this development is not inevitable. After all, "China" and "Taiwan" are not essential, pre-existing entities, but constructions. Taiwan Studies may thus have an impact on China Studies as well as vice versa.

The "Taiwan Academies" established by the KMT government seek to draw attention to Taiwan by representing Taiwan as the "major Chinese cultural centre" (Taiwan Academy n.d). Some observers have criticized this strategy as failing to highlight Taiwan's social and political experience as the feature that most effectively differentiates Taiwan from the PRC (Rawnsley 2009).

Similarly, the cultural policy of the Democratic Progressive Party has been characterized as deliberately "de-sinicizing" Taiwan by downplaying the elements of traditional Chinese culture in Taiwan (Chang 2004). Such discussions show how Taiwan Studies is a very contested subject and closely related to the question of identity. Academics can very easily become implicated in different nationalist politics. The Inter-Asia Cultural Studies project around the Taiwanese scholar Chen Kuang-hsin has deliberately tried to place Taiwan in multiple, alternative frames of reference so as to move away from narrow nationalist conceptions of identity and to develop new modalities or forms of knowledge (Inter-Asia Cultural Studies n.d.).

Vincente Rafael notes that "the regional only comes into view comparatively: vertically related to that which seeks to maintain and subsume it; such as the empire, the nation-state, or the metropole; and horizontally in a relation of complementarity and conflict with other regions" (Rafael 1999). The construction of Taiwan Studies as an area study with a strong comparative angle does not preclude research on Taiwan as a case study with regard to wider debates in the disciplines. For instance, how does the discussion on Taiwan identity fit into the wider global system of the post–Cold War period? Could Taiwan represent a new type of sovereignty and identity in an increasingly globalized world? There are many other areas in which Taiwan can contribute to theory building in the mainstream academia. At the same time, Taiwan as an area study with a comparative orientation can also pose new research questions. Taiwan Studies is thus not just a provider of "data" for the disciplines. Reflection on Taiwan Studies can help to understand more about the conditions and contexts in which knowledge and theories are produced and help to generate alternative frameworks. The most promising element here seems to lie in the multiplicity of Taiwan Studies institutions and the recognition and coordination of this multiplicity by Taiwan itself. The case studies of European and U.S. Taiwan Studies already show different constructions of the field and different perspectives on the subject of Taiwan. This can be further extended if Taiwan Studies in other regions of the world are included and support for such projects becomes diversified.

Notes

1. Interview with Thomas Gold, Berkeley, 23 June 2008.
2. Interview with Robert Ash, London, 20 July 2010.

References

Ahern, Emily. *The Cult of the Dead in a Chinese Village*. Stanford: Stanford University Press, 1973.

Alatas, Syed Farid. *Alternative Discourses in Asian Social Sciences: Responses to Eurocentrism*. Thousand Oaks: Sage, 2006.

Appadurai, Arjun. *Modernity at Large: Cultural Dimensions of Globalization*. Minneapolis: University of Minneapolis Press, 1996.

Burgess, Chris. "The Asian Studies Crisis: Putting Cultural Studies into Asian Studies and Asia into Cultural Studies". *International Journal of Asian Studies* 1, no. 1 (2004): 121–36.

Chang, Bi-yu. "From Taiwanisation to De-Sinification: Culture Construction in Taiwan since the 1990s". *China Perspectives*, 2004 <https://chinaperspectives.revues.org/438> (accessed 16 May 2016).

Cheah, Pheng. "Universal Areas: Asian Studies in a World of Motion". In *The Postcolonial and the Global*, edited by Krishnaswamy Regathi and John C. Hawley. Minneapolis: University of Minnesota Press, 2008.

Cumings, Bruce. "Boundary Displacement: Area Studies and International Studies during and after the Cold War". In *Universities and Empire: Money and Politics in the Social Sciences during the Cold War*, edited by Christopher Simon. New York: New Press, 1999.

Diamond, Sigmund. *Compromised Campus: The Collaboration of Universities with the Intelligence Community, 1945–1955*. New York: Oxford University Press, 1992.

Dirlik, Arif. "Asia Pacific Studies in an Age of Global Modernity". In *Remaking Area Studies: Teaching and Learning across Asia and the Pacific*, edited by Terence Wesley-Smith and John Goss. Honolulu: University of Hawai'i Press, 2010.

Fulbright Taiwan. "Foundation for Scholarly Exchange: Mission and History". n.d. <http://www.fulbright.org.tw/dispPageBox/CtEn.aspx?ddsPageID=FOSEENGAB&> (accessed 16 May 2016).

Gold, Thomas B. *State and Society in the Taiwan Miracle*. Armonk: Sharpe, 1986.

The Guardian. "LSE Director Resigns over Gaddafi Scandal". 3 March 2011 <http://www.theguardian.com/education/2011/mar/03/lse-director-resigns-gaddafi-scandal> (accessed 27 October 2013)

Harrison, Mark. *Legitimacy, Meaning and Knowledge in the Making of Taiwanese Identity.* New York: Palgrave Macmillan, 2006.

Hughes, Christopher. *Chinese Nationalism in the Global Era.* London: Routledge, 2006.

————. "Confucius Institutes and the University: Distinguishing the Political Mission from the Cultural". *Issues and Studies* 50, no. 4 (2014): 45–83.

Inter-Asia Cultural Studies. n.d. <http://www.inter-asia.org/> (accessed 23 October 2013).

Jacoby, Neil H. *US Aid to Taiwan.* New York: Praeger, 1966.

Kelly, John D., and Martha Kaplan. *Represented Communities: Fiji and World Decolonization.* Chicago: University of Chicago Press, 2001.

Kerr, George H. *Formosa Betrayed.* Boston: Houghton Mifflin, 1965.

Kirby, E. Stuart. *Rural Progress on Taiwan.* Taipei: Joint Commission on Rural Reconstruction, 1960.

Knapp, Ronald G. "The Geographer and Taiwan". *China Quarterly* 74 (1978): 356–68.

Kratoska, Paul, Henk Schulte Nordholt, and Remco Raben, eds. *Locating Southeast Asia: Geographies of Knowledge and Politics of Space.* Singapore: Singapore University Press, 2005.

Kurzman, Charles. "Cross-Regional Approaches to Middle East Studies: Constructing and Deconstructing a Region". *Middle East Studies Association Bulletin* 41, no. 2 (2007): 24–29.

Lampton, David M., Joyce A. Madancy, Kristen M. Williams, and Committee on Scholarly Communication with the People's Republic of China. *A Relationship Restored: Trends in US–China Educational Exchanges, 1974–1984.* Washington: National Academy Press, 1986.

Madsen, Richard. "Institutional Dynamics of Cross-Cultural Communication: US–China Exchange in the Humanities and Social Sciences". In *Educational Exchanges: Essays on the Sino–American Experience,* edited by Joyce K. Kallgren and Denis Fred Simon. Berkeley: Institute of East Asian Studies of the University of California, 1987.

————. *China and the American Dream: A Moral Enquiry.* Berkeley: California University Press, 1995.

Naquin, Susan. *Millenarian Rebellion in China: The Eight Trigrams Uprising of 1813.* New Haven: Yale University Press, 1976.

Ohlendorf, Hardina. "Building a New Academic Field: The Institutionalization of Taiwan Studies in Europe". *International Journal of Asia Pacific Studies* 13, no. 2 (2017): 115–40.

Osander, Anja. *Settings for Asian Studies in Europe and the USA: An Explorative Study.* A Publication of the Strategic Alliance. EIAS, IIA, IIAS, NLAS. Hamburg: Institut fuer Asienkunde, 2001.

Palat, Ravi A. "Fragmented Visions: Excavating the Future of Area Studies in a Post-American World". In *Beyond the Area Studies Wars: Towards a New International Studies*, edited by Neil L. Walters. Middlebury, VT: Middlebury College Press, 2000.

Rafael, Vicente L. "Regionalism, Area Studies, and the Accidents of Agency". *American Historical Review* 104, no. 4 (1999): 1208–20.

Rawnsley, Gary D. "Selling Democracy: Diplomacy, Propaganda and Democratization in Taiwan". *China Perspectives*, 2003 <http://chinaperspectives.revues.org/361?lang=fr> (accessed 16 May 2016).

———. "Taiwan Academies a Poor Strategy". *Taipei Times*, 14 September 2009 <http://www.taipeitimes.com/News/editorials/archives/2011/09/14/2003513215/3>.

Resnik, Julia. "Introduction: The Limits of Educational Knowledge and New Research Opportunities in the Global Era". In *The Production of Educational Knowledge in the Global Era*, edited by Julia Resnik. Rotterdam and Taipei: Sense, 2008.

Szanton, David L. "Introduction: The Origin, Nature and Challenges of Area Studies in the United States". In *The Politics of Knowledge: Area Studies and the Discipline*, edited by David L. Szanton. Berkeley: University of California Press, 2004.

Taipei CCAS. "Communication: The Stanford Center in Taipei". *Bulletin of Concerned Asian Scholars* 7, no. 4 (1975): 62–63.

Taiwan Academy. "About the Academy". n.d. <http://taiwanacademy.tw/ch/about/about.jsp> (accessed 27 October 2013).

Times Higher Education. "Uproar as SOAS Takes Iran Cash". 10 December 1999 <https://www.timeshighereducation.co.uk/news/uproar-as-soas-takes-iran-cash/149196.article> (accessed 15 May 2014).

Walker, Richard L. "Taiwan's Development as Free China". *Annals of the American Academy of Political and Social Sciences* 321, no. 1 (1959): 122–35.

Winks, Robin W. *Cloak and Gown: Scholars in the Secret War, 1939–1961*. New Haven: Yale University Press, 1996.

Wong, Joseph. "Past, Present and Future of Taiwan Studies: A View from North American Political Science". *Proceedings of the International Forum on the Past, Present and Future of Taiwan Studies beyond Taiwan: Europe, North America and Japan Compared*, pp. 61–68. Taipei: Institute of Sociology: Academia Sinica, 2010.

Part III

Asian Studies in Former Soviet States

8

Southeast Asian Studies in Russia: Agents against Structural Limits

Ekaterina Koldunova

Southeast Asian states and Russia are not often seen as natural partners or countries engaged in a tight web of interconnections. They lack the geographical proximity which usually drives such interconnections in the political, economic and intellectual spheres and creates a shared space, literally and figuratively, of mutual practices, narratives and academic discourses. Southeast Asia would also seem to have lower strategic appeal for Russia compared to the larger entities like China or India. Historically, the region was not a sphere of colonial expansion for Russia, nor had Russia and Southeast Asia enjoyed shared cultural features which could have generated mutual interest. However, Southeast Asian Studies in Russia has not only managed to take shape but has also resulted in several well-established academic schools focused on area studies, linguistics and international relations in the region.[1]

Southeast Asian Studies in Russia may be seen as falling into different periods — first, fragmented interest in the eighteenth and nineteenth centuries, then a well-grounded rise in the Soviet period, a dramatic decline in the 1990s, and more or less pragmatic stabilization in recent years. Geopolitical and structural factors shaped the background conditions for Southeast Asian Studies during each of these periods. The USSR's role as one of the geopolitical centres in the bipolar system during the Cold War presupposed its global reach both politically and intellectually. In contrast to this outreach, the early 1990s witnessed a sharp "shrinking" of Russian foreign policy. After the dissolution of the Soviet Union, Russia rapidly transformed from a power with a visible presence in all regions of the world, including Southeast Asia, to a state with limited economic capacity and internal structural problems. However, the intellectual asset of Southeast Asian Studies did not vanish overnight.

This chapter thus argues that it was mainly the geopolitical context of the Cold War that shaped Southeast Asian Studies in Russia (and the USSR). Though Southeast Asia was not a high geopolitical priority for the USSR relative to larger Asian countries like China or India, the logic of Cold War competition with the United States, which unfolded in virtually all parts of the world, provoked not only academic but also practical interest in this region. In the late twentieth century, when Russia's geopolitical involvement in Southeast Asia diminished, the community of Russian experts specializing on the region faced serious structural limits, but they tried during this period to preserve their knowledge network. The chapter explores the particular ways in which this scholarly network has managed to overcome several sets of constraints, namely ideological, geopolitical and those related to the current foreign policy debate in Russia. Ideological constraints represented themselves in the division of Southeast Asia into those states orientated as pro-Soviet or anti-Soviet during the Cold War, and consequently in a stronger emphasis on studying those countries which were more inclined to join the communist bloc. Geopolitical constraints include the intellectual outcomes of the dissolution of the Soviet Union, which resulted in an overall reduction in the geographical scope of Russian foreign policy analysis. Finally, the ongoing debate about Russia's Europe-or-Asia foreign policy priorities, including emphasis on larger partners such as China, also keeps Southeast Asian Studies as secondary at best.

Against the background of these general considerations, the chapter starts by tracing the origins of Southeast Asian Studies in

Russia. The following section critically evaluates the process of institutionalization of Southeast Asian Studies in the Soviet period as a result of the USSR's growing geopolitical influence. The final sections analyse the impact of the changing geopolitical and ideological circumstances on Southeast Asian Studies at the turn of the century. They also examine how the scholarly network managed to sustain itself intellectually and financially despite the constraints enumerated above.

Historical Roots of Southeast Asian Studies in Russia

Russia's emerging interest in Southeast Asia in the late eighteenth and the nineteenth century preceded the coming into being of Southeast Asian Studies in Russia. The first information about Southeast Asia in Russia appeared in the eighteenth century. At that time, the majority of publications about this region were translations from French, English or German. Thus, the earliest record of Vietnam in Russia dates back to 1783 when the Moscow University print shop published the sixth volume of Antoine François Prevost's *The General History of Voyages*, which contained a description of Tonkin (Sokolov 2007).

Starting from the late eighteenth century, Russia demonstrated growing interest in Southeast Asia. However, at that time this interest arose mainly from Russia's intention to assess the dynamics of the balance of power among the key colonial states in the region; primarily Great Britain and France, but also the Netherlands and Spain (Kolotov 2011). These were the European powers with whom Russia had to deal constantly in its European and Asian foreign policy. Consequently, it had to scrutinize closely their activities in various parts of the world, including Southeast Asia.

At the same time, Russia's interest in Southeast Asia was highly dependent on the internal situation in Russia and its changing perception of Siberia and the Far Eastern region's role in the country's overall development. In 1637, Russian explorers reached the Pacific Ocean. After that, the goal of consolidating Russia's Asian territories and securing access to the Pacific Ocean became an integral part of

Russia's domestic and foreign policy. As far back as 1722, the eminent Russian geographer Theodore Soymanov presented to Emperor Peter I a plan of reaching Northeast and Southeast Asia through the Arctic Ocean and Kamchatka (Kozlova 1986). Russian geographers were looking for ways to establish more profitable trade routes to these regions than the routes used by Great Britain and the Netherlands.

Expeditions led by Vitus Bering in 1725–30 and 1733–41 paved the way for further exploration of the Pacific coast as well as the Aleutian Islands, the Kuril Islands, Kamchatka and Alaska. The Russian-American Company, established in 1799 with the aim of developing new Russian territories, was looking for ways to start trade with Southeast Asia. Had it succeeded, the supply of goods from this region to Alaska and the Russian Pacific coast might have been more efficient than the delivery of these goods from the European part of Russia. Russian seafarer Ivan Krusenstern also supported the idea of establishing direct trade between the Russian Far East and Southeast Asia. In fact, it was during his round-the-world expedition that the Russian vessels *Neva* and *Nadejda* crossed the waters of Southeast Asia for the first time. He himself made a description of the Sunda Strait (Kruzenstern 1810). However, at that time Russian diplomacy was more active in looking for ways to expand trade with neighbouring China and Japan than in dealing with a distant region that would become an arena of growing contradictions among key colonial powers. Trying to establish a consulate in the Philippines in the 1820s, Russia faced serious competition with European and American companies and was not very successful in promoting its economic interests.

This rising colonial competition in the second part of the nineteenth century, nevertheless, made Russia pay more attention to Southeast Asian states. Being in conflict with Great Britain over spheres of influence in Persia and Afghanistan, as well as vigilant about Britain's actions in China, Russian foreign-policy planning also had to take into account Britain's position in Southeast Asia. On the one hand, the government was trying to pursue a cautious approach to Southeast Asian states, as the case of Burma[2] demonstrates. On the other hand, the emergence of Japan as a serious rival to Russia in the Asia-Pacific necessitated maintaining a balanced approach in relations with France.

Russia's growing economic interests in this region at the turn of the century made it impossible for Russia to avoid getting more tightly involved in regional affairs.

In the 1870s, making all possible attempts to escape complete colonization by Great Britain, Burma undertook several efforts to establish diplomatic relations with other European powers, including Russia. Burma first sought to resolve its differences with Russia over Rangoon's Armenian diaspora. Burma later attempted to engage Persia in mediation of this same issue. Afterwards, Burma even asked for help in establishing diplomatic ties with Russia from the prominent Russian chemist Dmitri Mendeleyev, who was staying in France at the time when a Burmese delegation visited there (Bulychev 2010). The Russian government avoided answering Burmese requests in order not to aggravate relations with Britain. At the same time, the Russian public learned quite a lot about Burma from publications issued in the nineteenth century by such Russian magazines as *Vokrug Sveta* (Around the World), *Severnyi Arkhiv* (Northern Archive), *Moskovskii Telegraf* (Moscow Telegraph) and others (Kozlova 1986).

Russo–Siamese relations developed more successfully than Russo–Burmese contacts. In the late nineteenth century, Siam[3] was the only country in Southeast Asia that managed to preserve formal independence amidst British and French aspirations to expand their colonial possessions in the region. Using a strategy of balancing between the great powers, Siam established its embassies in Britain and France and consulates in New York, Hamburg, Lisbon and some other European and Asian cities. The Siamese monarch King Chulalongkorn himself undertook enormous efforts to modernize the state and to assert its sovereignty internationally (Terwiel 2005; Brailey 2009). In these circumstances, Siam was also looking for ways to establish diplomatic ties with Russia, which was, on the one hand, one of the great powers, but, on the other, not interested in territorial expansion in Southeast Asia. At that time Russia was actively developing its fleet and the Pacific squadron. The period of debate about whether and in what way Russia should develop its navy, including its units in the Pacific Ocean, resulted in a relatively unanimous conclusion among the Russian political elite and the general public. In line with this conclusion, the anonymous article titled "Whether Russia Needs a Fleet?" published by the magazine *Vremia* (Time) argued that Russia should be proactive in building both its commercial and military abilities in the Pacific Ocean (*Morskoi Sbornik* 1863). Incidentally, the same issue of *Morskoi Sbornik* (Maritime Journal) also contained a detailed description of the journey undertaken by the Russian clipper *Gaidamak*, the first Russian ship to enter the Chao Phraya River, in 1863. Russian ships visited Bangkok again in 1874 and 1882.

In March 1891, the future Russian emperor Nicholas II visited Siam during his tour of the Far East. And, in 1897, King Chulalongkorn paid a visit to Russia as part of his European tour. During King Chulalongkorn's stay in Russia, the two parties agreed to establish diplomatic relations. A cordial reception, which the Russian emperor provided for the Siamese king, sent a signal to other European powers that they had to treat King Chulalongkorn equally (Koldunova and Rangsimaporn 2012). In 1897, when King Chulalongkorn was travelling around Europe, the Russian magazine *Vokrug Sveta* (Around the World) published an article about Siam. The author even compared Siam with Japan, which managed to "catch up and overtake Russia in cultural development" in only five decades (Gotval't 1897). The first Russian diplomatic representative to Siam, Alexander Olarovsky, during his stay in Bangkok composed a *Historical Review* about internal political development in Siam and colonial struggle in Southeast Asia (Kozlova 1986). This first-hand research enriched knowledge about this state in Russia.

In the 1890s, Russia established its consulates in Bangkok, Rangoon, Singapore, Batavia and Manila. In some places, like Singapore, Russian officials replaced local traders who had previously represented Russian interests. Sending information to St Petersburg, Russian consuls presented a more detailed picture of the political situation and daily life in Southeast Asia. In 1902, Modest Bakunin, Russian consul in Batavia between 1894 and 1899, published his book about Indonesia titled *Tropical Holland: Five Years on the Island of Java*[4] (Bakunin 2007). Earlier, in 1885, Russian engineer Emil Koriander conducted the first Russian research on the Indonesian economy (Koriander 1885).

Thus, as the previous analysis has demonstrated, Russian foreign policy towards Southeast Asia passed through several periods, beginning in the late eighteenth century. Cautious attention and a selective approach were the hallmarks of the first period, from the mid-eighteenth to the mid-nineteenth century. The Russian elite considered various projects to establish trade relations with Southeast Asia, primarily with the Philippines, trying at the same time not to be mired in problems with European colonial powers. Knowledge of Southeast Asia in Russia at that period was based either on European publications translated into Russian or on notes by Russian travellers and geographers. The late nineteenth century witnessed more active interaction between Russia and the region. Trade and information exchange intensified following the establishment of the diplomatic mission in Siam and consulates in other parts of the region. The period from the late nineteenth to the early twentieth century laid the foundations of Russian academic interest in Southeast Asia. Regrettably, Russia's defeat in the 1904–5 war with Japan and World War I interrupted this exchange for several decades.

Southeast Asian Studies in Russia during the Soviet Period

During the early Soviet period, first-hand knowledge of recent developments in the region came to Russia via the Comintern — the Communist International — and leaders of local communist parties. Thus, for example, the translations of Ho Chi Minh's writings reached a broad readership in Russia because of the Comintern's activities. In 1930, the Soviet government established the Institute of Oriental Studies in Leningrad (previously St Petersburg), uniting several centres of Asian Studies under its auspices. Actually, one can trace the institute's history back to the nineteenth century, when it existed under the name of the Asian Museum at the Imperial Academy of Sciences in St Petersburg. Academic life at the institute was somewhat turbulent in the period prior to World War II. On the one hand, the study of Asia received a new impetus; the government set the clear task of more active research to establish closer ties with Asian countries and to form a better understanding of ways to adapt the socialist experience to their development. On the other hand, acts of repression during the 1930s and World War II seriously weakened the institute (Institute of Oriental Studies 2013; Baziyanz 1993). In 1950 the Institute moved to Moscow, developed new fields of research and expanded structurally. In the mid-1950s, the new department of Southeast Asian Studies separated from the India department and launched the large-scale admission of doctoral students (Tyurin 2005). At that time, many prominent scholars who had laid the foundations of Russian/Soviet Southeast Asian Studies joined the institute as research fellows. These included Eduard Berzin, Vladimir Tyurin, Igor Mojeyko and Nodari Simonia. The key aim of the department was to initiate comprehensive research on Southeast Asia.

Southeast Asian Studies as an academic subfield took full institutional shape in Russia (and the USSR more generally) in the 1950s and 1960s. During the 1950s, two important centres of these studies, in Moscow and in St Petersburg/Leningrad, came into being and framed academic research and education on the history, politics, international relations and linguistics of Southeast Asia. In Moscow, the key institutions in this sphere were the Institute of Oriental Studies of the USSR Academy of Sciences, Moscow State Institute of International Relations of the Ministry of Foreign Affairs of Russia (later, MGIMO University[5]) and the Institute of Asian and African Studies of Moscow State University. Later on, the Institute of World Economy and International Relations and the Institute of Far Eastern Studies of the USSR Academy of Sciences also became actively involved in Southeast Asian Studies. In St Petersburg (Leningrad, 1924–91) during the Soviet period, Southeast Asian Studies developed in Saint Petersburg State University (Leningrad State University from 1933 to 1991). In the late 1980s and the early 1990s, the Far Eastern State University in Vladivostok also launched its first programmes in Vietnamese, Thai and Indonesian Studies.

These academic schools produced a series of fundamental academic publications about Southeast Asian countries and the region in general. One can claim that despite the ideological divisions in the world at that time, Southeast Asian Studies in Russia developed in line with the general international trend elsewhere: identifying Southeast Asia as a separate region and as a distinct object of study (Park and King 2013). Institutionalization of Southeast Asian Studies made it possible to examine the regional processes from international relations, historical, ethnographic and cultural perspectives. The research agenda of that period was quite extensive, and varied from geography, demography, ethnography, history, economy and international relations of the region to language and cultural studies. Inevitably, a considerable part of the research of that time scrutinized the internal political situation in the newly emerged independent states of the region, the politics of colonial and so-called "imperial" powers, and the formation and evolution of communist movements in Southeast Asia.

Figure 8.1 classifies books and articles published from 1959 to 1970 according to the following categories: history (ancient and middle ages, modern, post–World War II), economy, and national focus. The calculations presented in this figure use data from the bibliography of Southeast Asian Studies in the USSR (Larionova 1980). The studies included in the country-related categories cover academic research and translations from foreign languages, including those of Southeast Asian nations. The category "other topics" contains the writings by Karl Marx, Friedrich Engels and Vladimir Lenin that mention

FIGURE 8.1
Classification of Books and Articles by Topic and National Focus (1959–70)

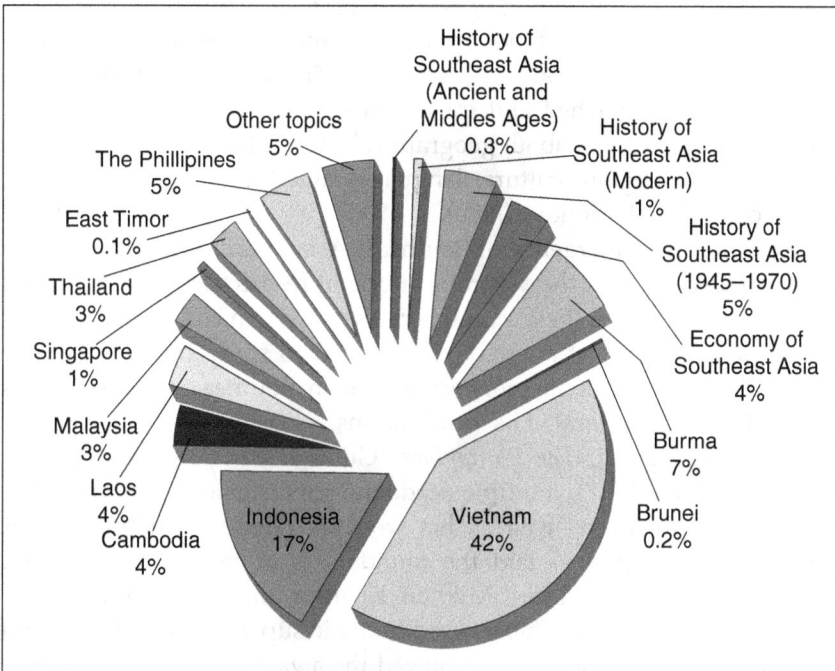

Source: Compiled by the author (based on Larionova 1980).

Southeast Asia, as well as other general publications related to the region in one way or another.

The figure indicates that the research works related to Vietnam, Indonesia and Burma took up the largest share of the country-study publications. The proportion of research on these three countries (66 per cent) reflects both the academic and foreign policy priorities of the USSR. The Soviet Union supported the Democratic Republic of Vietnam in its struggle for unification, provided economic aid to Burma in the 1950s to 1960s, and established close political and economic ties with Indonesia during Sukarno's presidency. However, one can hardly say that the ideological framework completely overshadowed the academic studies of Southeast Asia during the Soviet period. The ability to overcome ideological constraints was a result of a comprehensive approach to research on the region and its separate countries, scrupulous attention to the archives and historical sources, historical methodology that combined qualitative and quantitative methods, and aspiration to avoid the Eurocentric approach to history and international relations. These principles were among those particularly advocated by Alexander Guber, the founder of Indonesian, Filipino and Southeast Asian Studies in the USSR (Khaldin and Tsyganov 2004). In the decade of the 1960s, Soviet scholars published and translated more than 5,600 monographs, documents and articles about geography, history, ethnography, economic development, religion, culture, languages and healthcare in Southeast Asian countries (Larionova 1980).

Such a rapid emergence of Southeast Asian Studies could not have been possible without the vigorous efforts of researchers who advanced this discipline. Among these researchers, the already-mentioned Alexander Guber deserves special attention. He started to study Indonesia in the late 1920s and played a pioneering role in Southeast Asian Studies in the USSR in general. His publications — *Indonesia: Socio-economic Essays* (Guber 1932), *The Philippines* (Guber 1937), *Jozé Rizal* (Guber and Rykovskaya 1937), multiple academic papers, encyclopedia articles and book chapters, as well as his work as the academic supervisor for doctoral students — laid the foundations of the historical school of Southeast Asian Studies. Mikhail Khaldin and Vladilen Tsyganov mention that Alexander Guber was academic supervisor of 103 doctoral students. Twenty of them later achieved the award of Doctor of Science.[6] Students and followers of Alexander Guber — such as Eduard Berzin,

Dega Deopik, Georgiy Levinson, Vladimir Tyurin, Anton Uzyanov, Vladimir Vasiliev, Yuliya Levtonova, Valentina Dol'nikova and others — contributed to studies of Thailand, Vietnam, Burma, the Philippines, Malaysia and Indonesia in the USSR/Russia. As students of Southeast Asia, they knew each other most of their lives, thus constituting a scholarly network bound not only institutionally but also by personal relationships.

In addition to his research, Alexander Guber was an important figure in organizing Southeast Asian Studies in the USSR and presenting them in the international arena. He was deputy director (1950–54) and director (1954–56) of the Institute of Oriental Studies, gave lectures in Moscow State University, and was the major organizer of both the 25th International Congress of Asian and African Studies (1960) and the 13th International Congress of Historical Sciences (1970). Despite the limitations imposed on the humanities during the Soviet period (among them, the absence of full access to foreign literature), Alexander Guber and his students still managed to conduct research on international historical studies and Southeast Asian Studies in Europe and Asia. Alexander Guber himself was an active participant in international conferences held both in the USSR and abroad. In 1966–67, he spent time at Trinity College, Oxford. During his stay in Oxford he collected materials for a monograph he planned to write about the colonial powers' policies in Southeast Asia, but unfortunately managed to make only a draft of it before his death.

In the late 1970s and early 1980s, in addition to studies of single countries, the Institute of Oriental Studies accomplished several projects focused on Southeast Asia as an international region. Among these projects were several books, such as *Southeast Asia in World History* and Eduard Berzin's volumes on Southeast Asian history in the thirteenth to sixteenth and seventeenth to eighteenth centuries[7] (Rostovskiy and Vyatkin 1977; Levinson 1977; Berzin 1982, 1987). The authors of *Southeast Asia in World History* analysed the region as a system of communities/states which were evolving according to a certain historical logic and had some common features in terms of social, economic and political structures (Levinson 1977). The book had actually set itself the dual tasks of being a logical continuation of Daniel George Edward Hall's *History of Southeast Asia*[8] and to debate with Hall's assessments of the colonial period in the region's history. A series of publications focused on the

Association of Southeast Asian Nations (ASEAN) supplemented this kind of research (Khaldin 1983; Plekhanov and Rogojin 1985; Sulizkaya 1985), thus moving Southeast Asian Studies in the USSR away from focusing simply on those states in the region that were sympathetic to the Soviet model. Many of these publications were studies undertaken within the framework of a systemic approach to international relations. This approach became a hallmark of the Soviet school of the study of international relations, with the Institute of World Economy and International Relations of the USSR Academy of Sciences and Moscow State Institute of International Relations being two primary institutions which actively developed this approach (Maletin 1982).

Another group of research works made in the 1980s focused on political institutions, political regimes and authoritarian trends in Southeast Asian states. Alexei Drugov, Victor Sumsky, Nikolay Kalashnikov and some others analysed the evolution of political systems in Indonesia, Thailand, Singapore and the Philippines, the interplay between nationalism and political ideologies, and the role of the armed forces in the political systems of Southeast Asian states (Drugov 1989; Gurevich 1989; Sumsky 1987; Kalashnikov 1987; Fiodorov 1982). At the same time, Nikolay Maletin in MGIMO University extensively researched the foreign policies of Southeast Asian states (Maletin 1979, 1980, 1983). Economic researchers scrutinized general patterns and specific aspects of regional economies, the role of the Chinese diaspora in Southeast Asian countries' economies, and socio-economic models of capitalist Southeast Asian states (Chufrin and Shabalina 1983; Baryshinkova 1986; Simonia 1959; Bylinyak 1976). For the second part of the twentieth century, Moscow, St Petersburg (Leningrad) and Vladivostok established and developed academic schools to study the languages of all Southeast Asian countries. Graduates of these language schools, especially from MGIMO University, usually embarked on diplomatic careers with the Ministry of Foreign Affairs of the USSR and later of Russia.

The Soviet period saw the emergence, rise and institutionalization of Southeast Asian Studies in Russia/USSR, driven largely by the geopolitical context of the Cold War. The Cold War, on the one hand, spurred the development of this discipline in Russia/ USSR, but, on the other, imposed certain ideological constraints on studies of the region, evident in the overemphasis of certain countries such as Vietnam and Indonesia. Those who laid the foundations of the main Russian/Soviet schools in this field, however, developed genuine interest for the region among both academics and the public. Despite the lower priority of Southeast Asia in the Soviet–American geopolitical rivalry compared to Europe or Northeast Asia, the connection of Southeast Asian Studies with foreign policy as well as the Soviet Union's economic and military presence in the region added relevance to the field.

Asymmetry in Russian Foreign Policy in the 1990s: Implications for Southeast Asian Studies

Many of the factors fuelling academic and practical interest in Southeast Asia ceased to exist after the disintegration of the Soviet Union. In the early 1990s, post-Soviet Russia underwent a dramatic transformation from a world power with a visible presence and geopolitical interests in many regions of the world, including Southeast Asia, to a state with a limited economic capacity to project its power worldwide. Russia's foreign policy towards Asia at that time had secondary importance at best vis-à-vis Russia's relations with the West, while Southeast Asia was not even among those relationships in Asia that the Russian political elite still considered important. This circumstance had a negative impact on both Russia's relations with Southeast Asian states and Southeast Asian Studies as an academic field. Thus, in the 1990s, despite having a strong tradition and well-established schools, Southeast Asian Studies in Russia faced several significant challenges.

The domestic economic crisis that befell Russia after the collapse of the Soviet Union — combined with the area studies crisis of the 1990s, which was common to Russia and other countries — significantly weakened the institutional capacities of Southeast Asian Studies. A general view, which at some point became predominant at academic and governmental levels, was that foreign policy agencies needed more universal specialists rather than country-study specialists. In the situation of a narrower foreign policy perspective and globalization trends, the educational bureaucracy viewed the training of professionals focused on single countries as financially unjustified. This urge towards a more universalist approach to the education of history and international relations resulted in a radical reduction in the training of specialists on Myanmar, Laos, Cambodia and some other Southeast Asian states in Russian universities. For example, driven by financial considerations, MGIMO University, a premier Russian institution for training future diplomats, had to reduce the number of students enrolled in Southeast Asian Studies programmes to little more than a dozen every four years. In the previous decades, their number was two or three times bigger depending on the year of admission. MGIMO University also had to reduce Southeast Asian Studies to three programmes focused on Indonesia, Thailand and Vietnam, while previously the University used to train specialists on Myanmar, Cambodia, Laos and the region in general as well. Due to the financial situation in the education and research spheres, the 1990s did not witness many newcomers to Southeast Asian Studies in academic institutions.

Paradoxically, despite all the political and economic turbulence in the early 1990s, Russia still witnessed quite a lot of publications on Southeast Asia and ASEAN during this period (Levtonova 1993; Chufrin and Bylinyak 1994; Chufrin 1995). Obviously, some of these publications were released as a result of research initiated in the previous decade. In 1998, to revive intellectual discussions about Southeast Asia, the Centre of Southeast Asia, Australia and Oceania of the Institute of Oriental Studies started to publish an annual review which covered the most recent events in the region. This review and related annual conferences were among the few opportunities to support professional development and intellectual exchange within the community of Southeast Asian researchers in the 1990s. These included annual conferences devoted to Alexander Guber in the Institute of Asian and African Studies at Moscow State University, annual conferences on Vietnamese studies in the Institute of Far Eastern Studies of the Russian Academy of Sciences, and occasional conferences in St Petersburg and Vladivostok.

Foreign policy constraints which influenced Southeast Asian Studies in the early 1990s resulted from limited geopolitical and economic interest in the region. In the late 1990s, however, Russia started to reassess its Asian foreign policy and counted more on its relations with such major regional powers as China and India. In fact, above all, it was Russian foreign minister (1996–98) and later prime minister (1998–99) Yevgeny Primakov's idea of a Russia–China–India triangle and the necessity to deal with an economically rising China that inspired a more balanced approach to the Western and Eastern directions in Russian foreign policy. Primakov embodied the successful case of a foreign policy and intelligence practitioner with a strong academic background. Heading the Institute of Oriental Studies (1977–85) and the Institute of World Economy and International Relations (1985–89), he interacted a lot with Asianists abroad, such as Robert Scalapino and Leo Rose at the University of California, Berkeley. With Primakov's arrival in the Russian Foreign Ministry, a somewhat more active foreign policy in Southeast Asia followed his efforts to shift Russian geopolitical priorities towards Asia and away from the West. Partly due to these efforts, in the first decade of this century, new interest in Southeast Asia brought to the forefront a research focus on ASEAN, an organization central to the overall Asia-Pacific regional institutional architecture. Mired in domestic political and economic turbulence, Russia turned out to be a latecomer to many regional processes in the Asia-Pacific. Consequently, ASEAN as a core institution driving most of these processes became particularly important for Russia as a geopolitical partner, not only in Southeast Asia but also in the Asia-Pacific in general.

International Relations and World Regional Studies in Russia: Is There a Place for Southeast Asia?

Currently, Southeast Asian Studies in Russia are witnessing two main trends. The first is preservation of the schools of Southeast Asian Studies and maintenance of the concept of Southeast Asia as a separate object of study. A number of recent publications on the history and current economic and political developments of Southeast Asian states illustrate the continuing visibility of this academic subfield (Efimova 2001; Sumsky 2003; Mosiakov and Tyurin 2004; Tyurin 2004; Mazyrin 2007; Bektimirova and Dol'nikova 2009; Tyurin and Tsyganov 2010; Vasiliev 2010; Mosiakov 2010; Simonia 2012). ASEAN and the analysis of its development are helping to keep Southeast Asia as an object of academic study in Russia, if not of full-scale educational programmes (Maletin 2007; Kobelev, Lokshin and Maletin 2010).

The growing institutional and geographic diversification of Southeast Asian Studies in Russia and the increasing number of international projects of Russian and Southeast Asian academic institutions have brought some positive developments to this field. The recent projects include several joint publications of Singapore's Institute of Southeast Asian Studies (ISEAS) and the Institute of World Economy and International Relations of the Russian Academy of Sciences (Chufrin and Hong 2007; Chufrin, Hong and Teo Kah Beng 2006). Another example of this kind is the comparative research of economic reforms in Russia, China and Vietnam made by the Centre of Vietnamese and ASEAN Studies in the Institute of Far Eastern Studies (Ostrovsky and Do Tien Sham 2012). In fact, Vietnamese studies, especially in Saint Petersburg State University and in the Institute of Far Eastern Studies, remain currently the most structurally solid subfield among Southeast Asian country studies in Russia, demonstrating certain continuity from the Soviet period. Financing provided since 2007 by the Russian Humanitarian Science Foundation and the Vietnamese Academy of Social Sciences for joint Russo–Vietnamese projects and Vietnamese studies in Russia reinforces this trend. For the past six years the foundation and the Vietnamese Academy of Social Sciences have already supported almost twenty research projects and expeditions focused on historical, linguistic, economic and political studies of Vietnam (RHSF 2014). Joint business councils, for example, with Malaysia, and friendship societies, like the ones with Indonesia or Myanmar, became yet another source of occasional financial support for research, scholarly networking and publications.

The ASEAN Centre established in MGIMO University in 2011 as a cooperative effort of the ASEAN–Russia Dialogue partnership also aims at supporting Southeast Asian Studies. Not being a fully academic agency, the centre nevertheless undertakes visible action to support networking between Russian and Southeast Asian scholars through joint conferences, roundtables and publications, and to enhance academic cooperation between Russian and Southeast Asian academic institutions. Among the latter are ISEAS, the Diplomatic Academy of Vietnam, and the Centre for Policy Analysis of the Ministry of Foreign Affairs of the Republic of Indonesia. *ASEAN–Russia: Foundations and Future Prospects*, a recent publication prepared by the centre in cooperation with ISEAS, is the most comprehensive research in this sphere published outside Russia (Sumsky, Hong and Lugg 2012).

The second current trend is the growing practice of locating the analysis of Southeast Asian political and economic processes in a broader macro-regional context (Chufrin 2004; Voskressenski 2010;

Voskressenski, Koldunova, Kireeva and Lunev 2014). This trend defines the organization of educational programmes on international relations and world regional studies as well as recent academic research in this field. The emphasis on studies of international regions and the connection between domestic and international processes in Asia, on the one hand, and global transformations, on the other, became a way to preserve Asian Studies, including Southeast Asian Studies, amidst challenges to classical area studies. Moreover, such an approach intensified the analytical and comparative focus of those specializing on Southeast Asia and enabled them to explain regional developments against the background of global geopolitical and geo-economic shifts. World regional studies programmes, however, have not replaced traditional Southeast Asian Studies programmes. Rather, they coexist with those programmes, which are still in effect in Saint Petersburg State University and in the Institute of Asian and African studies. The constellation of these programmes also reflects the scope and focus of PhD topics and current research on Southeast Asian Studies. Single country studies remain the focus of a limited number of dissertations in history, political science and economics, while the general trend in international relations and political science is to look more closely at regional or macro-regional developments. Thus, for example, according to the Russian State Library website, in 2004–14 only eleven doctoral candidates defended dissertations focused specifically on political, historical or socio-economic development in Vietnam, eight in Indonesia, four in Thailand, three in Malaysia, three in the Philippines, and one in Myanmar (RSC 2014).[9] The number that defended theses for Doctor of Science degrees came to just four cases within the same period. The number of PhD dissertations on Southeast Asia and developments in the region against the background of international political and economic transformations in the Asia-Pacific is three times higher, and has a tendency to grow.

Both transformations discussed above correspond to the international debate about the concept of Southeast Asia, which is facing a critical reassessment worldwide (Huxley 1996). They also reflect the current state of area and world regional studies in Russia as academic and educational fields. Area studies research is now becoming a rare academic choice, giving way to broader and more region-focused professional specializations. However, the coexistence of the two mentioned trends contributes to institutional, intellectual and geographical diversification and framing of Southeast Asian Studies in Russia.

Conclusion

The previous analysis has demonstrated that Southeast Asian Studies in Russia has gone through several periods. The eighteenth and nineteenth centuries demonstrated Russia's interest in the region, which, however, was not substantiated by political or economic presence. The Cold War competition with the United States created the geopolitical context that spurred the development and institutionalization of Southeast Asian Studies in the USSR; in many aspects similarly to the development of this academic field in the United States. The Soviet period saw a rapid increase in the number of academic schools in this field, with a specific focus on countries such as Vietnam, Indonesia and Burma.

The breakup of the Soviet Union was a serious challenge to Southeast Asian Studies in Russia, resulting in the discipline shrinking both institutionally and in terms of the number of people involved in it. However, the schools established in the Soviet period did not vanish completely. Southeast Asian Studies during the Soviet period generated fundamental research, which today remains an intellectual asset for those engaging in the discipline. Moreover, the generation of scholars who started to work in the 1970s and 1980s, during the late Soviet period, remained active as professionals in the subsequent decades. Many of them had strong personal enthusiasm and interest in Southeast Asian Studies and were willing to convert it into academic research, scholarly networking and teaching, even in the turbulent 1990s.

At the beginning of this century, the widening scope of Russia's foreign policy beginning with Yevgeny Primakov's geopolitical concepts of balancing the West with Russia's relations with Asia contributed to keeping some continuity (like Vietnamese studies) and bringing change to Southeast Asia Studies. A good example of this change might be a research focus on ASEAN, originally an anti-communist organization but now one of Russia's important foreign policy counteragents in the Asia-Pacific. Studies of regionalism, macro-regional processes in the Asia-Pacific, and the political and economic impact of global trends on Southeast Asia have been other vibrant directions of Southeast Asian

Studies over the past decade. In the educational sphere, a new academic discipline of world regional studies has provided the opportunity to overcome the crisis of area studies and to preserve Southeast Asian Studies as a valuable part of Asian Studies in general.

Notes

1. This chapter does not cover the academic tradition of Buddhism studies, studies of Islam, or cultural or ethnographic studies of Southeast Asia. Nevertheless, the beginning of these studies in Russia, including the academic research of the Theravada tradition in Southeast Asia, goes as far back as the second half of the nineteenth century.
2. I use the term "Burma" here and in later parts of this chapter to refer to the country in the period prior to 1989.
3. I use the term "Siam" to refer to the country prior to 1939.
4. This book has been republished several times, most recently in 2007.
5. Up until 1994, MGIMO University functioned as the Institute of International Relations. In 1994 the institute gained the status of a university.
6. A Soviet/Russian academic degree which follows the degree of Candidate of Sciences, a rough analogue to a Doctor of Philosophy degree (Khaldin and Tsyganov 2004, pp. 121–22).
7. Berzin's third book, which covers the period from ancient times up to the thirteenth century, was published in 1995 (Berzin 1995).
8. The Russian translation of Hall's *History of Southeast Asia* appeared in the USSR in 1958, three years after its publication in Britain.
9. These figures do not include doctoral candidates from Southeast Asian states studying in Russia.

References

Bakunin, Mikhail. *Tropicheskaia Gollandiia. Piat' let na ostrove Iava* [Tropical Holland: Five years on the Island of Java]. Moscow: Minuvshee, 2007.

Baryshnikova, Olga. *Ekonomika Filippin v nastoiashchem i budushchem* [The Filipino economy nowadays and in the future]. Moscow: Nauka, 1986.

Baziyanz, Ashot. *175 let Institutu vostokovedeniia (1818–1993)* [175th anniversary of the Institute of Oriental Studies, 1818–1993]. Moscow: Institut vostokovedeniia, 1993.

Bektimirova, Nadejda, and Valentina Dol'nikova. *Al'ternativnye puti demokratizatsii: na primere Kambodzhi i Tailanda* [Alternative paths to democratization: The cases of Cambodia and Thailand]. Moscow: LENAND, 2009.

Berzin, Eduard. *Iugo-Vostochnaia Aziia v 13–16 vekah* [Southeast Asia in the 13th–16th centuries]. Moscow: Nauka, 1982.

———. *Iugo-Vostochnaia Aziia i ekspansiia Zapada v 17 – nachale 18go veka* [Southeast Asia and the expansion of the West in the 17th and early 18th centuries]. Moscow: Nauka, 1987.

———. *Iugo-Vostochnaia Aziia s drevnikh vremen do 13 veka* [Southeast Asia from ancient times to the 13th century]. Moscow: 'Vostochnaia literatura' RAN, 1995.

Brailey, Nigel. *Imperial Amnesia: Britain, France and "The Question of Siam".* Dordrecht: Republic of Letters Publishing BV, 2009.

Bulychev (Mojeyko), Kir. *Mech generala Banduly* [The sword of General Bandula]. Moscow: Eksmo, 2010.

Byliniak, Stanislav. *Valiutnye problemy i ekonomicheskii rost razvivaiushchikhsia stran* [Currency problems and economic growth in the developing countries]. Moscow: Nauka, 1976.

Chufrin, Gennady, ed. *Iugo-Vostochnaia Aziia: parametry bezopasnosti v kontse 20 stoletiia* [Southeast Asia: The parameters of security at the end of the 20th century]. Moscow: Institut vostokovedeniia, 1995.

———, ed. *Vostochnaia Aziia: mezhdu regionalizmom i globalizmom* [East Asia: Between regionalism and globalism]. Moscow: Nauka, 2004.

Chufrin, Gennady, and Stanislav Byliniak, eds. *ASEAN v sisteme mezhdunarodnykh ekonomicheskikh otnoshenii* [ASEAN in the system of international economic relations]. Moscow: Nauka, 1994.

Chufrin, Gennady, and Mark Hong. *Russia–ASEAN Relations: New Directions.* Singapore: Institute of Southeast Asian Studies, 2007.

Chufrin, Gennady, Mark Hong, and Teo Kah Beng, eds. *ASEAN–Russia Relations.* Singapore: Institute of Southeast Asian Studies, 2006.

Chufrin, Gennady, and Galina Shabalina, eds. *Sverkhmonopolii v Iugo-Vostochnoi Azii* [Super-monopolies in Southeast Asia]. Moscow: Nauka, 1983.

Drugov, Alexei. *Politicheskaia vlast' i evoliutsiia politicheskoi sistemy Indonezii (1965–1988)* [Political power and the evolution of the political system in Indonesia, 1965–1988]. Moscow: Nauka, 1989.

Efimova, Larissa. "New Evidence on the Establishment of Soviet–Indonesian Diplomatic Relations (1949–1953)". *Indonesia and the Malay World* 29, no. 85 (2001): 215–33.

Fiodorov, Vasiliy. *Armiia i politicheskii rezhim v Tailande* [Army and Thailand's political regime]. Moscow: Nauka, 1982.

Gotval't, V. "'Prazdnik plat'ia' v Siame" [A "dress fest" in Siam]. *Vokrug Sveta* [Around the World] 27 (1987) <http://www.vokrugsveta.ru/vs/article/7605/> (accessed 31 May 2017).

Guber, Alexander. *Indoneziia. Sotsial'no-ekonomicheskie ocherki* [Indonesia: Socio-economic essays]. Moscow, 1932.

———. *Filppiny* [The Philippines]. Moscow: Sozekgiz, 1937.

Guber, Alexander, and Olga Rykovskaya. *Khose Risal'* [Jozé Rizal]. Moscow: Zhurnal'no-gazetnoe ob'edinenie, 1937.

Gurevich, Emma. *Politicheskaia sistema sovremennogo Singapura* [Political system of contemporary Singapore]. Moscow, 1989.

Huxley, Tim. "Southeast Asia in the Study of International Relations: The Rise and Decline of a Region". *Pacific Review* 9, no. 2 (1996): 199–228.

Institute of Oriental Studies. *Istoriia Instituta vostokovedeniia: sovetskii period* [History of Institute of Oriental Studies: Soviet period] <http://www.ivran.ru/about-institute/58> (accessed 31 May 2017).

Kalashnikov, Nikolai. *Evoliutsiia politicheskoi sistemy Tailanda* [The evolution of the political system in Thailand]. Moscow: Nauka, 1987.

Khaldin, Mikhail. *ASEAN bez illiuzii* [ASEAN without illusions]. Moscow: Mejdunarodnye otnosheniia, 1983.

Khaldin, Mikhail, and Vladlen Tsyganov. "Guber – osnovopolozhnik otechestvennoi istoricheskoi nauki po Indonezii i Filippinam" [Guber: The founder of Russian historical studies of Indonesia and the Philippines]. In *Akademik A.A. Guber: istorik i lichnost'. K 100-letiiu so dnia rozhdeniia. Vospominaniia, rechi, stat'i* [Academician A.A. Guber: Historian and person. On the occasion of the centenary of the birth of Alexander Guber. Memoirs, speeches, articles], pp. 110–26. Moscow: Muravei, 2004.

Kobelev, Evgeny, Georgy Lokshin, and Nikolay Maletin, eds. *ASEAN v nachale XXI veka: Aktual'nye problemy i perspektivy* [ASEAN in the early 21st century: Problems and prospects]. Moscow: Forum, 2010.

Koldunova, Ekaterina, and Paradorn Rangsimaporn. "Russia–Thailand Relations: Historical Background and Contemporary Developments". In *ASEAN–Russia: Foundations and Future Prospects*, edited by Victor Sumsky, Mark Hong, and Amy Lugg, pp. 160–72. Singapore: Institute of Southeast Asian Studies, 2012.

Kolotov, Vladimir. "Evropeiskie derzhavy v Iugo-Vostochnoi Azii do nachala KhKh veka. Rossiia i Iugo-Vostochnaia Aziia" [European powers in Southeast Asia up to the early 20th century: Russia and Southeast Asia]. In *Rossiia i Vostok: fenomenologiia vzaimodeistviia i identifikatsii v novoe vremia* [Russia and Orient: The phenomenology of interaction and identification in the modern times], pp. 359–74. St Petersburg: Saint Petersburg University, 2011.

Koriander, Emil. *Torgovo-statisticheskii ocherk Iavy, v sviazi s budushchnost'iu russkoi torgovli v Indiiskom okeane* [Trade and statistics essay on Java, in relation to future Russian trade in the Indian Ocean]. St Petersburg: The printing house of V. Demakova, 1885.

Kozlova, Maria. *Rossiia i strany Iugo-Vostochnoi Azii* [Russia and Southeast Asian States]. Moscow: Nauka, 1986.

Kruzenstern, Ivan. *Puteshestvie vokrug sveta v 1803, 4, 5 i 1806 godakh. Po veleniiu ego Imperatorskogo Velichestva Aleksandra Pervogo, na korabliakh Nadezhda i Neva, pod nachal'stvom flota kapitan leitenanta, nyne kapitana vtorogo ranga, Kruzenshernta, Gosudarstvennogo Admiralteiskogo Departamenta i Imperatorskoi Akademii Nauk Chlena* [Round-the-world Journey in 1803, 4, 5 and 1806 years. As ordained by His Imperial Majesty Alexander I, on the ships Nadejda and Neva, under the command of Navy captain lieutenant, currently the frigate captain Kursenstern, a member of State Admiralty Department and Imperial Academy of Sciences and Arts]. St Petersburg: Morskaia tipografiia, 1810 <http://az.lib.ru/k/kruzenshtern_i_f/text_0030oldorfo.shtml> (accessed 31 May 2017).

Larionova, Olga. *Bibliografiia Iugo-Vostochnoi Azii (1959–1970): Sovetskaia literatura na russkom iazyke original'naia i perevodnaia* [Bibliography of Southeast Asian studies (1959–1980). Soviet Literature in Russian, original and translated]. Moscow: Nauka, 1980.

Levison, Georgy, ed. *Iugo-Vostochnaia Aziia v mirovoi istorii* [Southeast Asia in world history]. Moscow: Nauka, 1997.

Levtonova, Yulia ed. *ASEAN v sisteme mezhdunarodnykh politicheskikh* otnoshenii [ASEAN in the system of international political relations]. Moscow: Nauka, 1993.

Maletin, Nikolay. *Vneshniaia politika Indonezii (1959–1972)* [The foreign policy of Indonesia, 1959–1972]. Moscow: Institut mezhdunarodnykh otnoshenii, 1979.

———. *ASEAN v sisteme mezhdunarodnykh otnoshenii* [ASEAN in the system of international relations]. Moscow: MGIMO, 1982.

———. *Vneshniaia politika Filippin* [The foreign policy of the Philippines]. Moscow: MGIMO, 1983.

———. *Vneshniaia politika Tailanda (1945–1983)* [The foreign policy of Thailand, 1945–1983]. Moscow: MGIMO, 1986.

———. *ASEAN: chetyre desiatiletiia razvitiia* [ASEAN: Four decades of development]. Moscow: MGIMO-Universitet, 2007.

Mazyrin, Vladimir. *Reformy perekhodnogo perioda vo V'etname (1986–2006)* [Reforms of the transition period in Vietnam, 1986–2006]. Moscow: Klyuch-S, 2007.

Morskoi sbornik [Maritime Journal]. "Kritika i bibliografiia: Nuzhen li Rossii flot?" [Critique and bibliography: Whether Russia needs a fleet?]. *Morskoi sbornik* 5 (1863): 1–5.

Mosiakov, Dmitry. *Istoriia Kambodzhi. XX vek* [History of Cambodia: The 20th century]. Moscow: Institut vostokovedeniia, 2010.

Mosiakov, Dmitry, and Vladimir Tyurin. *Istoriia Iugo-Vostochnoi Azii* [History of Southeast Asia]. Moscow: Vostochnyi universitet, 2004.

Ostrovsky, Alexander, and Do Tien Sham. *Sravnitel'nyi analiz obshchikh chert i osobennostei perekhodnogo perioda v Rossii, Kitae i V'etname* [Comparative analysis of common and specific features of the transition period in Russia, China and Vietnam]. Moscow: Forum, 2012.

Park Seung Woo and Victor T. King. "The Historical Construction of Southeast Asian Studies and the Emergence of a Region". In *The Historical Construction of Southeast Asian Studies: Korea and Beyond*, edited by Seung Woo Park and Victor T. King, pp. 1–42. Singapore: Institute of Southeast Asian Studies, 2013.

Plekhanov, Yuriy, and Alexander Rogojin. *Ekonomika i politika ASEAN* [Economy and politics of ASEAN]. Moscow: Mysl', 1985.

RHSF (Russian Humanitarian Science Foundation). "Arkhiv podderzhannykh proektov RGNF" [Archive of the projects supported by RHSF] <old.rfh.ru/index.php?option=com_content&task=category&sectionid=12&id=102&Itemid=231&limit=50&limitstart=0> (accessed 10 June 2016).

Rostovskiy, Sergei, and Anatoly Vyatkin, eds. *Iugo-Vostochnaia Aziia: problemy regional'noi obshchnosti* [Southeast Asia: Issues of regional commonality]. Moscow: Nauka, 1977.

RSC (Russian State Library). Electronic catalogue <www.rsl.ru/ru/s97/s339/> (accessed 10 June 2016).

Simonia, Aida. *M'ianma: perekhod k rynochnoi ekonomike (1988–2011)* [Myanmar: A transit to market economy, 1988–2011]. Moscow: Institut vostokovedeniia, 2012.

Simonia, Nodari. *Naselenie kitaiskoi natsional'nosti v stranakh Iugo-Vostochnoi Azii* [The Chinese populations in Southeast Asia]. Moscow: Institut mezhdunarodnykh otnoshenii, 1959.

Sokolov, Anatoly, ed. *Russkie vo V'etname: ocherki i putevye zametki (XIX – nachalo XX veka)* [Russians in Vietnam: Essays and travellers' notes, the 19th – early 20th centuries). Moscow: 'Vostochnaia literatura' RAN, 2007.

Sulizkaya, Tatiana. *Strany ASEAN i mezhdunarodnye otnosheniia v Iugo-Vostochnoi Azii* [ASEAN member states and international relations in Southeast Asia]. Moscow: Nauka, 1985.

Sumsky, Victor. *Natsionalizm i avtoritarizm: politiko-ideologicheskie protsessy v Indonezii, Pakistane i Bangladesh* [Nationalism and authoritarianism: Political and ideological processes in Indonesia, Pakistan and Bangladesh]. Moscow: Nauka, 1987.

———. *Fiesta Filipina: reformy, revoliutsiia i aktivnoe nenasilie v razvivaiushchemsia obshchestve* [Fiesta Filipino: Reforms, revolution, and active non-violence in a developing society). Moscow: Vostochnaia literature, 2003.

Sumsky, Victor, Mark Hong, and Amy Lugg, eds. *ASEAN–Russia: Foundations and Future Prospects.* Singapore: Institute of Southeast Asian Studies, 2012.

Terwiel, Barend Jan. *Thailand's Political History: From the Fall of Ayutthaya in 1767 to Recent Times*. Bangkok: River Books, 2005.

Tyurin, Vladimir. *Istoriia Indonezii* [History of Indonesia]. Moscow: Vostochnyi universitet, 2004.

———. "Slovo o druge" [A word about friend]. In *Iugo-Vostochnaia Aziia v 2004 g.: Aktual'nye voprosy razvitiia* [Southeast Asia in 2004: Issues of development], pp. 6–8. Moscow: Institut vostokovedeniia, 2005.

Tyurin, Vladimir, and Vladlen Tsyganov. *Istoriia Malaizii. XX vek* [History of Malaysia: The 20th century]. Moscow: Institut vostokovedeniia, 2010.

Vasiliev, Vladimir. *Istoriia M'ianmy/Birmy. XX* vek [History of Myanmar/Burma: The 20th century]. Moscow: Institut vostokovedeniia, 2010.

Voskressenski, Alexei, ed. *Bol'shaia Vostochnaia Aziia: mirovaia politika i regional'nye transformatsii* [Greater East Asia: World politics and regional transformations]. Moscow: MGIMO-Universitet, 2010.

Voskressenski, Alexei, Ekaterina Koldunova, Anna Kireeva, and Sergei Lunev. *Mirovoe kompleksnoe regionovedenie* [World regional studies]. Moscow: Magistr, 2014.

9

India Studies in Soviet Lithuania: Approaching Asia from Outside the Establishment

Valdas Jaskūnas

Asian Studies as a constituent of area studies has constantly been framed by the discourse of a nation-state both as an object of study and as the subject generating demand for such knowledge. In particular, it holds true to nation-state debate in area studies which questions methodology, as well as the organizational principles of area studies based on the concept of the nation-state. However, the predominantly outward orientation of Western Asian Studies, preoccupied with post-colonial discourse, has given less attention to frameworks and strategies of engagement with Asia from the perspective of non-colonial nations in Europe or of those deprived of statehood and sovereignty through occupation, as was the case with the Baltic states in 1940. What is specific about engagement with Asia in these stateless countries is that, instead of producing knowledge in the service of the state, the local academies and in particular the cultural activists set out to appropriate orientalist knowledge for the construction of national identity aimed at resisting the colonial regime.

Lithuania is a clear example of a European nation which, since the late eighteenth century, more than once experienced the loss and regaining of statehood. The epoch of more than six centuries of early statehood, which began in the early thirteenth century, ended with the Third Partition of the Polish-Lithuanian Commonwealth (also known as the Commonwealth of Two Nations) by Russia, Prussia and Austria in 1795. Established in 1569, the commonwealth was a confederal state where Lithuania and Poland maintained their statehood. The collapse of Lithuania's political life was the result of its losing its status as an active state in the region — a position it had held since the early eighteenth century. The Third Partition marked the beginning of a stateless period under Russian rule which lasted for over a hundred years. After the abolition of the Russian monarchy and the subsequent Bolshevik Revolution, the Lithuanian Council, or *Taryba*, proclaimed the declaration of independence on 16 February 1918. The period of interwar independence lasted until the de facto Soviet annexation of Lithuania in 1940, although the loss of political status as a state had already been determined on the eve of WWII when the USSR and Germany signed a non-aggression pact, known as the Molotov–Ribbentrop Pact, on 23 August 1939. The pact included secret protocols whereby Moscow and Berlin divided their spheres of interest within the region. Five decades of Soviet occupation — following the years of the Nazi regime from 1941 to 1943 — lasted until 1990, when the Declaration of Restoration of the Independence of the Lithuanian State was passed by the elected Supreme Soviet of Soviet Lithuania on 11 March (Kiaupa 2005, pp. 152–68).

This chapter thus sets out to explore the case of engagement with India on the marginal zones of colonial formations, such as twentieth-century Lithuania under Soviet occupation, by addressing the rather hybrid orientalist tradition of imagining and knowledge of India, which gained currency in the society preoccupied with the reframing of national identity. The idea of Lithuania's links with India was modelled on linguistic affinity between the Lithuanian language and Sanskrit established in nineteenth-century comparative linguistics. During the years of Soviet oppression this not only contributed to long-term fascination with this country but also raised profound interest in ethnic Lithuanian culture, which proved to be an effective and socially engaging framework of identity transmission.

However, the loss of statehood immediately before WWII resulted in ideological restrictions on Soviet Lithuania's educational policies and on study of "distant foreign countries" at the universities of the Soviet periphery, to which Lithuania was relegated. In this political environment, dissemination of knowledge about India almost disappeared from the university and was taken over by non-academic institutions. The Lithuanian–Indian Society for Friendship, despite meagre contacts with India, served as camouflage for expressions of supressed national identity. This examination of a specific orientalist framework in Soviet Lithuania, on a broader scale, aims to address questions about contributions of the academies of stateless nations to the post-WWII Asian Studies enterprise and the role of non-academic institutions in generating interest about Asia within particular ideological environments.

Launching Projects of Oriental Studies in Lithuania

Early projects of establishing Oriental Studies in Lithuania date back to the early nineteenth century. As a part of the Russian Empire, Lithuania had to submit to the imperial education system, although living memories of the Polish–Lithuanian Commonwealth were a driving force in culture for generations, perhaps until the 1830s. The cultural environment of post-disintegration of the commonwealth was stimulated by the statesmen's strategies of rebuilding an independent state — the idea cherished till the unsuccessful November Uprising in 1830–31. Hence, the initial projects of Oriental Studies evidently had a political rationale. My argument is that questioning the establishment of Oriental Studies as merely the outcome of the imperial or nation-state politics of knowledge of the rest of the world may help to disclose the multifaceted nature of this establishment. Hence, the launching of projects and subsequent development of Oriental Studies in Lithuania and at Vilnius University in particular is a case that illustrates the nationalist discourse within the establishment of area studies relevant to a stateless nation in pursuit of constructing both political and national identity.

The date of 1 June 1810 marks the inception of Oriental Studies at Vilnius University (then Imperial Vilnius University) with the decision passed by the University Senate to appoint Julius Klaproth (1783–1835) professor and chair for Oriental languages and literatures (Mejor 2009). The idea of studying Oriental languages academically was already in the air at the beginning of the century. Correspondence between Prince Adam Jerzy Czartoryski, the curator of Vilnius University, and Sir William Jones, the founder of the Asiatic Society of Bengal, indicates that initial attempts to start Oriental Studies go back to the late eighteenth century, i.e., the last years of the republic of both nations. At the same time, a project of an Asiatic Society (Academie Asiatique) in Russia designed on the pattern of the Oriental Academy in Vienna was also discussed. The students of this academy were supposed to study Eastern languages, such as Tatar, Turkish, Arabic, Persian, Mongolian, Tibetan, Manchu and Chinese, as well as the customs and laws of Asian peoples. The academy was intended to spread information about Europe among the peoples of Asia by publishing books in Oriental languages and to make Eastern cultures better known in the Russian empire by the annual publication of translations.

Taking into consideration the political situation of the region in the early nineteenth century, it seems improbable that such a pioneering institution of Oriental Studies would have been launched in a province of the Russian Empire rather than in the capital city. In the end, Julius Klaproth, the scholar of Chinese and other Oriental languages, apparently chose not to take the newly established chair for which he had been nominated. The reasons for this might have been political. It is known that in the same year (1810), the project of the Asiatic Academy had already been worked out by Count Sergey Semionovich Uvarov (Ouvaroff) (1786–1855), the then honourable member and later president of the Russian Academy of Sciences. Klaproth was also engaged in this project in compiling the syllabi on Indian literature, Chinese and Manchu literatures and Arabic, Persian, Turkic and Tatar literatures. The idea finally was realized with the establishment of the Asiatic Museum at the Russian Academy of Science in St Petersburg in 1819, which was later transformed into the Institute of Oriental Studies, the present Institute of Oriental Manuscripts.

A new idea of establishing a Chair of Oriental Studies at Vilnius University came about in 1822, with a new candidate to take the position of professor, Józef Sękowski (1800–1858). Before being nominated for the professorship, Sękowski was sent in 1819 on a trip to the Near East with a university grant to enable him to undertake a practical study of languages and to broaden his knowledge of local cultures, returning in October 1821. In 1822 he was elected "extraordinary professor of Oriental languages" by the University Council. Unfortunately, this time the initiative of Vilnius University did not meet with approval at a higher political level. Minister of Religious Affairs and National Education, Prince Alexander Golitsyn, in a letter dated 29 July the same year, informed the university curator that Józef Sękowski would instead be granted a position at the College of Foreign Affairs in St Petersburg (Mejor 2009).

After 1822, academic life at Vilnius University came under strict supervision from imperial bureaucrats because of social discontent and civil unrest fuelled by semi-official groups that involved academics of the university. These included the Philomaths, Philarets and Brotherhood of Rascals (Shubravts). The unrest led to the official closure of the university in 1832, which affected many talented young graduates, who were forced to pursue their academic careers in Russia. Among them was the originator of Mongol Studies in Russia, Józef (Osip) Kowalewski (1801–78), who was exiled to Kazan, where he took up the study of Eastern languages, especially Mongolian. His contemporary, Antoni Muchliński (1808–77), undertook a state service career in St Petersburg and entered the Faculty of Eastern Languages at the university there. Very likely an academic career developed for another graduate of Vilnius University, the noted scholar of northern Iranian peoples and literatures, Alexander Chodzko (1804–91). His interest in Eastern cultures began while he was a student and active member of a circle of young philologists. It was developed when he entered the education department of spoken languages at the Ministry of Foreign Affairs in St Petersburg, where interpreters of Eastern languages for Russian missions to Iran and Turkey were educated.[1]

The early history of Oriental Studies in Vilnius, when seen from the point of view of structured demand for such knowledge in the early nineteenth century, proves to be quite logical. Given that the initiative of starting Oriental Studies brought Vilnius and imperial St Petersburg into competition, the course of events comes as no surprise: the establishment of Oriental Studies fostered by Russia's imperial ambitions found better support and secured more funds for implementation in St Petersburg than in Vilnius. Obviously, the rationale for the establishment of Oriental Studies was set in the colonial agenda of Tsarist Russia, as it was with major powers across Europe. Vilnius University, soon closed for almost a century, was not destined to contribute to these politics of knowledge.

New initiatives for structuring Oriental Studies in Lithuania emerged, after almost a century, in the early twentieth century, meeting the demands of the nation-state established in 1918. The period between the world wars saw little enthusiasm for the Oriental Studies which had been taking shape at the University of Lithuania (since 1933, Vytautas Magnus University) in Kaunas, the temporary capital of Lithuania.

The fact that Oriental Studies generated little interest within local academia could be explained by the overwhelming nationalist concern within the inherited multicultural society. The nodal point around which Oriental Studies centred was Biblical Studies informed from the endeavours of archaeologists, philologists, linguists and theologians, which was divided into the fields of Jewish and Egyptian Studies. Two leading scholars at the university were an Egypt-focused archaeologist, Marija Rudzinskaitė-Arcimavičienė (1885–1941), and a Semitist, Khaim-Nakhman Shapira (1894–1943). Rudzinskaitė-Arcimavičienė started teaching in 1922 at the Faculty of Humanities the course of History of Ancient East, which comprised the history of Semitic peoples, Persia and Egypt. The course was offered to students of History, Semitic Studies, and Greek and Latin languages and literatures. Khaim-Nakhman Shapira, a scholar of Jewish Hebrew literature and a son of the chief rabbi of Kaunas, held the Semitic chair at the University from 1922 to its closure in 1940. He lectured on a range of subjects, with a major focus on Jewish culture, to educate teachers for Jewish schools. Other courses included the Arabic language, Syriac language, comparative grammar of Semitic languages, and even a course on the Qur'an.[2]

Still, Semitic Studies and Egyptology were not the only fields representing the Orient. University records show that students of comparative linguistics were able to choose the course of Sanskrit. The first professor of Sanskrit was an honorary doctor of the university, Adalbert Bezzenberger (1851–1922), former rector and professor of comparative linguistics and Sanskrit at Königsberg University. He was able to teach for perhaps no longer than half a year before his death in October 1922. The course was taken over by the Swiss linguist and lexicographer Alfred Senn (1899–1978). Among Senn's students happened to be future professor of comparative linguistics Ričardas Mironas (1908–79), the key figure of Soviet-period Indian studies in Lithuania.

Despite the regular presence of Sanskrit in the university curriculum prior to 1940 — the year of Soviet occupation — it was not developed into a structured Indian Studies course. Yet, it could be considered one of the key elements in mobilizing the national identity of early twentieth-century Lithuania, marked with fundamental political and social shifts. Derived from linguistic affinity between Sanskrit and Lithuanian languages, the idea of Lithuanian–Indian ties obsessed the minds of pre-WWII intellectuals and evolved into a nationalist mythology of shared cultural heritage. Thus, before turning to the orientalist discourse of Soviet Lithuania that provides the main arguments for discussing out-of-the-establishment orientalism during Soviet times, I will seek to explore the notion of inward orientalism — a common cultural legacy of stateless nations in East and Central Europe.

Inward Orientalism: Building the Identity of a Stateless Nation

The concept of orientalism originated in the magnum opus of Edward Said. *Orientalism* (1978) played a major role in reshaping understanding of the premises of Western perceptions of the Orient, drawing on examples of British and French imperialism. Said's analysis of orientalism underlined its outward orientation. However, orientalism as a discourse of power may have also an inward direction, which is relevant for a society in need of an interpretative framework to resist the Other. Sheldon Pollock's (1993) and Robert Cowan's (2010) contributions on Indo-German identification established an understanding of orientalism as being directed inwards. Such an understanding of orientalism, which provides a framework for identity-construction analysis, has been applied to the encounter with India in Central Europe (see Strnad 2007; Hříbek 2012), so it stands as a working hypothesis to analyse the case of Lithuanian fascination with India that intensified during the period of lost statehood.

Lithuania and other small and non-imperial nations from Eastern and Central Europe share a similar set of representations of India, which is based on an imagined identity that includes a notion of superiority. The Orientalist legacy across this region demonstrates that engagement with India was "constructed not on the premises of otherness and inferiority but, on the contrary, the premises of identity and equality ... as a site for projection of our collective self down imaginary history and as a possible source of legitimacy for our own claims to independent national statehood" (Hříbek 2012, p. 48).

This model of inward orientalism was developed in Germany as "the late eighteenth and nineteenth-century German proponents of Indian wisdom ... brought to the study of Sanskrit texts their own search to establish a set of German national origins that were independent of the Graeco-Roman and Judeo-Christian traditions" (Cowan 2010). In Lithuania this Germanized model of inward orientalism gained currency in the stateless cultural environment. The links of the Lithuanian language with Sanskrit, which entered the academic scene with its discovery by the German linguist Franz Bopp (1791–1867), had crucial significance for the further construction of Lithuanian national identity along similar lines: of an India-as-a-cradle-of-civilization theory which encompassed similar linguistic ties between Sanskrit and the languages of the Slavs.

At the turn of the twentieth century, the linguistic affinity between Lithuania and India developed in similar directions, which in one way or another contributed to the hypothesis of an Indo-European homeland. The location of the Indo-European homeland in Asia, suggested by the discovery of the Hittite Empire and the deciphering of its language in 1915, gained in popularity among Lithuanian intellectuals and enhanced arguments for the origin of Lithuanians being from Asia Minor. In the period between the world wars, marked by the first independence of the country (1918–40), the idea of an Indo-European homeland underwent a transformation, with India taking a prominent place. Although Indo-European linguistics endowed the Lithuanian language with great antiquity, it drew its arguments from the affinity of the Baltic and Slavonic languages, that did not apply in the context of the political conflict between Lithuania and neighbouring Russia and Poland.[3] Fascination with India became a recurrent topic in pre-WWII Lithuanian literature. It played upon the issue of cultural affinity and explored numerous Indian notions such as philosophical idealism. Literary production ranged from renderings of Indian texts, such as the hymns of the *Rigveda* by the national poet Maironis (1862–1932) and the *Bhagavadgita* by Vilhelmas Storostas-Vydūnas (1868–1953) to the *Pratjekabuda*, a philosophical story (1913) by Vincas Mickevičius-Krėvė (1882–1947), an outstanding writer and academic (Tamošaitis 1998).

The intellectual movement that appealed more to nationalist sentiment and entrenched nationalistic identity with oriental associations was soon reinforced with religious concepts, which helped to transform linguistic linkages into assumed religious kinship between ancient India and the Paganism of pre-Christian Lithuania. One of the chief proponents of the revival of Lithuanian paganism by connecting it with Hinduism was the writer, philosopher and playwright Vilhelmas Storostas-Vydūnas, from Prussian-dominated Lithuania Minor. Through his writings, although never explicitly in practice, he stimulated interest in pagan customs and provided an ideological foundation for Lithuanian resistance to foreign domination and cultural assimilation.

Vydūnas's engagement with the Orient started while studying German translations of Indian philosophy and led him to deep fascination with the Vedanta school of philosophy and other Indian spiritual traditions, which brought him into association with German theosophy in Leipzig. In theosophy he believed he had come across ideas of intentional movement towards the spiritual liberation relevant to developing better resistance against national assimilation for his compatriots in Russian-dominated Lithuania. Moreover, theosophy supplied him with the idea of a religiosity which propagated no primacy of any religion and simultaneously helped to downplay the hegemony of Christianity. For Vydūnas it was appealing to look for inspiration in the pagan religion of Lithuanians which he believed to be the setting wherein national values originated. The culture of

Hinduism, in the form of Indian philosophy, especially its idealistic trend, convinced him that moral revival of the nation based on national values might be possible through human liberation (Bagdonavičius 2000).

Imagination about India ranging from scholarly speculation to religious idiosyncrasy was a key issue that foreshadowed the national awakening movement in Lithuania down to the late years of the Soviet regime. Therefore, we might argue that inward orientalism has relevance to questioning the experience of the oppressed society where the Other stands for an oppressor of the national identity. The experience of Soviet Lithuania proves that inward orientalism of the stateless nation was primarily driven by linguistic and literary engagement. There are striking parallels with orientalist encounters within other totalitarian societies: in a Central European country such as Czechoslovakia that had an established tradition of Oriental Studies, the focus on the study of languages and production of literary translations was the prerequisite for partly salvaging Oriental Studies (Hříbek 2012, p. 47). So, the literary nature of inward orientalism, approached from the discourse of national identity, supports questioning the universal applicability of the Saidian notion of orientalism as framed by the outward British and French political discourse.

Linguistic and Literary India: Legacy of Ričardas Mironas

The period from 1939 to the late 1970s features incoherent and partly structured interest in India Studies in Lithuania, which was mainly focused on Sanskrit language and literature meant as a prerequisite for comparative linguists. The only person to have continuously taught Sanskrit and Indian literature since 1944 was Ričardas Gabrielius Mironas (1908–79), a 1933 graduate from Vytautas Magnus University in Kaunas. Educated as a linguist leaning to Sanskrit studies, he played a major role in post-WWII Soviet Lithuania academia in incorporating Indian Studies into the curriculum.[4]

The career of Mironas as a Sanskritist started just after his graduation from the Faculty of Humanities at Kaunas Vytautas Magnus University in 1933 with a thesis on comparative Sanskrit–Lithuanian linguistics. Immediately after graduation he was sent to Paris with a grant from the Ministry of Education of Lithuania. There he spent three years (1933–36) at the Institute of Indian Civilization at l'École pratique des hautes études (EPHE) in the Sorbonne. He studied under the supervision of Émile Benveniste with the tutorial assistance of Jules Bloch, Louis Renou, Sylvain Lévi, Alfred Charles Auguste Foucher and Nadine Stchoupak. During his final year of study, Mironas worked on the translation of *Rigveda* hymns. After his return to Kaunas, these annotated translations into Lithuanian were published as *Twelve Hymns of the Rigveda* (Kaunas 1939). This was followed by a few translations of classical Sanskrit literature, such as the first act of the *Abhijnanashakuntala* by Kalidasa and fully translated *Panchatantra* stories published posthumously in 1990.

Mironas's academic career provides a sound example of the attitude towards Oriental Studies in Soviet Lithuania. After the battlefront moved westward and the work of the Vytautas Magnus University in Kaunas resumed, Mironas addressed university authorities with the proposal to teach India-related subjects. Disappointingly, the new establishment and the Soviet politics of higher education did not entitle universities in the Soviet republics to run area studies, so plans to introduce Indian or Sanskrit studies had to be given up. Although Mironas kept teaching the basic Sanskrit course as an optional subject for comparative linguists till his premature death in 1979, Indian studies or translations from Sanskrit were secondary in importance to research in comparative linguistics and translations of Latin and Ancient Greek classics. To promote studies of Sanskrit language and literature, Mironas in the early 1960s prepared the manuscript of a Sanskrit handbook of over five hundred pages, along with a Sanskrit–Lithuanian vocabulary consisting of 6500 words — the first didactic tool on an Indian subject ever produced in Lithuanian. However, publication of the handbook was deliberately delayed and never realized.

The changing attitude towards Indian studies during the early years of the Soviet regime in Lithuania is exemplified by the account of Mironas's submission of his doctoral thesis, specifically termed, Dissertation of the Candidate of Science in the Soviet Union.[5] Mironas was granted the status of Candidate of Science in Philology on 27 February 1948 with the defence of his dissertation on "Translation of Aeschylus' drama *Prometheus Bound*". The option for an ancient Greek tragedy as a topic for the dissertation seems to be rather a matter of concession. Records of official documentation since 1944 prove that Mironas had been working on a thesis related to Sanskrit linguistics. Mironas changed the topic of his dissertation several times, from "The Tropes of the *Rigveda*" — the idea born while still in Paris working under Louis Renou — to "The equivalent forms of Sanskrit noun and pronoun inflection in Lithuanian morphology" which he submitted to the Faculty of Philology Council. However, in subsequent years the suitability of the topic must have been evaluated negatively, resulting in the consequent change of subject to that of ancient Greek drama.

Institutionalizing Cultural Encounter: Activities of the Lithuanian–Indian Friendship Society

Oriental Studies in the Soviet Union were a highly politicized and centralized enterprise, with centres in Moscow and Leningrad and five republican institutes of the Soviet "own Orient" in Tashkent (Uzbekistan), Dushanbe (Tajikistan), Tbilisi (Georgia), Yerevan (Armenia) and Baku (Azerbaijan). The network of Oriental institutes in the southernmost Soviet republics, in proximity to Turkey, Iran, Afghanistan and Pakistan, had a political rationale, since the principal purpose of these establishments was to monitor political developments in these Muslim neighbouring countries (Kemper 2011, p. 11). Other Soviet republics, including Lithuania, were deprived of the possibility of carrying out Oriental Studies and research.

In the absence of a structured academic body of Oriental Studies in Soviet Lithuania, there were still other forms of encounter with the Orient supported by the official establishment. One of the channels to increase intercultural awareness was enhanced by Soviet cultural diplomacy. Soviet cultural diplomacy was organized through the Union of Soviet Societies for Friendship and Cultural Relations with Foreign Countries (henceforth, USSF), founded in 1958 to replace the All-Union Society for Foreign Cultural Exchange. The union worked as a network of the central and branch societies in the Soviet republics. The Lithuanian Society for Friendship and Cultural Relations with Foreign Countries (LSF) was launched in January 1959.

There were two reasons for the new Soviet framework for cultural relations with foreign countries: the slow emergence of proletarian revolutions in post-colonial countries across the world, and changing domestic attitudes towards internationalization. The latter were reshaped by the course of nationalities policies, especially those towards the Soviet republics of Central Asia and the Caucasus. In 1958 the Soviet nationalities policy underwent robust reconsideration. This was prompted by the programme of de-Stalinization launched by Nikita Khrushchev, which in turn emancipated the suppressed nationalism that had been hard to explain both at home and abroad. If Lenin and Stalin's policy of indigenization (*korenizaciya* or "in-rooting") privileged domination of the titular nation in a given territory, Khrushchev replaced it with the idea of a supranational Soviet people. Strengthened with the rhetoric of "brotherly alliance", this notion actually introduced a hierarchical interpretation of national and ethnic identities. Two terminological collocations — "internationalism" and "friendship of nations and nationalities" — were in use to negotiate relations between Soviet nations. Internationalism presupposed a hierarchical dimension and the submission of any Soviet nation to the greater Russian one, and hence entailed the legitimized concept of Russification; whereas friendship of nations addressed horizontal relations between nations and nationalities across the Soviet Union.

Such internationalism understood in hierarchical terms has permeated Soviet cultural diplomacy as well. Its agenda promoted internationalist activities, which were usually carried out through the involvement of the communist organizations in different countries. In the case of Soviet–Indian friendship, the recipient organization in India was the Communist Party of India (CPI) and its branch sections in different states.

By 1975 the USSF comprised sixty-three societies with different foreign countries. The Society of Soviet–Indian Cultural Relations, established in 1958, began expanding as a follow-up to the visit of the prime minister of India, Mrs Indira Gandhi, to the USSR in April 1966 — evidently the mutually taken decision reflecting the changing political climate in the region after the Sino–Indian conflict in 1962. In the late 1960s and 1970s, the Soviet government frequently prioritized diplomatic relations with India from among the non-socialist countries, despite the fact that the CPI was not only in opposition but also sometimes even subject to persecution. The USSF was based on a strictly supervised network of the branch societies in different Soviet republics. The first branch society of Soviet–Indian friendship was established in 1966 in the port city of Odessa (Ukraine SSR), which had a consulate general of India. Later it was followed by the societies in Kirghiz SSR (1967), Azerbaijan (1968), Irkutsk Region (1972), etc. Lithuania was among the first, with the establishment on 18 February 1967 of the Indian section of the Lithuanian Society for Friendship and Cultural Relations with Foreign Countries (henceforth, Lithuanian–Indian Society). From twenty-eight founding members, among whom Vilnius University teachers and students made a majority, it increased to a body of thirty-five members by the end of the year. The Sanskritist Ričardas Mironas was elected its chairman with folklorist association activist Jonas Trinkūnas his deputy. As officially stated, the major objective of the society was to acquaint Lithuanian society with the literature and culture of both ancient and contemporary India and to spread knowledge of the cultural achievements of Soviet Lithuania in India.

From the very beginning following the adoption of the official cooperative framework, the society established links with Orissa as a partner state. The first Indian delegation — headed by Mangaldas Jagjivandas Shah, vice-president of the Bombay branch of the CPI-controlled India–Soviet Cultural Society (ISCUS) and the professor of psychology from Utkal University, Rathanath Rath, a member of the National Council of ISCUS — visited Vilnius in August 1967. In following years both parties exchanged delegations, but the members of the Lithuanian–Indian Society were not frequently represented in Lithuanian delegations. Mironas was on the delegation headed by the minister of higher and professional secondary education of Soviet Lithuania, Henrikas Zabulis, which left for India in March 1969.[5] In Orissa, Mironas delivered a few public lectures at the Sanskrit College in Puri and at Utkal University. In Calcutta, he met the Bengal linguist Suniti Kumar Chatterji (1890–1977), the author of the book *Balts and Aryans in Their Indo-European Background* (Simla 1968), with whom Mironas had had communication since Chatterji's visit to Vilnius in 1964.

In 1968 Lithuania welcomed the first delegation of ISCUS from Orissa led by the communist activist Sarat Patnaik, member of the National Board of ISCUS, and the journalist Janaki Ballav Patnaik (b. 1927), then the editor of two newspapers and the monthly journal *Pourusha*, fellow of the senate of Utkal University and later chief minister of Odisha (1980–89 and 1995–99) from the Indian National Congress.

The Lithuanian–Indian society notably differed from other sections of the LSF in that it aimed first to cooperate with the countries from the socialist camp and — no less important — to establish links with Lithuanian diasporas. It should be noted that, although Soviet societies of friendship primarily operated as instruments of cultural diplomacy, in the Soviet totalitarian state they also served to build up networks of surveillance at home and spying abroad. The archive of the LSF provides comprehensive documentation of the activities managed by the societies: apart from information concerning cultural exchange and the promotion of Soviet cultural achievements, usually in a self-congratulatory manner, it also contains files of the lists of hand-picked Soviet embarking tourists or delegations; completed questionnaires; autobiographies; recommendations from their work places; detailed reports on the tours, including personal meetings; and statistics on foreign tourists and groups visiting Lithuania.

In contrast to other similar sections of the LSF that usually were organized from the top down, the Lithuanian–Indian Society happened to be the result of an initiative by a group of intelligentsia predominantly related to Vilnius University. Despite very few contacts with and virtually no travel to India, the activities of the society raised a high degree of interest among the people from academic, cultural and artistic circles.

The home activities of the newly established society were predominantly educational and focused on public talks on topics of Indian culture, literature and art, or literary gatherings where translations of extracts from Sanskrit texts were read out. It is no surprise that such an educational agenda must soon have turned into a more ideologically laden internationalist one which facilitated channelling Soviet propaganda to India. A constant voluminous supply of Soviet promotional material to Orissa was, noticeably, not reciprocated by the Indian side, which aroused disappointment among Lithuanian activists.

Internationalist agenda-setting instead of the promotion of "friendship of nations and nationalities" is evidently one of the paradoxes of Soviet cultural diplomacy embodied by the "societies of friendship". Soviet cultural diplomacy from the late 1950s displayed an increasing Kremlin concern about internationalist framing of ethnicity and national culture, which worked to downplay or deny the cosmopolitan and multilingual characteristics of both multicultural states. It is likely that the formal organization of Soviet–Indian friendship establishing links between Soviet republics and Indian states, such as Lithuania–Orissa or Azerbaijan–Gujarat, should have encouraged the possibility of communicating national or regional culture, but an internationalist framing kept it minimized and subject to constant misinterpretation.

As an example, at the USSR–India friendship symposium in Moscow held in June 1973, the question of teaching Indian languages was raised by the chairman of the Lithuanian–Indian Society, Ričardas Mironas. He proposed that widely spoken Indian state languages be taught and learned not only in Moscow and Leningrad (nowadays St Petersburg) but also at the universities of Soviet republics. In particular, he advocated for the framework of teaching at the universities of a particular Soviet republic the language of an Indian partner state. Indeed, Mironas had a strong argument for promoting the idea of Oriya being taught in Lithuania, as by that time he had already compiled the *Oriya–Lithuanian Vocabulary*, with Sanskrit and Hindi equivalents published in 1972. Albeit such suggestions were hardly even discussed, as practice showed. The very formulation of the question was rather provocative since it was well known that the teaching and learning of Asian languages and related subjects was highly politicized and delegated only to certain institutions.

A number of questions about this situation could be raised. How could the Lithuanian–Indian Society, given the vague contacts with India, afford sustainable activity? Did those activities elaborate only on the mythology of the cultural affinity, or were there other forms of engagement? As a matter of fact, from the very beginning the Lithuanian–Indian Society became a shelter for more overt expressions of national sentiment and ethnic culture shared with the increasing ethnocultural movement centred around the association *Ramuva* established in the early 1960s. Officially it was devoted to collecting folklore from rural communities for scientific ethnographical purposes and the preservation of cultural heritage; but, unofficially, its activists shared a common appreciation for pagan religious elements. It is no surprise that many members of the society were active members of Ramuva, among them Jonas Trinkūnas, the vice-chairman of the society as well as one of the leaders of Ramuva.[7] Thus, the major event organized under the umbrella of the society in the year of its inception, 1969, had little to do with India proper — the ancient pagan summer solstice feast (Lith. *Rasa* or *Joninės*) on the mounds of Kernavė, the ancient capital of the medieval Lithuanian state.

After a few years of deliberation and surveillance, the reaction of the Soviet regime to the nationalist and religious outburst of the ethnocultural movement was rigorous. The noted trial of the so-called "Folklorists' case" in 1973 resulted in five active members of the ethnocultural movement being sentenced to imprisonment. Around one hundred were interrogated and prosecuted for anti-Soviet agitation and propaganda as well as copying and circulating underground literature. Jonas Trinkūnas, leader of Ramuva, was prosecuted for underground activity and punished by dismissal from his doctoral studies at Vilnius University. He had to take employment in the countryside, chiselling tombstones.

Conclusions: Orientalism of the "Parallel Society"

The different forms of encounter with India in Soviet Lithuania, put into a wider context, bear many characteristics of an alternative society, or even border on disobedience. Social disobedience under the Soviet regime has been a recurrent topic in post-Soviet scholarship. Post-socialist scholarship has suggested the term "parallel society" to describe structurally such networks of ideological resistance. Post-independence Lithuanian scholars of sociology largely draw upon two social networks of disobedience in Soviet Lithuania: the Catholic underground and the ethnocultural movement (Ramonaitė 2011). Along with these two, the subculture of the hippies is sometimes classed by anthropologists as another form of disobedience to the Soviet regime.

Largely due to a lack of research, post-Soviet Lithuanian scholarship on alternative social networks has not taken into consideration another form of social disobedience generally associated with fascination with the Orient, which was interpreted as mental deviation by Soviet psychiatry. Orientalism in this respect bears very similar features to the Catholic underground and ethnocultural movements in embracing a religious and cultural orientation. The latter has already been drawn upon while dealing with the activities of the Lithuanian–Indian Society and the academic career of Ričardas Mironas. The former, still awaiting deeper investigation, has been represented by numerous religious movements, such as the Lithuanian Roerich Society or newly established Buddhist communities that have coordinated their activities with allied communities in Russia, especially in Buryatia. What is specific about orientalist engagement in comparison with alternative movements in Soviet Lithuania is that it had a more distinct international dimension, which is still rather underestimated in Lithuanian historiography of subcultures. Otherwise, orientalism might be considered an instrumental framework of national identity formation — a common feature of all social movements of disobedience traceable within the stateless society of Soviet Lithuania.

My working hypothesis for further exploration of orientalism within the stateless Soviet society, therefore, rests on consideration of engagement with the Orient as a strategy of "resistant identity", to put it in Castells' (1997) terms, enacted within the wider conceptual framework of a "parallel society" pertinent to a totalitarian state. Given the main point of divergence from the theory of social movements, disobedience as a form of resistance in totalitarian society is a social practice based on sociality established from the top. Hence, any semi-official or alternative participation bears a resistant character, even if it does not contradict dominant institutions. As has been shown, engagement with India in Soviet Lithuania can be approached both from institutional and social network analysis. In this regard, fascination with the Orient is hardly distinguished from other social networks, such as ethnocultural or religious ones.

To sum up, inward orientalism as a strategy paired with the revival of national identity is a particular feature of Lithuanian orientalism which it shares with other Central and Eastern European stateless and/ or non-imperial discourses. Examining the specific framework of social and academic interest in India within Soviet Lithuania leads us to a notion of orientalism that gains currency within the "parallel society" driven by an encounter with the Other from within society rather than outside it.

Notes

1. For more on the early history of Oriental Studies in Lithuania, see the special issue of the journal *Acta Orientalia Vilnensia* 10, nos. 1–2, "Studying the Orient in Lithuania" (2009).
2. In April 2017 Dr Khaim-Nachman Shapira was granted posthumously the Memory Diploma of Vilnius University under the Recovering Memory initiative, which commemorates and pays respect to staff and students of Vilnius University who were expelled from the university by the totalitarian regimes and their local collaborators. Shapira was deprived of his academic career by the Soviets in 1940 as a consequence of closure of the Department of Semitology and killed three years later by the Nazis because of his Jewish nationality (for more on the Recovering Memory initiative, see http://www.vu.lt/en/about-us/history/recovering-memory).
3. Later, Marija Gimbutas (Lith. Gimbutienė; 1921–94), an American scholar of Lithuanian origin, launched the hypothesis of the Indo-European homeland in the steppes of South Russia, where Kurgan culture prevailed between 5000 and 3000 BC. Her work was continued by her student James P. Mallory.
4. The academic career of Ričardas Mironas is henceforth documented with reference to the very thoroughly maintained collections of personal documents kept at the Department of Rare Books and Manuscripts of Martynas Mažvydas National Library of Lithuania (fund no. F133) and the Department of Manuscripts of Vilnius University Library (fund no F128), as well as a personnel file kept at the Vilnius University Archive.
5. The Candidate of Science was the first postgraduate scientific degree in the Soviet Union.
6. Other members of the delegation were the opera singer Valentinas Adamkevičius, the Baltic psaltery player Bronė Simonaitienė and the Lithuanian reed player Kazys Budrys.
7. In 1991 Jonas Trinkūnas (1939–2014) openly declared the religious purposes of Ramuva's folkloristic movement and launched a revivalist religious organization, Romuva, named after the ancient Baltic sanctuary (Ramuva being camouflage of its name) to express its pagan religious orientation. Trinkūnas's many years of leadership in Romuva were honoured with the bestowal of the title *Krivis*, the high priest of Romuva in 2002. See Strmiska (2012, p. 133–32).

References

Bagdonavičius, Vaclovas. "Vydūnas: The Essential Features of his Philosophy". In *Lithuanian Philosophical Studies*, vol 2, *Lithuanian Philosophy: Persons and Ideas*, edited by Jūratė Baranova, pp. 87–104 (Cultural Heritage and Contemporary Change, Series IVA, Eastern and Central Europe, vol. 17; General Editor: George F. McLean). Washington, DC: The Council for Research in Values and Philosophy, 2000.

Castells, Manuel. *The Power of Identity*. Malden: Blackwell, 1997.

Cowan, Robert. *The Indo-German Identification: Reconciling South Asian Origins and European Destinies 1765–1885*. Rochester, NY: Camden House, 2010.

Hříbek, Martin. "Czech Indology and the Concept of Orientalism". In *Understanding India: Indology and Beyond*, edited by Jaroslav Vacek and Harbans Mukhia, pp. 45–56. Orientalia Pragensia 18. Acta Universitatis Carolinae. Philologica 1, 2011. Prague: Charles University in Prague, Karolinum Press, 2012.

Kemper, Michael. "Introduction: Integrating Soviet Oriental studies". In *The Heritage of Soviet Oriental Studies*, edited by Michael Kemper and Stephan Conermann, pp. 1–25. Abingdon: Routledge, 2011.

Kiaupa, Zigmantas. *The History of Lithuania*, 2nd ed. Vilnius: Baltos lankos, 2005.

Mejor Marek. "Early history of Oriental Studies at Vilnius University". *Acta Orientalia Vilnensia* 10, nos. 1–2 (2009): 15–28.

Pollock, Sheldon. "Deep Orientalism? Notes on Sanskrit and Power beyond the Raj". In *Orientalism and the Postcolonial Predicament: Perspectives on South Asia*, edited by C.A. Breckenridge and P. van der Veer, pp. 80–96. Philadelphia: University of Pennsylvania Press, 1993.

Ramonaitė, Ainė. "'Paralelinės visuomenės' užuomazgos sovietinėje Lietuvoje: katalikiškojo pogrindžio ir etnokultūrinio sajūdžio simbiozė" [Germinal 'parallel society' in Soviet Lithuania: Symbiosis of Catholic underground and ethno-cultural movement]. In *Sajūdžio ištakų beieškant: nepaklusniųjų tinklaveikos galia*, edited by Jūratė Kavaliauskaitė and Ainė Ramonaitė, pp, 33–58. Vilnius: Baltos lankos, 2011.

Strmiska, Michael F. "Romuva Looks East: Indian Inspiration in Lithuanian Paganism". In *Religious Diversity in Post-Soviet Society: Ethnographies of Catholic Hegemony and the New Pluralism in Lithuania*, edited by Milda Ališauskienė and Ingo W. Schröder, pp. 125–50. Farnham, Burlington, VT: Ashgate, 2012.

Strnad, Jaroslav. "India as Reflected in Czech Consciousness in the Era of the National Revivalist Movement of the Nineteenth Century (ca. 1800–1848)". Special issue: "India – 60th Anniversary of Independence Celebration Issue", *Archiv orientální* 75, no. 3 (2007): 279–90.

Tamošaitis, Regimantas. *Kelionė į laiko pradžią: indų idealizmas, Vydūnas, Krėvė* [Travelling to the beginning of time: Indian idealism, Vydūnas, Krėvė], Mokslo darbai series: Literatūra 35. Vilnius: Pradai, 1998.

Part IV

Inter-Asian Gazes

10

Indian Understandings of Asia

Brij Mohan Tankha

Modern Indian academic interest in East Asia has a multilayered context. Historical connections built through the movement of ideas and material objects were decisively reshaped during the colonial period so that these earlier linkages were always in tension with the colonial construction of the "East". These ways of understanding created tensions and ambiguities in Indian engagement with countries in East and Southeast Asia. The writing of India's past was an enterprise carried out under British supervision, but also in resistance to it. In this enterprise, India's historical relationship with Asia played an important role in highlighting the unique qualities of Indian civilization — ideas that continue to shape contemporary thinking and, perhaps, account for the lack of an "Asian" boom in Indian intellectual circles.

India has yet to witness studies of Japan or China comparable to what has occurred in Europe, the United States and many other countries. That is not to say that Asian countries have not been studied, or that there is no sustained engagement with these countries. Rather, it is to suggest that this "past" has been marginalized or forgotten, and recovering this history provides a way of relocating India as part of a larger regional community. In this chapter I argue that Indian "understandings of Asia" have a different and layered history, and exploring these provides a way of thinking about knowledge production and its relationship to both civil society and the state.

I begin the chapter by first discussing the idea of Asia and the historical development of modern Indian conceptions of Asia. I look at four defining moments. The first is the pre-modern basis for Indian engagement, which began to change sometime in the early eighteenth century. The second came during the late nineteenth and early decades of the twentieth centuries when Indian intellectuals engaged directly with China, Japan and other parts of the Asian region. This first modern engagement, often in colonial capitals, grew out of the anti-colonial struggle and resistance to Western intellectual domination, where the idea of "community" was on resistance. In fact, often India was projected as the core element of "Asia". The third moment was in the year of independence, the Asian Relations Conference held in New Delhi. This could be called an "Afro-Asian" moment, for it built on the idea of resistance that included not only geographical Asia but all the former colonized territories. The fourth and current phase started around the mid-eighties as the gradual opening of the Indian economy brought foreign collaboration, particularly Japanese. Then, from the late 1990s, Korean and Chinese ties created a new demand for expertise as well as greater flows of people and information between India and these countries, a period of the rediscovery of Asia. I conclude by considering why, even as East Asia is coming centre stage, "Asian Studies" continues to be relatively marginal in the universities.

Can We Talk of "Asia"?

Does Asia have either cartographic or intellectual boundaries; does it refer to a supra-regional community bound by spiritual, social and cultural affinities? Or is it merely "this enmapped place [which] has never been more than a simulacrum of something that has no substance" (H. Haratoonian, quoted in Dirlik 1997), an invention of orientalism and inseparable from Euro-American power over Asia (Said 1978). Geographical boundaries are drawn on the basis of political and intellectual principles and are not merely markers for natural boundaries. Yet, these constructed identities and territories are not illusory. Increasingly, the notion of an Asian community has become common currency. Politicians and intellectuals within Asia use terminology that comes straight out of the orientalist lexicon, and yet they use it to underline their differences.

In India, geostrategic compulsions have played a role, but these have been overlaid with often conflicting ideas that come out of a history with origins in the spread of Indic civilization and Buddhism, a history that was reworked to argue for a cultural and non-violent expansion in the colonial period. To this was added the various layers formed by those in opposition to it, the émigré nationalist and revolutionary networks fighting for independence. I think it is more productive to think of overlapping zones: the East Asian, South Asian, West Asian and the Russian zones bound not just by culture but also by an intertwined history of intellectual engagement, commerce and conflicts. These zones overlap and intermingle in various ways, but they do carry a history that also sets them apart as well.

The idea of India has been shaped through a complex history of interactions that have been marginalized during the colonial period as a notion of India as a self-contained civilization was formed. This myth of India as a nation of "eternal standstill" has obscured the extensive links India has had with the outside world. This myth of self-containment overlooked, erased and marginalized the vast networks of trade, communication and the movement of people that had linked India to the outside world and contributed to the creation of its history and culture.

The critique of colonialism laid the foundation for a new understanding of Asia, but one that drew on earlier ideas as well. I consider five approaches to an engagement with Asia: those of Aurobindo Ghosh, Rabindranath Tagore, the Greater India Society, M.N. Roy, and J. Nehru. Each of these played an important role in shaping the Indian mental map of Asia, then and now. In the aftermath of independence, these ideas formed the bedrock on which political and intellectual strategies were conceived. However, already a new element was entering the scene, the fight against communism, which merged with the need to study China after the 1962 border war.

Aurobindo Ghose: Being Asian and Modern

Aurobindo Ghose (1872–1950) — radical nationalist, poet and later philosopher of a new way of life — exercised a decisive influence on Indian thought. What is salient here is that his analysis, as reflected in his early political writings, was grounded within an Asian perspective (Tankha 2011). His ideas were premised on the idea that each civilization had certain long-term historical characteristics. Japan was an example of successful development, but, he pointed out, China was also changing, and the only reason that India could not advance in equal measure was because she was enslaved. Far from seeing a stagnant or unchanging Asia, Aurobindo argued that Asian nations had sources of strength greater than those of the European nations, and therefore their ability to resist and transform was correspondingly greater. To understand these sources of strength, he said, it was important to recognize that the political ideals of the West were not the mainsprings of the political movements of the East (Ghose, 16 March 1908).

Aurobindo's view was a syncretic vision based on the fusion of Islam and Vedanta; the ideal of equality in Islam was brought together with the divine unity of man and spirit expressed in the Vedanta. Politically, this led him to question the European theory of rights, arguing that any movement of Asian democracy must discard this illusion of following Europe. Asia cannot forget its past, he wrote, "for it is the dharma of everyman to be free in soul. It is this ideal that differentiates the soul of Asia from that of Europe."

Aurobindo's vision of Asia included East Asia as well as Persia and Turkey. Each embodied certain civilization characteristics: the Japanese have a "patriotic spirit and imitative faculties" and the Chinese strength lies in "grand deliberation, the patient thoroughness, the irresistible organization of China" (Ghose, 1 April 1908). It is the Indian genius that gets his fulsome praise, however, for he sees in it "an all embracing intellect, her penetrating intuition, her invincible originality", and his belief that if "[t]he genius of Japan lies in her imitation and improvement, that of India [lies] in origination" (Ghose, 9 April 1908). He also examines and comments on the constitutional movements in Persia and Turkey and notes that their strength lies in "the preservation of their nation's individuality and existence while equipping themselves with the weapons of the modern strength for survival" (Ghose 1909). Given the climate in which these countries were operating, Aurobindo argued that in the initial phase of transformation the army or a few strong men would ensure internal stability, as in Turkey or Japan.

Aurobindo's ideas worked within a colonial frame of "Asia", even as he questioned many of the premises on which this was based. He essentialized national characteristics that he saw as growing out of a long civilization practice. But, more importantly, his idea of modernity linked social equality with the need to preserve the unity of the secular and religious. He saw an Asia where the secular and religious had not been fractured as offering the possibility of creating a modernity based on different principles. This search for an alternative modernity offered by Aurobindo has been central to later intellectual debates. His ideas provide a path to thinking about India and Asia that is neither a spatial construct nor one that uses the standard of European modernity, but is the product of a search for universal principles.

Tagore: Search for a Cultural Ideal

Rabindranath Tagore was a multifaceted personality whose literary output in a range of genres has made him the preeminent poet and philosopher of modern Bengal. He became the first Asian to win the Nobel Prize for literature, in 1913. Tagore travelled widely between the years 1878 and 1932, visiting some thirty countries in five continents, to lecture and raise money for his university. Among the countries he visited and wrote on were China and Japan.

Perhaps the earliest modern work on China was the trenchant critique of the opium trade written by the twenty-year-old Tagore in 1881. "The Death Traffic in Opium" published in the Bengali magazine *Bharari* (no. 98, May 1881) was, it should be noted, in print well before the now standard academic works on the opium trade. The effect of the trade on both India and China was pernicious, as it forced people to grow opium instead of food crops and led to both a rise in addiction as well as an increase in the severity of famine when crops failed. This common suffering as an impact of Western colonialism underlay the understanding of Tagore and his contemporaries.

Rabindranath Tagore first went to Japan in 1916, and his views of Japan provide one perspective, a leitmotif, that runs through Indian ideas regarding East Asia. Tagore was enthralled by Japanese culture and the aesthetic principles that seemed to him to govern daily life. His trip was also important for the contacts he made. He invited Okakura Tenshin and Japanese artists to Shantiniketan. These interactions played out in both India and Japan across a broad range of areas. But let me note just two examples to suggest the richness of this interaction. Okakura Tenshin wrote two of his seminal English books while in India, *The Ideals of the East* (1903) and *The Awakening of Japan* (1904), and the draft of another which was not published until after his death. The sustained dialogue between Abanindranath Tagore (1871–1951) and Nandalal Bose (1882–1966) with Japanese artists such as Yokoyama Taikan (1868–1958) and Arai Kanpo (1878–1945), who came to India in 1916–18, led to experiments as each learnt from the other in their common search for a new visual language. Similarly, the interaction between Chinese and Indian artists helped to create new styles of expression and new ways of seeing.

Yet, Tagore was also critical of Japan. Even before his arrival there he was uneasy about Japanese policies. His unease lay with his understanding of nationalism as the source of modern conflict and his search for an alternative way to build a society that allowed human beings to develop their full potential. His basic aversion to nationalism as the source of evil won him praise from thinkers such as Romain Rolland (1866–1944), but it also brought criticism in India.

Tagore saw Japan's strength in the way she had preserved the old while accepting the new, and this ability, he argued, was a gift she had given Asia. Japan's strength, according to him, lay not in nationalism but in her aesthetic sensibility embedded in social life. This sensibility drew its strength from a long and rich past, and the mental training that was integral to this sensibility had helped to create a mental mobility that enabled the Japanese to learn European ways with astonishing speed and allowed them to build an industrial society and adopt modern ways with little resistance. Japan was successful, in his thinking, because adopting an industrial civilization was not just a matter of factories and products but of accepting a new way of thinking, a new mental framework. Japan had done this because it could learn a new way of being.

However, Tagore found an absence of any spiritual basis in Japanese civilization, and this, he felt, was a serious limitation that circumscribed her achievements. Here he compared India and Europe as sharing a common bond of spiritual devotion that transcended national boundaries and made it possible to share common ideals. Tagore's thinking was diametrically opposed to Okakura Tenshin's celebration of the nation and national strength, and it was a powerful influence on the way many Indians came to think of China and Japan.

The desire for independence in India sent many into exile and study abroad where they came into contact with similar exiles from other parts of the colonized world. They helped each other to develop an understanding of the situation in their respective countries that was not completely mediated by the Western world. By the 1920's, Nehru had been in contact with Chinese leaders. He met Kuomintang delegates in Brussels in 1927 and agreed to cooperate and exchange information. Nehru and the Congress had objected to the use of Indian troops in China since the Opium Wars. The activities of the Ghadar Party (Party of Revolution) in China between 1925 and the 1930's, particularly when Indian troops were used against the Chinese in 1925, helped to bring China into the Indian consciousness. In China there was also interest in India. In Nanjing, on the initiative of the Dai Jitao (1891–1949), an India–China Friendship Association had been established. There was also a growing interest in Gandhi and the Non-Cooperation movement. The influence of Marxism and the growth of the communist movement and the Comintern led to greater support for the Chinese. Chiang Kai-shek (1887–1975) visited India and was extremely well received by Indian leaders, including Nehru. India also sent a medical mission to the Chinese Communists to show their support for the war against Japanese aggression.

It was in this environment that Calcutta University established a Chinese language department in 1918. Japanese Buddhists had also been coming to India, with Buddhist monk Kitabatake Doryu being the first in 1883, and by 1902 there were Japanese studying in Calcutta University. Tagore established Cheena Bhavana (China House) in his Shantiniketan after a trip to China and Japan and persuaded Tan Yun-shan (1898–1983) to join the institute and inaugurate Chinese studies in India. The main areas of interest at this time were Buddhism, languages, art and literature, and historical ties between China and India.

M. Visvesvaraya: Looking East

One of the early visitors to Japan was Swami Vivekananda, who stopped on his way to the World Congress of Religions in 1892 and was impressed with Japanese use of Western science and technology. A closer study of Japan was made by M. Visvesvaraya (1860–1962), who went there in March 1898 and again in 1919.

M. Visvesvaraya was an engineer by training who made important contributions to developing new technologies in water management. Later, as an administrator in the state of Mysore, he took steps to build educational institutions and promote economic development. Visvesvaraya was among the earliest in India to look at Japan. What interested him was the Japanese policy of developing the infrastructure of schools, transport and communications to actively support industrialization. Economic orthodoxy argued that the market would do this, and was against state intervention. Visvesvaraya went to Japan in March 1898 and conducted a close study of the country. (On his first trip he spent three months travelling to Tokyo, Kyoto and other parts, then in 1919 he made a second trip, along with Sir Vithaldas Damodar Thackersey and Mulraj Khatau, both noted industrialists. They went via Ceylon, Hong Kong and Shanghai. Visvesvaraya spent three months in Japan and then went on to the United States and Canada.)

Visvesvaraya was convinced that education was the key to economic development. The principal need for a country, he argued, was to increase production and so raise the standard of living of the people, provide education for all, spread enlightenment and finally train the people so that their capacity for initiative and enterprise would be raised (Tankha 2003).

To quote one example from his writings: "Since all industrial progress in Japan has been achieved in comparatively recent years she offers to India the most direct and valuable lessons obtainable in material advancement and reconstruction." The nation, he argued, was the most "effective unit of combination for securing to the people composing it the maximum benefit from their aggregate activities and efforts", and therefore India must cherish this spirit of nationalism and patriotism.

The Greater India Society: India's Cultural Empire

The Greater India Society, established in 1926, was a product of the cultural nationalists in Bengal who sought to find in India's past the strengths of her civilization, a civilization that had radiated its culture in a benevolent and benign manner (Tankha 2011). The noted historian Sir Jadunath Sarkar (1870–1958) was president of this society and some of its most prominent members included historians R.C. Majumdar (1888–1980), Phanindranath Bose and Kalidas Nag (1891–1966) and the philologists Suniti Kumar Chatterji (1890–1977) and P.C. Bagchi (1898–1956). They were influenced by the writings of the European orientalists, particularly the French Indologist Sylvain Levi, and by the then ongoing excavations at Angkor Wat.

This society and the views it represented were not just the product of European orientalism, but arose from, and were shaped by, the cultural milieu of Bengal and the desire to strengthen society and build the basis for a new nationalism. The cultural nationalists underlined the superiority of India civilization through their exploration of Indian influence in Southeast Asia. This served to show both its superiority over the West — which was an example of rapacious colonialism — as well as the strengths of Hinduism, perceived as weak and unable to resist both the so-called Muslim invasions and British imperialism.

Kalidas Nag, one of the leading proponents of India's cultural empire, wrote that,

> foreign propaganda has always tried to prove that Indian people and civilisation grew in "splendid isolation". Yet, from the earliest phase of her documented history India was in constant touch with all the principal currents, racial and cultural, of Asia. Some of the Asian folks have penetrated peacefully, others have rushed into our body politic; but all of them have contributed substantially to the development of our state and society and the enrichment of our cultural heritage, literary, artistic and philosophical. (Nag 1957)

Benoy Kumar Sarkar: A Republican Polytheist

Benoy Sarkar (1887–1949) was a brilliant polymath. Though recognized as one of the pioneers of sociology in India, he is not much remembered today. A scholar with an astonishing range of interests, including sociology, economics, history, religion and literature, he wrote in Bengali, English, German and Italian. He travelled widely, going around the world from 1914 to 1925. He wrote *The World Today* (Varttaman Jagat) (1914–25), a collection of articles based on his extensive travels in Europe, the United States, Hawaii, Japan, Korea, Manchuria, and China. His ideas of Asia were further developed in *The Futurism of Young Asia* (1922), where he argued that Young Asia, as he called it, was born in 1905.

Sarkar came to adulthood in the same political climate as Aurobindo during the tumultuous years of the Bengal partition in 1905. Sarkar rejected the Europe–Asia dichotomy as well as the notion of racial differences in favour of a medieval–modern dichotomy. In this regard the West was not an equal and homogeneous space, he argued, nor did the East lack secular, life-affirming traditions. He also emphasized that Euro-America had also been equally "primitive" or "unscientific" till the end of the eighteenth century, so modern ideas were new and equally revolutionary for Europeans as well as Asians. Sarkar advanced what today would be called a critique of Western orientalism, saying that it was based on differing standards and prejudice. He argued that industrial civilization would bring about a convergence, so that, while countries may lag behind, they would ultimately develop and achieve parity.

Young Asia, he argued, was born of contact with the modern West, and the idea of progress, industrialization and antipathy to foreign domination, intervention and coercion were helping to shape it. New ideas of the East drew inspiration from earlier achievements in culture, economics and politics, but they were also a product of modern scholarship and Western education. A major point to come out of his extensive comparisons of India, China and Japan was to underline the fact that societies were moving in the same direction, so sociology and policymaking should focus on how to hasten this process.

In looking for Asian unity, Sarkar argued against basing it on cultural practices or trade links. He constructed an argument that first defined the historical background. He argued that the idea that

Buddhism was dead in India and preserved in China and Japan was historically wrong. First, religion in India had changed between the fourth and sixth centuries when Chinese pilgrims came to India and took back Buddhist teachings. Second, the two — Buddhism and Hinduism — could not be viewed as different. His study of folk religions in the three countries showed the similarities in the function of the local gods — Avalokiteswara or jizo — worshipped in China and Japan were the same as those in India, and so he pointed out that the people's creative energies had transformed religion into a secular activity for the realization of happiness on earth. The conclusion he drew was that the shared rituals point to the importance of polytheism in Asian psychology. Polytheism for Sarkar was far more rational than Western monotheism, and he argued in support of republicanism in politics and polytheism in religion.

Sarkar (1916) writes,

> It is this psychological groundwork that makes Asiatic Unity a philosophical necessity in spite of ethnological and linguistic diversities. The unity is thus more fundamental than has hitherto been recognised by historians. This intercourse between members of the San-Goku established by the Buddhist missionary work or by commercial activity and diplomatic relations has only supplied additional connecting links. But the chief point to be noticed is that, Buddhism or no Buddhism, international relations or no international relations, the three nations of Asia had a common mentality. That commonness is deeper than what can be supplied by actual coming and going – in fact, absolute, as contrasted with the relative, which is born of political or commercial contact. (pp. 279–80).

The cultural unity of Asia was thus based on a dynamic and people-centred unity, not on idealized conceptions of grand traditions. However, with the spread of an industrial civilization, these were in a process of change and ferment. The changes so initiated were creating not just regional but global links and transforming ways of thinking. He saw that Asia was being united in new ways as the old isolations were breaking down. So, for instance, even in religious matters there was an exchange of ideas, so people were becoming familiar with hitherto foreign religious practices.

M.N. Roy: From Communism to Radical Humanism

M.N. Roy (1886–1954) was inspired by both the militant ideas of Lala Lajpat Rai (1865–1928) and by Swami Vivekananda's (1863–1902) mission of serving the poor, and he went abroad to seek help for Indian independence. He helped to found the Communist Party of Mexico in 1917 and came to the attention of Lenin, who accepted his alternative thesis that the revolution would first occur not in the developed countries but in the colonies. Roy became advisor to Stalin and, as the Comintern perspective was that the starting point for revolution in India was China and not Persia or Afghanistan, Roy was assigned the task of spreading revolutionary consciousness among Indian troops and of maintaining the joint front between the Kuomintang and the Communist Party of China. Roy helped to establish schools in Tashkent to prepare for the coming revolution.

In China, Roy worked to implement the Comintern line of maintaining a joint front, but Mao Zedong began organizing peasant resistance and training cadres in Hunan as the Kuomintang was restricting Communist activities and suppressing them. While Michael Borodin supported Chiang, and called for Mao to stop, Roy disagreed and wanted to "deepen before broadening"; that is, to intensify peasant activity, which would force reactionary elements to leave the Kuomintang and give the Communists a free hand. He supported Mao's strategy of creating a peasant army, but was recalled by Stalin. The Kuomintang purged the Communists and Mao launched the Autumn Uprising in Hunan and then began the Long March. In 1930 Roy wrote *Revolution and Counter Revolution in China*, an account of the political situation informed by both his analytical rigour and close observation as a Comintern agent.

M.N. Roy escaped from Stalinist Russia and later returned to India. He is a remarkable figure and representative of many exiled nationalists and radicals who went abroad and worked for national independence. Examples of organizations they established include the India Independence League in Japan and the Ghadar Party (Party of Revolution), which functioned from the United States but was also present in other parts of the world, such as China. The party created networks between Indians and local communities. These overseas groups — in China, Japan and Southeast Asia — later played an important role in working with the Indian National Army, created with Japanese support and led by Subhash Chandra Bose. M.N Roy's approach differed from that of

Gandhi and Nehru as it was based on a communist platform, but he grounded his thinking in the conditions within India and China, not accepting Western Marxist formulations at face value. In that sense, as well, he represents a new way of thinking about India, the Asian region, and the wider world, in ways that do not compartmentalize or seek to draw "imperial boundaries" (to quote W. van Schendel) as "Asian Studies" seeks to do. He sought to address the dilemma that continues to haunt the left (van Schendel 2002).

Jawaharlal Nehru and Asia: A Vision of Asia

Jawaharlal Nehru worked hard to promote ties with Asian countries, particularly China. He first met Chinese political leaders at the International Conference against Imperialism organized by the Comintern in Brussels in 1927. Nehru and the Congress supported China against Japan, and in 1938 Nehru helped to send a medical unit to provide medical assistance to Chinese fighting the Japanese. While working to build relations with Asian countries, Nehru was dismissive of the importance of Japan. In his conception of world history, he saw Japan as a peripheral nation and argued that its history had become important only in modern times. Japan's victory over Russia aroused pride in Asia, not only because of the defeat of a Western power but also because it demonstrated the need to assimilate new ideas, as the victory was the result of Japan successfully adopting Western science and technology.

After independence, Nehru was instrumental in convening the Asian Relations Conference in Delhi in 1947, where he said,

> Apart from the fact that India herself is emerging into freedom and independence, she is the natural centre and focal point of the many forces at work in Asia. Geography is a compelling factor, and geographically she is situated as to be the meeting point of Western and Northern, Eastern and South-east Asia.... Streams of culture have come to India from the West and the east and been absorbed in India.... At the same time, streams of culture have flowed from India to distant parts of Asia. If you would know India you have to go to Afghanistan and Western Asia, to Central Asia, to China and Japan and to the countries of South-East Asia. There you will find magnificent evidence of the vitality of India's culture which spread out and influenced vast numbers of people. (quoted in Hay 1970, pp. 254, 294)

Here, again, India is the natural centre of Asia because it is the influence of Indian civilization that has shaped and formed the other parts of Asia. There is never any sense of how these beliefs and ideas changed and transformed in their travels, and what entered India is seen to be absorbed without changing the essential elements that form India. It is not how these inward flows have reshaped the South Asian region nor how ideas emanating from here have, in turn, been reshaped as they were taken up by people in other parts of the world.

While it is not possible here to deal with the history of India's relations and interactions with China in the years before independence in detail, it does provide the context for the post-independence policies of Nehru and the Congress in recognizing the Peoples Republic of China, the launching of Panchsheel and Non-Alignment, and convening the Asian Relations Conference. The conference was held in March–April 1947 in New Delhi to build the bonds of brotherhood among Asian nations. This larger concern with rebuilding an independent India underlies the vision expressed in K.M. Panikkar's, *Asia and Western Dominance*, a book conceived of in Portugal and finished in Peking, where he was India's ambassador, and which represents a modern nationalist vision of Asia transformed by European modernity. The Indian School for International Studies was established in 1948 as a direct result of the conference. It was headed by A. Appadorai and had an East Asia Division. It was intended to serve as training ground for specialists who would be taken into the Foreign Service and other policymaking bodies of the government. In Delhi University the study of Chinese began in the Department of Buddhist Studies in 1958

War and the Creation of Area Studies

In the immediate aftermath of Indian independence, a meeting of Commonwealth foreign ministers led, in 1950, to the establishment of the Colombo Plan. Largely funded by the United States and initially proposed by K.M. Panikkar, the Indian ambassador to China, to combat communism in Southeast Asia, the Colombo Plan primarily focused on cooperation to transfer technology and skill development between the member states. But it also led to the development of language training programmes, for instance in Japanese.

The 1962 conflict with China was a watershed for greater research on China and initiated the process of building up expertise within the government. Here the main focus was on foreign policy and security issues. The foundations for "Area Studies" were in effect laid during this second stage. Academic institutions included the Centre for Chinese Studies, Delhi University, initially headed by Tan Chung, then in 1964 by V.P Dutt (later, Japanese was added, and then the Korean language and Korean studies, and the centre was renamed the Department of East Asia Studies). The Indian School of International Studies became part of Jawaharlal Nehru University. The Ford Foundation provided funding and scholarships to send Indian scholars to some of the leading universities. Funding by the Japan Foundation came much later, in the mid-seventies; till then there was some limited funding under the Colombo Plan and through Japan's Ministry of Education. The Japan Foundation was established to promote intellectual and cultural exchange between Japan and the United States; it was part of Japan's "soft diplomacy". Funding to other parts of the world was limited, and very few scholarships were given in India initially. The Ford grants finished, but the Japan Foundation's activities have increased. There are a few places outside Delhi where it is possible to study China or Japan up to the doctoral level, such as Vishwabharati and Benares Hindu University.

In the mid 1980's greater economic interaction led to an increase in demand for the Japanese language and this, in turn, contributed to a growing interest in contemporary Japanese policies, particularly foreign policy, security and economic policies. Similar changes have occurred in Chinese Studies as relations with China began to improve after China's reforms, but they really picked up momentum from the 1990s. The demand for Chinese translators and interpreters in trade and industry fuelled the growth of language programmes. There has also been an increase in academic exchange, allowing scholars to study in Chinese universities and carry out field trips. Access to Chinese data has become easier.

The point to note is that the China and Japan study programmes in Delhi University, though supported by Ford grants, did not work as traditional area studies departments. They tried to combine language and disciplinary expertise. So students with postgraduate degrees from the social sciences were accepted for research degrees and required to do language-training programmes. In some cases students had participated in these language programmes as part-time courses. However, the student intake was always very low, so the department changed tack and introduced a postgraduate degree course in East Asian studies. This resembles the traditional "area studies" approach of combining language training and courses in various aspects of society, culture and politics. It remains to be seen whether this is a turn for the better, but there are certainly more students joining the programme.

The Post 1990s: The Indian Academy Looks Outwards

A look at the changes in funding, even over the last eight years, in the Department of East Asian Studies in Delhi University shows that there has been a substantial increase, but the total amount still remains relatively small.

TABLE 10.1

Amounts Sanctioned by UGC to East Asian Studies, University of Delhi, 2004–12
(100,000 rupees)

Sanctioned for the Financial Years under the Following Heads	2004–9	2009–12
Building	1.00	10.00
Office equipment and furniture	3.00	4.00
Books and journals	3.00	5.00
Field work (25% for students for the 2009–12 period)	5.00	15.00
Seminars/symposia/conferences/international seminars/faculty/projects	3.50	10.00
Visiting faculty	2.00	6.00
Operational expenses and contingency	2.00	5.00
Publications	2.00	5.00
Total	21.50 (US$33,486)	60.00 (US$96,704)

The scale of funding and the size of departments specializing in the study of China and Japan have been very small. They are even smaller for some other areas, even those as economically and politically important as West Asia or the former USSR, and even though Indian academic and other interactions have a long and dense history. Indian universities have had very few student exchanges or joint programmes with foreign universities. Since 2000 they have begun to increase. One illustration of this is the memorandums of understanding (MOUs) that Delhi University has signed with foreign universities. In the period 1998–2012, Delhi University has signed 3 with Oceana (signed between 2007 and 2010), 8 with North America (2003–10), 24 with Europe (1999–2010), 1 with Africa (Sudan, 2004), and 25 with Asia (1 each with Iran, Afghanistan, Uzbekistan, Nepal, China and Taiwan; 5 with Japan; and 14 with South Korea [1998–2010]). These MOUs allow for faculty and student exchange, but not all of them are necessarily functioning regularly. What it does illustrate is that Delhi University has many MOUs with Asian universities and that South Korea has been the most vigorous in establishing these links.[1]

The Benaras Hindu University has 41 MOUs, of which 9 are with Asian Universities. All of them were signed between 2005 and 2012. To put this into perspective, Tokyo University has 45 MOUs with China alone, of which 3 are with Peking University and only 7 with India.

Related to these limited exchanges is the restricted interest Indian universities have for foreign students. The bulk of the foreign students are from the neighbourhood, including the Tibetan refugee population in India. In 2007–8, foreign students seeking admission to various undergraduate and postgraduate courses offered by Delhi University were from Nepal, Afghanistan and Tibet. A large number of students from Vietnam and Thailand applied to Buddhist Studies and language programmes. Students from Sri Lanka and Mauritius usually come to study science subjects.[2]

In 2012, Delhi University admitted more than 1,400 international students, the most the university has ever admitted. That number was up from 1,200 the year before, which was the previous high. Students are still mostly from Nepal, Tibet, Afghanistan and Vietnam, but now Korea as well.[3]

In contrast, in 2010–11 there were 103,260 Indian students studying in the United States, and even 100 studying in Poland. There are just 500 Indian students studying in Japanese universities, and over 9,000 in China — over 90 per cent of these are studying for an MBBS (Bachelor of Medicine, Bachelor of Surgery) degree, because it is cheaper there.[4]

Conclusion: New Directions in Studying Asia

India's long engagement with the East Asian region has taken place largely, but not completely, outside the "area studies" or "Asian Studies" approach. Its "failure" is the product of a number of reasons, partly to do with a lack of resources — a failure of the government in not recognizing the importance of such programmes. But even Indian students who have gone abroad for further studies rarely enter programmes on Japan or China. In common with other developing countries, the emphasis has largely been on studying languages rather than in engaging in studying these countries. There has also not been any "boom" such as happened in the United States and Europe. But outside the academy or within disciplines there has been a continuing engagement with China and Japan that grows out of, and develops on, the approaches in pre-Independence India. The increased interaction between India and East Asia over the last few decades has once again opened the possibilities of greater intellectual exchange outside the "area studies" framework.

I would like to end by pointing to two very different examples to illustrate how these exchanges are taking place. In September 2000, a separatist group known as the Revolutionary People's Front banned the screening of Hindi films in the Indian state of Manipur, along with stopping the distribution of all Hindi satellite channels there. Hindi films were denounced as a form of cultural imperialism. Hindi films were undermining Manipuri culture. This had unexpected consequences, as the cultural space was soon occupied by the Korean satellite channel, Arirang TV. Korean actors have become role models, food and fashion have taken the Korean route, and large sections of the young have grown up watching Korean language films and soaps so that they have acquired a familiarity with the Korean language. Many of these young Manipuris even do formal Korean courses. This has happened in just a decade.

The second example I would like to offer is the West Heavens project launched by a group of intellectuals in China. It "aims to untangle and compare the different paths of modernity taken by India and China, to facilitate high-level communication between the two countries' intellectual and art circles, and to promote interaction and cross-references between the two countries through social thoughts and contemporary art. Since 2010, the project has organized more than 100 events including forums, exhibitions, film screenings and workshops, as well as publishing more than 10 books."

To break out of the East/West or China/West dichotomies, it has organized this forum of intellectual exchange because "[f]or more than a century, challenges of imperialism and capitalism have forced India and China to develop political strategies that have profoundly transformed both societies. To share this experience is valuable for Indians and Chinese alike." It sees India as a country that has faced similar challenges, but with which it has a shared past, hence the title West Heavens referring to India as the land from where Buddhism came.

In conclusion, I think it is important to note that much of the production of knowledge on Asia is now taking place in civil society, outside the academy, and that it is not just driven by the demands of the state. The end of "Asian Studies" is, in that sense, another sign of the rise of Asia.

Notes

1. <http://www.du.ac.in/fileadmin/DU/Academics/international_collaboration/List_of_MoUs.pdf>.
2. <http://www.hindu.com/2007/06/18/stories/2007061810870300.htm>.
3. <http://magazine.delhiuniversity.com/?p=2794>.
4. <http://www.chinapost.com.tw/china/national-news/2013/08/20/386832/Aspiring-medical.htm>.

References

Dirlik, Arlif. "No Longer Far Away: The Reconfiguration of Global Relations and Its Challenges to Asian Studies". In *Unsettled Frontiers and Transnational Linkages: New Tasks for the Historian of Modern Asia*, Comparative Asian

Studies no 19, edited by Leo Douw. Amsterdam: VU University Press, 1997.

Ghose, Aurobindo. "Asiatic Democracy". *Bande Mataram*, 16 March 1908. Reprinted in *Sri Aurobindo Birth Centenary Library*, vol. 1, *Bande Mataram Early Political Writings*, pp. 757–60. Pondicherry: Sri Aurobindo Ashram Trust, 1972.

――――. "India and the Mongolians". *Bande Mataram*, 1 April 1908. Reprinted in *Sri Aurobindo Birth Centenary Library*, vol. 1, *Bande Mataram Early Political Writings*, pp. 812–17. Pondicherry: Sri Aurobindo Ashram Trust, 1972.

――――. "The Asiatic Role". *Bande Mataram*, 9 April 1908. Reprinted in *Sri Aurobindo Birth Centenary Library*, vol. 1, *Bande Mataram Early Political Writings*, pp. 842–45. Pondicherry: Sri Aurobindo Ashram Trust, 1972.

――――. "Facts and Opinions". *Bande Mataram*, 9 October 1909, pp. 230–31, 247–48.

Hay, Stephen N. *Asian Ideas of East and West: Tagore and His Critics in Japan, China and India*, Cambridge, MA: Harvard University Press, 1970.

Nag, Kalidas. *Discovery of Asia*. Calcutta: Institute of Asian African Relations, 1957.

Said, Edward W. *Orientalism*. New York: Vintage, 1971.

Sarkar, Benoy Kumar. *Chinese Religion through Hindu Eyes: A Study in the Tendencies of Asiatic Mentality*. Shanghai: The Commercial Press, 1916.

Tankha, Brij. "Japanese Studies in India: Mapping the Contours". In *Asian Research Trends*, pp. 47–61. Tokyo: Centre for East Asian Cultural Studies, The Toyo Bunko, 2003.

――――. "Aurobindo Ghose: The Logic of Asia 1908–09". In *Pan-Asianism: A Documentary History*, vol. 1, *1850–1920*, edited by Sven Saaler and Christopher W.A. Szpilman. Plymouth, Devon: Rowman & Littlefield, 2011.

――――. "The Greater India Society: Indian Culture and an Asian Federation". In *Pan-Asianism: A Documentary History*, vol. 1, *1850–1920*, edited by Sven Saaler and Christopher W.A. Szpilman. Plymouth, Devon: Rowman & Littlefield, 2011.

Willem van Schendel. "Geographies of Knowing, Geographies of Ignorance: Jumping Scale in Southeast Asia". In *Environment and Planning D: Society and Space* 20 (2002): 647–68.

11

South Seas Chinese in Colonial Classifications

Huei-Ying Kuo

Between the nineteenth and early twentieth centuries, British Singapore was a popular destination for migrants. The ample supply of labour helped the British develop the port city as a midway point between India and China. By the turn of the twentieth century, the proliferation of trading networks that converged in the port city also turned it into an emporium of British textiles. Later, after the 1910s, when Japan launched its agenda of southward advance to the region known today as Southeast Asia, Tokyo journalist Inoue Kiyoshi spent a year touring the region and concluded that Singapore was "the threshold of the South Seas" (Inoue K. 1913, pp. 17–65).

South Sea — or *nanyang* in Chinese and *nan'yō* in Japanese — was the term the Chinese and Japanese adopted to refer to the region generally called Southeast Asia in the post-war years. My choice of naming the region South Seas was to emphasize the contested responses to the changes in the region generated from the imposition of the British free-trade imperialism in the long nineteenth century. As pointed out by Prasenjit Duara, the British system intensified "some of the old relationships and generat[ed] new linkages between the cities (and hinterlands) of Aden, Bombay, Calcutta, Singapore, Hong Kong and Shanghai as enterpôts and financial centers for Asian trade" (Duara 2010, p. 964). The rise of Japanese power in the late nineteenth century, however, challenged the British imperial regional formation. Japan looked at the South Seas — including the natural resources, markets and land — as its economic frontier. The Japanese pan-Asianism thus entailed an anti-imperialist tone from the beginning (Duara 2010, pp. 969–73). Therefore, regardless of the formation of the Anglo–Japanese alliance that lasted between 1902 and 1923, and despite the fact that the initial goal of southward expansion of the Japanese was primarily economic, not territorial, tension between the two empires was inherent. Both the Anglo–Japanese economic competition in the South Seas and the white supremacy of racial disparagement against the non-white Japanese accounted for the final military confrontation in the Pacific War (Best 2002; Horne 2005).

The role of the Chinese overseas residing in the South Seas in general and in Singapore in particular was key to understanding the Anglo–Japanese rivalry. Existing studies on Chinese reactions to the Japanese expansion to the South Seas have pointed out that Chinese anti-Japanese nationalism surged after the late 1920s (Akashi 1970; Yen 1989; Yong 2014). The Chinese anti-Japanese movements in the South Seas developed concomitantly with the replacement of British market share in the region by Japanese interest after the late 1920s. And given that both British and Japanese wholesalers would count on the retailing networks that the Chinese operated, the commercial competition was not only between the British and Japanese but among the various Chinese business networks (Kuo 2011, 2014). This was the historical background against which the Japanese conducted a series of surveys to classify the Chinese migrant communities and business groups in the region.

In her analysis of the colonizers' tactics to shape the social and cultural order of a colonial society, Ann Stoler pointed out the quintessential role of colonial knowledge construction. Through the imposition of the approved "qualified knowledge" upon the colonial subjects, colonial control became a hidden power, under the guise of spreading objective information and universal theses (Stoler 2008). Above all, the system of colonial censuses and other surveys was key to creating an epistemological height from which colonial subjects could voluntarily adopt the colonizer's views to define themselves. The colonial census presented the boundaries developed from the mutually unintelligible languages, the religious practices and native places of origin as objective, fixed and static gaps. In reality, however, the social distance among the migrants was variable and would change constantly.

How did an incumbent colonial power like Great Britain construct the "qualified knowledge" on Chinese migrants in Singapore? And how did Japan confront the British colonial status quo and the British–Chinese alliances through its own "qualified knowledge"? This chapter compares the diverse British and Japanese classification systems for Chinese in Singapore. The British colonial censuses of the Straits Settlements were the principal data used to interrogate the British systems. The Japanese sources came from the writings of Japanese intellectuals and colonial officers on the Chinese residing in or coming from Fujian and Guangdong in South China, from where the majority of Chinese in colonial Singapore traced their paternal ancestral roots.

The different types of sources that presented the British and Japanese understandings of the Chinese in the South Seas reflected the divergent positions between the two imperialist powers in Asia. As colonizer of the Malay Peninsula and Hong Kong, the British in the nineteenth century governed the Chinese communities in Singapore through the "divide and rule" policy. But after Chinese nationalism turned to an anti-imperialist position in the 1920s, the British colonial census changed to view the Chinese as an integrated group. In contrast, the Japanese challenger had to deal consistently with the divergent Chinese reactions to its southward expansion. Japan thus learned to make use of the social cleavages that prevailed in the Chinese communities in the South Seas. The surging Chinese anti-Japanese movements accentuated the Chinese social divide. Emphasizing the difference between the British shifting perspectives (from the divided to the unitary Chinese "racial group") and the Japanese consistent view of the fragmented Chinese people and civilizations, I argue that the difference should be understood by the different places between the two empires in their capitalist expansion to the South Seas in the interwar years.

The rest of the chapter is organized as three main sections. The first shows how the British colonial system changed its codification of the Chinese, from various speech-group "tribes" to a singular Chinese race. The second considers the Japanese discourses on the differences between the Chinese in Southeast Asia and those in the China homeland. In addition to highlighting similarities and differences between the British and Japanese classification systems, the conclusion emphasizes the importance of the context of inter-imperialist competition for understanding these different colonial views of the Chinese.

From Plural to Singular Chinese Group: The Chinese in British Colonial Censuses

The British secured the Malay Peninsula by waging wars against the local sultans and the neighbouring Siamese and Dutch powers, and developed it by attracting migrants to dredge harbours and to open up fields for tropical plantation. By 1867, Singapore was incorporated as a British Crown Colony under the direct supervision of the Colonial Office in London. To become financially independent from the metropolis of London, the British regime of the Straits Settlements authorized local Chinese residents, many of them Baba Chinese who had assimilated with local Malay culture and society, to solicit labour migration from China. The British also granted exclusive rights for the Chinese labour recruiters to sell opium and run brothels and gambling dens. These sustained the reproduction of the labour power, as the new migrants found it hard to save money to leave their jobs. Because these labour recruiters would then pay revenues to the British, the patronized Chinese labour recruiters and opium sellers were thus called revenue farmers. Nonetheless, frequent fights among the Chinese revenue farmers, particularly among those competing for the monopolization of the opium trade, became a serious issue that troubled the British (Trocki 1990).

In 1877 the British authority of the Straits Settlements set up the office of Chinese Protectorate and appointed William A. Pickering (1840–1907) as the first protector. Pickering's credentials came from his mastering several southern Chinese languages, skills that he obtained from a decade of service at the Chinese maritime customs offices in Fuzhou, Hong Kong and Formosa (Taiwan). Sitting at his office at North Canal Street (later moved to Havelock Road), Pickering witnessed the rampant Chinese gangster fights. Cross Street, close to his office, was also known as Hai San Street, which marked the notorious domination of the Hai San gangsters of that area. Pickering concluded that the existence of Chinese secret societies was a source of problems for the Chinese. He presented this conclusion at general meetings of the newly established Malayan Branch of the Royal Asiatic Society in 1878. The "Chinese problem" soon became an urgent task for the British colonial office in Singapore (Choy 1984/85). Pursuing this idea, Pickering issued the society ordinance that required all Chinese societies to register with the government (Mak 1981). Not all agreed with this diagnosis, however. One critique came from Jonas Daniel Vaughan (1825–91), police magistrate of the Straits Settlements since 1869 (Foster 1885, p. 480). Vaughan considered Pickering's approach "a popular error". The root of the fighting, in Vaughan's view, came from the conflicts among speech groups. Vaughan thus proposed to "limit the immigration of Chinese to the Straits from one province in China and peace would be the result" (Vaughan 1879, p. 96). This was never adopted by the British authorities of the Straits Settlements, the Federation of the Malay States or the Unfederated Malay States. Hokkien migrants from southern Fujian, Teochew from eastern Guangdong, Cantonese from the core of the Pearl River Delta of Guangdong province, Hakka from the mountainous border between Guangdong and Fujian, Hainanese from Hainan Island, as well as Hokchiu and Hokchin from northern and coastal Fujian continued to migrate to the British territories. In these migrant communities, the division among mutually unintelligible Chinese languages continued.

Chinese communal leaders became intermediary managers for the British colonial order. The British authority recruited representatives from each major speech group to sit in the Chinese Advisory Board (est. 1890). The idea of classifying the Chinese by their linguistic differences was the norm in colonial surveys. The British census report of the Straits Settlements (Singapore, Malacca and Penang) in 1871 classified the Chinese population of the Straits Settlements into two groups: Chinese and Cochin-Chinese. The category of Chinese contained 86,649 males and 17,287 females, which included both migrants from China and Peranakan Chinese, who had assimilated with the local Malay societies for generations of overseas settlement. The category of Cochin-Chinese, which ceased to exist in the following decennial census reports, was composed of 86 males and 8 females (McNair et al. 1871, p. 6).

The decennial census reports revealed the British views on the composition of local Chinese communities, as well as those communities' relationships with their homelands in China. In the following census report, compiled in 1881, the British grouped the Europeans and Americans of the settlement into 19 "nationalities". These included Americans, Austrians, Belgians and British, among others. At the same time, the category applied to classify the Chinese was "tribe". The 6 main tribes included Hokkiens, Hylams, Kehs, Macaos, Straits-born, and Teochews (Straits Settlements 1881, pp. 5–6). The census of 1891, under the supervision of E.M. Merewether, listed 5 main nationalities, including Europeans and Americans, Eurasians, Chinese, Malays and other Natives of the Archipelago, as well as Tamils and other Natives of India (Merewether 1892, p. 2).

Though Merewether now put the Chinese under one common generic category of nationality like the Europeans, he continued to apply the concept of "tribe" to understand the divided Chinese communities. In his classification, the 6 main tribes now included Cantonese (which substituted for the term "Macaos" used in the 1881 report a decade earlier), Hokkiens, Hylams, Khehs (spelled as "Kehs" in the earlier report), Straits-born, and Teochews (Merewether 1892, pp. 10–11). At the same time, the inspector believed that "race" should be a more objective term than "nationality", as the latter "conveyed a false impression of the information which was intended to be filled in" (Merewether 1892, p. 8). Alongside the change, in the census of 1901, "races" and "nationalities" became two interchangeable categories used to distinguish the Europeans and Americans from the Eurasians as well as the Chinese (Innes 1901, pp. 2, 15). It was in the next census report of 1911 that race became the sole criterion to frame the Chinese migrants and their descendants in the British territory. "Straits-born Chinese" and "China-born Chinese" were listed as two different "races", together with Eurasians, Europeans, and Kindred Races, Indians, Jawi Pekans, Malays of the Peninsula, and Malays of the Archipelago (Marriott 1911, section on Age and Sex, table IV, 2). The category was further broken into several subcategories of Chinese speech-groups. Designated as "Chinese dialects", these speech groups included Cantonese, Hailam, Hokkien, Kheh, Teochew (spelt as Teochhiu) and others (Marriott 1911, Language, table V, 3). The category of Straits-born Chinese was not among these groups. The number of Straits-born Chinese was cited as the 17,882 Chinese who were Malay speakers in the Straits Settlements (Marriott 1911, Language, Table V, 3).

The 1921 Census, under the supervision of J.E. Nathan, was different from the previous reports in the following ways. First, Nathan took the local Malayan boundary as the centre of his analysis. This is shown by his changing of the categories for the birthplaces of the ethnic Chinese. He kept the category of "Chinese born in British Malaya" while replacing the "Chinese China born" with "Chinese born elsewhere". The latter category lumped together those Chinese migrants born in China, Burma, Siam, Netherlands India, or elsewhere outside British Malaya (Nathan 1922, p. 95). This change marked the shift of the focus from the mainland homeland of these southward Chinese migrants to the distinction between being local-born or foreign-born Chinese. At the same time, for those local-born Chinese, most of whom were based in Malacca, he applied the view of the linguist W.G. Shellabear that they possessed an idiosyncratic language, Baba Malay, which "differs from the language of the Malays, because it uses a number of Chinese words, mispronounces many Malay words, is ignorant of others, and employs a wonderful 'pidgin' idiom" (Nathan 1922, p. 77). This resulted from long-term social interactions between the earlier Hokkien migrants and the local Malay population.

Second, Nathan focused on the top five Chinese speech-groups in the colony: Hokkien, Cantonese, Teochew, Kheh, and Hailamhe. He also adopted the view of A.M. Pountney, the superintendent of the 1911 census in the Federated Malay States, about the emphasis on the incompatibilities among the speech groups. In Pountney's words: "The word dialect as generally applied to the language spoken by the various Chinese tribes is so far a misnomer as to give rise to considerable misconception of the vast difference between the various so-called dialects. Between what may be called the major dialects or, preferably, the principal languages of China, e.g., the Mandarin, the Cantonese, the Hokkien, etc., lies as great a difference as between European languages, and, though these major dialects range themselves into groups as do European languages, it is scarcely an overstatement to say that there are as many different languages in China, and as many different dialects of those distinct languages, as there are languages and dialects in Europe" (Nathan 1922, p. 78). The implication is that the Chinese of different languages should be treated as different and not the same "race".

Nathan's report emphasized the distinctive boundary between the local Malayan Chinese vis-à-vis Chinese from the outside as well as the fragmentation of the Chinese communities. These understandings, however, changed a decade later. In the survey that followed, C.A. Vieland, the superintendent of the 1931 census, pointed out the limit of considering "race" as a useful concept to classify people: "the word 'race' is used, for lack of a more appropriate term, to cover a complex set of ideas of which race, in the strict or scientific sense, is only one small element. It would be of little use to the administrator or the merchant to attempt a classification of the population by race in the ethnographic sense, to say nothing of the fact that any such tentative classification would be highly controversial" (Vieland 1932, p. 73). Nonetheless, he believed that adopting this notion of "race" would be a judicious blend, for practical ends, of the ideas of geographic and ethnographic origin, political allegiance, and racial and social affinities and sympathies" (Vieland 1932, p. 73). He thus treated "race" as a nominal category without any substantial indication of its ontological ground. The "six main racial heads" in Malaya and Brunei were "Europeans (including Americans and all white races), Eurasians, Malaysians, Chinese, Indians and 'Others'" (Vieland 1932, p. 74). By putting the various Chinese speech groups (of which he counted seven) as one singular Chinese "race", he illustrated the trend of the making of a unitary Chinese identity through the adoption of Mandarin as the medium of instruction in local Chinese schools. In his words, "it may be anticipated that, as this movement becomes increasingly effective, the special problems confronting the census authority in the case of the Chinese population of Malaya will progressively diminish, but it remains to be seen in what manner and degree linguistic assimilation will affect the discrimination between the 'tribes' and necessitate a different 'racial' classification" (Vieland 1932, p. 78). Believing that Mandarin education might integrate the Chinese communities, Vieland no longer distinguished the category of the Straits-born Chinese from other Chinese populations. The registration of Baba Chinese was merged with the category of Hokkien. In short, at the end of the open policy for Chinese migrant workers to land in the British colony in the South Seas, the colonial regime saw the Chinese inside and outside China as one unitary group, or at least a singular group in the making through Mandarinization. The British assumption mirrored the development of Chinese nationalism, which imposed the sanction of Chinese nationalism on Chinese overseas.

Vieland's concern about the imminent influence from mainland China to the Chinese in Malaya reflected awareness by the British of accelerating mainland Chinese partisan mobilization in their territories at this juncture. Sir Cecil Clementi, the governor of the Straits Settlements at the time when Vieland compiled the census data, was known for his suppressive policies against all China-oriented activities in the colony. As the Baba Chinese in general lost their communal leadership to those China-born Chinese in both the Hokkien and Teochew circles in the 1920s, the new leaders developed a stronger commitment to China-oriented affairs than allegiance to the local British regime (Kuo 2014, ch. 3). For those Baba Chinese who strived to continue the communal influence, the connection with partisans in China was crucial. One example was Teo Eng Hock's engagement of the organization of the Kuomintang (Chinese Nationalist Party; hereafter KMT) in Malaya. On 5 February 1930, when Clementi had just assumed his position in Singapore, he convened a meeting with Teo regarding his dual identity:

> You have ... been British for two generations, and no doubt if you went to China you would claim British protection, you would register yourself in British Consulates in China as a British subject, and yet here in Singapore, you become a member of a Chinese political society, the Kuomintang. So you endeavor to have a double allegiance. There is a Chinese phrase for this. They call it Leung t'au sha "double-headed snake."[1]

Clementi's comment shows how the British looked at the consolidation among the Chinese groups as an inevitable trend, and a trend that marked the betrayal of the Baba Chinese. The British understanding reflected their concern over the mobilization of anti-Japanese nationalism from mainland China to the colony throughout the long 1930s.

The Many Chinese "Races" in Japan's Southward Advance

In contrast to the concern by the British to sustain their control over the territories of Malaya, Brunei and Hong Kong, the initial Japanese motivation to understand the differences among the Chinese in the South Seas in general and in Singapore in particular was to export Japanese industrial products to overseas markets. The Japanese surveys on the Chinese communities in the South Seas thus covered the political territories of Singapore, the Federated Malay States, Dutch East Indies and beyond. In addition, as Japan before 1935 was not a colonial power but an aspiring investor in the South Seas, the Japanese surveys of the Chinese business and migration networks in the region appeared in various sources: pan-Asianists' propaganda, commercial surveys of Japanese banks and ad hoc organizations for Japan's southward business expansion, and Japanese travellers' accounts of the region, among others.

To be sure, in contrast to the case for the British, the vast area of the Japanese South Seas was not new to Japan. In the Azuchi Momoyama period (1573–1615) and the early Tokugawa period before the 1630s, Japanese *daimyos* (feudal barons) would issue licences for merchants to navigate to the South Seas, where the Portuguese, the Dutch, the French and the Chinese as well as local traders gathered for trade. The Japanese referred to these southern business encounters as *nanban bōeki*, literally meaning trade with southern barbarians. And the Japanese overseas settlements in the South Seas developed at this juncture were called *Nanyō Nihon machi* (South Seas Japanese quarters). Within a decade after the visits of the American "black ships" that forced Japan to end the seclusion era, in 1861, Japanese scholars had translated the Chinese writing of world history and geography, Xu Jiyu's *Ying Huan Zhi Lue* (world geography; originally published in 1849; translated by Shun'yō Inoue et al. 1861). But in the early Japanese surveys of the region, presented in the books of Shiga Shigetaka and Suzuki Keikun published between 1887 and 1893, geographical interest in the South Seas was limited to the southern Pacific, and not including the region surrounding Singapore (Peattie 1987; Suzuki 2009).

Japanese attention to the Chinese in the region started with the Pan-Asianist search for a Chinese "hero" who could rescue China from Western encroachments. For example, in Inoue Masaji's graduate thesis submitted to the Tōkyō Senmon Gakkō, the precursor of the Waseda University, he pointed out that the "three million of southern Han Chinese overseas" constituted the key to China's revival (cited in Kuo 2015). By this, he specifically referred to the anti-Manchu republican revolution supported by Han Chinese from the six southern provinces: Guangdong, Guangxi, Hunan, Hubei, Zhejiang and Fujian. It is worth noting that Inoue was a disciple of Arao Sei, an advocate of mid-Meiji Japan's expansionist policy and the founder of the Ni-Shin bōeki (Japan–China Trade Research Institute; est. 1880) for the promotion of economic ties between China and Japan. Inspired by Arao Sei's commitment to prevent the further dismemberment of China, Inoue supported the Chinese revolutionaries Tang Caichang and Sun Yat-sen (Kuo 2015). Shortly thereafter, in 1901, the Japanese governor-general in Taiwan, Kodama Gentaro, sheltered the Cantonese Christian and first Chinese graduate from Yale University, Yung Wing, for Yung's involvement in the aborted constitutional reforms in Qing China (Yung Wing 1909, pp. 113–36). In Tokyo, the metropolis of the Japanese Empire also became a haven for revolutionaries and constitutional reformists alike; most of them also southerners: Sun Yat-sen, Hu Hanmin, Wang Jingwei, Kang Youwei and Liang Qichao from Guangdong, Zhang Taiyen from Zhejiang, Song Jiaoren and Huang Xing from Hunan (Bergére 1998). The fruit of the southern Chinese revolutions was the triumph of the anti-dynastic revolution in October 1911.

The collaboration between the Japanese Pan-Asianists and the southern Chinese revolutionaries and reformists was the background against which Japanese intellectuals started to construct the thesis about the divided Chinese civilization. Among the first presentations of such a tenet was in Tanaka Zenryū's *Taiwan to minami Shina* (Taiwan and South China). He demarcated the boundary of southern China by the provinces south of the Yangzi River in Zhejiang, Fujian, Guangdong, Guangxi, Yunan and Guizhou. He argued that, compared with the central Chinese and northern Chinese, the southern Chinese were in the "infant stage" of civilizational development. The plentiful uncultivated land and barbarian people would allow the southern

Chinese to have the greatest potential for future development (Tanaka Z. 1913, cited in Kuo 2015, p. 158). It is worth noting that Tanaka's observation was based on his decade-long service at the Buddhist temple of Higashi Honganji in Quanzhou, Fujian (Nakauchi 1942, pp. 22–28). The temple belonged to the Japanese Buddhist sect of Shinshū Ōtani-ha, which started its missionary work of reformist Zen Buddhism in Fujian in 1898, when Qing China guaranteed Japan the privileged right of the province, including Qing's guarantee of not ceding Fujian to any foreign country. The Higashi Honganji also handled non-religious programmes such as providing courses in Japanese, mathematics, Confucian classics, world geography and history (Kan 2011).

Japanese appreciation of the southern Chinese and the notion of the divided Chinese civilization also affected Japanese colonial governance in Taiwan. A Japanese colonial survey in Taiwan in 1904 states that "most Taiwanese were Chinese immigrants from the Hokkien area in southeastern Fujian, therefore we can use the Hokkien customs as a means to understand the customs in Taiwan" (Kuo 2015, pp. 156–57). Beginning in the 1910s, Japan used the shared Hokkien ties across the Taiwan Straits to extend its economic influence to the South Seas, especially to the ports where the Hokkien merchants were dominant. In 1912 the Japanese charter bank in Taiwan, the Bank of Taiwan, opened the first overseas bank in Singapore. Tokyo also began to set up and sponsor the operation of regular southbound shipping routes by way of Taiwan and Java to Singapore. In April 1919 the Osaka Mercantile Steamship Company established a direct shipping line between Jilong and Singapore. To deepen its understanding of the Chinese in the South Seas, in 1914 the Bank of Taiwan organized a survey tour to investigate trade and the financial system in the South Seas. In the following year, Inoue Masaji, who became an entrepreneur of a rubber plantation in Johor from 1910, as well as Japanese politicians including Uchida Kakichi, chief of Home Affairs, the Taiwan office of the governor-general (Taiwan Sōtokufu) and Den Kenjirō from the Japanese Diet, founded the South Sea Association (SSA; Jpn. *Nan'yō kyōkai*) in Tokyo. It was an ad hoc organization for Japan to collect commercial data and to promote the sale of Japanese merchandise in the South Seas. The SSA opened its first overseas branch in Taiwan in the same year, followed by the Singapore branch in 1916. In Singapore, the SSA officers also set up a commercial showcase to display Japanese goods and to train Japanese interns for trading in the south. Kimura Matsutarō, a graduate of Kyoto University and a bureaucrat of the Office of the Governor-in-General, Taiwan, was its first director. Accordingly, either through mobilizing Taiwanese Hokkien speakers or through recruiting Japanese colonial officers with Taiwan experience to work in Singapore, Japan made use of the Hokkien ties to plug into the South Seas markets (Kuo 2011; Kuo 2014, pp. 94–97).

Against this backdrop, Japan looked at the differences among the southern Chinese speech groups, such as those between Hokkien and Cantonese, as evidence for the thesis of a multitude of Chinese civilizations. For example, in 1919 Koku Ryōgo, who directed the missionary work of the Higashi Honganji in Amoy and Zhangzhou, Fujian, explained the success of the South Seas Hokkien, especially those from the Quanzhou area, by the idiosyncratic "Hokkien racial trait": the mixture between the southward Han migrants and the indigenous non-Han people in the region.[2] "Because of the barren land, enterprising spirit was prevalent there. Both men and women worked assiduously and diligently. They were thus more successful in overseas emigration" (Koku 1919, p. 45). It is worth noting that both the qualities that defined the unique characters of the Quanzhou Hokkien — the mixture of Han and non-Han racial stocks as well as active engagement in the South Seas trade and migration — were also documented in the survey of the Cantonese in Guangdong and Guangxi compiled by the Bank of Taiwan in 1923 (Taiwan Ginkō Chōsa-ka 1923, p. 2).

In response to the fragmented Chinese politics after the fall of the Qing Empire in 1911, Japanese Sinologists found it imperative to investigate the ethnic and cultural differences between northern and southern Chinese. Naitō Konan (1866–1931) — a member of the Japanese East Asian Common Culture Association (Jpn. *Tōa Dōbunkai*) — presented a notable thesis about the break in China's history after the transition from the Tang (681–907) to the Song (960–1279) when the nomadic tribes from the north destroyed the Tang state. After that, the political framework of a centralized state no longer existed in China, while the interests of the commoners began to shape China's politics (Egami 1992, pp. 54–56). This thesis can be understood by the inevitable shift of China's economy from the north to the south, from the Yellow River plain to the south of the Yangzi River after the Tang and particularly in the Song. Around the same time, another Sinologist, Fujita Toyohachi (1869–1929), advanced the thesis of north–south dualism to analyse the changing genres of Chinese literature throughout history (Fujita 1943). Another notable Japanese Sinologist, Kuwabara Jitsuzō, published an article that emphasized the rise of southern Chinese cultural influence after the Song dynasty. This article also points out the absolute dominance of southern Chinese intellectual development during the Qing, according to the percentage of qualified scholars passing the Confucian civil examinations (Kuwabara 1925). In line with the interest of reckoning the differences within the generic Chinese category, in 1931 the colonial bureaucrat Kobayashi Shinsaku further differentiated the southern Chinese between those newly arrived in the South Seas and those earlier settlers. He emphasized the biological changes that the Chinese underwent after settling in the South Seas: new migrants from China, or the China-born new migrants (Jpn. *shinkyaku*; literally, "new guests"), were more diligent than the Malay-born creolized Baba Chinese who had settled in the South Seas and assimilated with the Malays for generations (Kuo 2015, p. 170n63).

One of the most prolific writers about the South Seas Chinese sojourners in the wartime era was Ide Kiwata (1880–1960?).[3] Ide, a graduate of political science from Tokyo University, was a Japanese colonial bureaucrat in Taiwan. He joined the research cluster of the Department of Ethnology and Anthropology at Taipei Imperial University. *Nan'pō Dozoku* (Southern native customs), the official newsletter of the department, was among the venues where Ide published his work. For example, between 1931 and 1934 the journal published his articles about the customs and cultures of various ethnic groups in Southwestern China. These included Yao, Miao and Luo people in Yunnan and Guangxi, Tibetans in the Tibetan area, and the Tanka people in Guangdong (Ide 1931, 1933a, 1933b, 1934). He later developed a general thesis about the southern Chinese racial groups (Jpn. *minami shina minzoku*): the dominant southern speech-groups such as the Hokkien and Cantonese should be considered as divergent racial groups — not only between themselves but also with the generic Han Chinese category (Ide 1940b).

Such an argument differed from the self-identification among most Hokkien and Cantonese speakers. Both groups claimed their quintessential Han Chineseness, and both traced their ancestral roots back to the Yellow River plain. The discourse was that the southward migration took place several times in history, including the century following the fall of the Han dynasty in the third century, the fall of the Western Jin in the fifth century, the fall of the Tang dynasty in the tenth century and the fall of the North Song in the twelfth century. Ide recognized the Chinese history of the nomad–Han tensions, but he argued that the southern part of China in Fujian and Guangdong had been populated with indigenous people when the Han arrived, and the Han migrants had also assimilated with indigenous southern peoples for several generations. The southern Chinese — in Ide's terms the Fujian "race" and the Guangdong "race" — were thus closer to the southern indigenous groups than the northern Han (Ide 1938a, pp. 25–36; Ide 1938b, pp. 34–44; Ide 1939b; Ide 1940b, pp. 34–40). It is worth noting that Ide did not look at the southern indigenous peoples as inferior groups to the Han Chinese. He cited the work of the Chinese anthropologist Xu Songshi, *Yuejiang liuyu renmin shi* (History of the people of the Yue River basin), in particular. Xu, a Hakka scholar, traced the southern roots of the residents of Guangdong and Guangxi from the Miao, Yao and Tong peoples. And these southern peoples, like their northern counterparts in the Yellow River plain, contributed to the making of Chinese civilization six thousand years ago. Ide later translated Xu's work into Japanese and published it under the title *Minami Shina minzoku-shi* (History of southern Chinese people) in 1941 (Kuo 2015, p. 172).

Against the backdrop of Japan's military preparedness to confront Western colonial powers in Asia, a faculty member of Taipei Imperial University, Kuwata Rokurō (1894–1987), attributed the expansion of Western powers from the sixteenth century to the end of business, cultural and diplomatic exchanges between the southern Chinese and Persians, Arabs and Indians that started from the Chinese Tang dynasty. After that juncture, to manage and continue their maritime trade, southern Chinese had to be in contact with the Western colonizers in the region (Kuwata 1940, pp. 22–26).

In Ide's view, the overseas migration of southern Chinese contributed to the making of South Seas Chinese. Ide provided rich reports on the political dispositions among South Seas Chinese in the Dutch East Indies, French Indochina, the Philippines and British Malaya in the Pacific War (Ide 1939*a*, 1940*a*). Throughout the wartime period, Ide repeatedly criticized the Japanese official policy that treated the South Seas Chinese as enemies of the Japanese empire. He argued instead the importance for Japan to protect Chinese overseas interests in the Japanese Greater East Asian Co-prosperity Sphere (Kuo 2015, p. 173). After the Japanese Occupation of Singapore, Ide stated that the Chinese overseas in Singapore changed their political position "one hundred and eighty degrees" during the development of the Greater East Asian War. At the beginning of the war, Chinese overseas rallied to the KMT regime; but now, many prominent Chinese overseas leaders have turned to support the Japan-led Greater East Asian Co-prosperity Sphere (Ide 1943, pp. 5–6). And compared with the Euro-American colonial policies, Japan identified with local interests and was willing to prepare the indigenous people for national autonomy (Ide 1943, p. 10). In retrospect, as the Japanese *sook ching* purge took forty thousand lives, among those Chinese participating in the national salvation movements in previous years (Heng 1988, p. 37), Ide's emphasis on the possibilities for Chinese–Japanese cooperation can be viewed as his attempt to enhance Japanese understanding of the southern Chinese.

Conclusion

Comparing the two different systems on the classification of the Chinese in Singapore, this chapter points out the different approaches that set up the parameters for the British and Japanese colonizers to engage with the Chinese overseas. Each system of classification entails not only the understanding of the dynamics of the South Seas Chinese communities, but also the very notion of the relationship between the Chinese inside and outside China. I argue that the differences between the British and Japanese systems of classification should be understood by the different roles and interests of these two imperialist powers in their connections with the South Seas Chinese.

In the late nineteenth century, the British colonial censuses of the Straits Settlements classified the Chinese by their mutually unintelligible languages. The goal of the British at that time was to patronize a select group of Chinese to govern the inflow of new migrants from China on behalf of colonial interests. But, after the 1920s, while keeping the old matrix of racial classification, the British began to put the elitist Baba Chinese under the same category of the Chinese race as those new migrants from China. This reflected the fading influence of the Baba and the British view about surging Chinese nationalism and the influence of Mandarin education. For the British, the growing Chinese anti-Japanese nationalism in the 1930s was inspired by mainland Chinese politics. In the colonial censuses in the 1930s, the category of Chinese became an encompassing framework that represented the Chinese within and without the territorial boundary of the Chinese state. In contrast, the pre-war Japanese surveys not only separated the southern Chinese from the central and northern Chinese, but also presented the different speech-groups among the southern Chinese as different races.

The contrasting views between the British and Japanese classifications could be understood by their respective positions in sustaining their imperialist agendas against Chinese nationalism. For the British, the incumbent colonizer, the principal policy concern over the Chinese was to incorporate and to domesticate the existing Chinese social and economic networks into the British colonial framework of "indirect rule". The British thus considered the Singapore Chinese' connection with mainland China a threat to the colonial status quo, and highlighted the connection by lumping different Chinese speech-groups within the singular framework of the Chinese "race". For Japan, the late-rising imperialist power, the strategy was to extend its influence in Fujian and Taiwan to the South Seas. The divided Chinese networks thus helped Japan isolate some anti-Japanese Chinese groups while working with the others. The pan-Asianist activists and colonizers like Inoue Masaji, Tanaka Zenryō and Ide Kiwata could not stop the Japanese *sook ching* purge. Their understanding of the intricate differences among the southern Chinese, however, created space for Chinese–Japanese collaboration. The collaboration was certainly precarious, but it nonetheless created substantial ground to restore the local order after the British withdrew.

Stoler has pointed out that the implementation of the colonial census was more for the purpose of political domination. It was also for the colonizers to construct "qualified knowledge" about the colonial subjects in the hope of achieving "epistemic supremacy" that would eventually fix the racial hierarchy between the colonizers and their subjugated subordinates. In the body of research on ethnic Chinese in the South Seas, most of the well-cited sources include the prolific publications of Victor Purcell (1896–1965). With his experiences as a colonial administrator in British Malaya, Purcell follows the British colonial framework that classifies the Chinese by their differences along the native-place and dialect ties that originated in China. His main idea was that overseas Chinese communities in the South Seas were a continuity of the Chinese in China. The studies of Maurice Freedman (1920–75), G. William Skinner (1925–2008) and Constance Mary Turnbull (1927–2008), to a large extent, all continue this perspective. This approach, in the words of William G. Skinner, was to see South Seas Chinese societies as "a window on China proper" (Skinner 1979, p. xiii).

In the post-war years, while the assumption of British colonial censuses evolved into the epistemological foundation for the intellectual inquiry about the South Seas Chinese communities, the Japanese racial accounts on the Chinese became an oft-neglected subject. Does this mean that Chinese speech-group differences are no longer relevant to understanding the Chinese overseas communities dispersed from southern China? In post-colonial Singapore, the official language was English. The "Speak Mandarin Campaign" after 1979 emphasized the replacement of southern languages (called dialects) by Mandarin, whose phonetic basis was the Beijing tone. In Taiwan, Mandarinization subjugated the use of the Taiwanese Hokkien. Even in Hong Kong, which continued to be under British governance until 1997, the policy of "biliterate trilingualism" — the use of English and Chinese as the two written languages and English, Mandarin, and Cantonese as the three spoken languages — nonetheless could not discourage Chinese parents from sending their children for English education.[4] Regardless of intentional official suppression (such as in Singapore and Taiwan) or voluntary choice, the southern Chinese speech-group identity continues to affect all these societies. The resilient southern-speech-group ties can manifest in the following cases: the intentional neglect among Singaporean parents of the official policy of registering children's names according to Mandarin but not Hokkien, Cantonese or Teochew pronunciation (Trocki 2006, p. 153); the benefit of using Taiwanese Hokkien in different levels of political elections in Taiwan (Heylen and Sommers 2010); and the protests of the Hong Kong people over Beijing's agenda of privileging Mandarin while marginalizing Cantonese in education (Simpson 2010). The continuing influence of the southern languages in these communities points out that the differences among the southern Chinese speech-groups could not be commensurate with unitary Chineseness. The oft-neglected Japanese system of classifying the Chinese, with its emphasis on the disaggregated roles among these speech-groups in the inter-imperialist rivalry, could shed light on pervasive assumption about a singular Chineseness and the overarching influence from mainland China towards Chinese overseas communities.

Notes

1. FO 371/14728/2083, Government House meeting between Sir Cecil Clementi and 17 office-bearers of the British Malaya Head Branch of the Chinese Nationalist Party, 20 February 1930 (cited in Yong and McKenna 1990, p. 251).
2. He estimated that "40% of [the] local population were Han Chinese, and the rest were descendants of the ancient Min people. However through 2,000 years of assimilation, the mixture with Han racial blood became universal here" (Koku 1919, p. 45).
3. The year of Ide's death is based on Kaneko (1980, p. 73). Kaneko, however, stated that he only had fragmented information about Ide's life after retiring from Takushoku University in 1953. He became a university lecturer after obtaining a doctorate in economics from Tokyo University in 1940.
4. In 1958 about 55 per cent of students were enrolled in English-language secondary schools, and the percentage jumped to 92 per cent in 1988 (Chao 2002. p. 284).

References

Akashi, Yōji. *The Nanyang Chinese National Salvation Movement, 1937–1941*. Kansas: Center for East Asian Studies, the University of Kansas, 1970.

Bergère, Marie-Claire. *Sun Yat-sen*, translated by Janet Lloyd. Stanford, CA: Stanford University Press, 1998.

Best, Anthony. *British Intelligence and the Japanese Challenge in Asia, 1914–1941*. London: Palgrave McMillan, 2002.

Choy Chee Meh. "History of the Malaysian Branch of Royal Asiatic Society, 1877–1983". BA thesis, Department of History, National University of Singapore, 1984/85.

Egami Nami'o. *Tōyō gaku no keifu*. Tokyo: Taishūkan Shoten, 1992.

Foster, Joseph. *Men-at-the-Bar: A Biographical Hand-List of the Members of the Various Inns of Court, Including Her Majesty's Judges, Etc.* Ithaca: Cornell University Library, [1885] 2009.

Fujita Toyohachi. *Tōzai kōshōshi no kenkyū: Nankai-hen*, edited by Hiroshi Ikeuchi. Tokyo: Ogiwara Seibunkan, 1943.

Helen, Ann, and Scott Sommers. *Becoming Taiwan: From Colonialism to Democracy*. Harrassowitz, 2010.

Heng Pek Koon. *Chinese Politics in Malaysia: A History of the Malaysian Chinese Association*. Oxford: Oxford University Press, 1988.

Horne, Gerald. *Race War! White Supremacy and the Japanese Attack on the British Empire*. New York: New York University Press, 2005.

Ide Kiwata. "Seinan shina dozoku shiryō, ichi". *Nan'pō Dōzōku* 2, no. 2 (April 1933*a*): 41–50.

———. "Seinan shina dozoku shiryō, ni". *Nan'pō Dōzōku* 2, no. 3 (October 1933*b*): 29–44.

———. "Unnan no dozoku nit suite". *Nan'pō Dōzōku* 3, no. 2 (November 1934): 47–60.

———. "Fukken Minzoku to Nan'yō Kakyō". *Nan'yō Kyokai Zasshi* 24, no. 5 (1938*a*): 25–36.

———. "Minami Shina no tenbō to so no taisaku". *Tōyō* (October 1938*b*): 34–44.

———, "Nan'yō kakyō no dōkō tsuite". *Tōyō* 42, no. 5 (1939*a*): 120–27.

———. "Kanton minzoku to kakumei go seisen no sui'i". *Nanshi Nan'yō* (November 1939*b*): 1535–50.

———. "Nan'yō kakyō saikin no dōkō to shōrai". *Tōyō* 43, no. 1 (1940*a*): 88–95.

———. "Nan'yō no kakyō". *Umi wo koeru* (October 1940*b*): 34–40.

———. "Shōnan-dō no seiseku to shōrai no shimei". *Umi wo koeru* (May 1943): 2–10.

Innes, J.R. *Report on the Census of the Straits Settlements, Taken on the 1st March 1901*. Singapore: Government Printing Office, 1901.

Inoue Kiyoshi. *Nan'yō to Nihon*. Tokyo: Taishō-sha, 1913.

Kan Zheng Zong. "Mingzhi shiqi Zhenzong dagu pai [Shinshū Otani-ha] zai liang an de huo dong" [Activities between cross-straits during the Meiji Era (1873~1912)]. *Yuan Kuang Journal of Buddhist Studies*, no. 17 (October 2011): 99–125.

Kaneko Fumio. "Personalities in the History of Japanese Coloniaism: Kiwata Ide". *Historical Studies of Taiwan in Modern Times*, no. 3 (1980): 67–85.

Kuo Huei-Ying. "Social Discourse and Economic Functions: The Singapore Chinese in Japan's Southward Expansion, 1914–1941". In *Singapore in Global History*, edited by Derek Heng and Syed Muhd Khairudin Aljunied. Amsterdam: Amsterdam University Press, 2011.

———. *Networks beyond Empires: Chinese Business and Nationalism in the Hong Kong–Singapore Corridor, 1914–1941*. Leiden: Brill, 2014.

———. "Learning from the South: Japan's Racial Construction of Southern Chinese, 1895–1941". In *Race and Racism in Modern East Asia: Interactions, Nationalism, Gender and Lineage*, edited by Rotem Kowner and Walter Demel. Leiden: Brill, 2015.

Kuwabara, Jitsuzō. "Rekishi jyō yori kansuru minami shina no kaihatsu". In *Tōyōshi ronsō: Shiratori Hakushi kanreki kinen*, edited by Shiratori Kurakichi and Ikeuchi Hiroshi. Tokyo: Iwanami Shoten, 1925.

Kuwata Rokurō. "Nan Shi bunka no shi deki kaiko". *Nanpō Dōzōku* 6, nos. 1–2 (March 1940): 1–26.

Mak Lau Fong. *The Sociology of Secret Societies: A Study of Chinese Secret Societies in Singapore and Peninsular Malaysia*. Kuala Lumpur: Oxford University Press, 1981.

Marriott, Esq. H. *Report of the Census of the Colony of the Straits Settlements, 1911*. Singapore: Government Printing Press, 1911.

McNair, J.F.A., C.B. Waller, and A. Knight. *Miscellaneous Numerical Returns: Straits Settlements Census Reports and Returns, 2nd April 1871*. Singapore: Straits Settlements Government Press, 1871.

Merewether, E.M. *Report of the Census of the Straits Settlements Taken on the 5th, April, 1891*. Singapore: Government Printing Press, 1892.

Nakauchi Hideo. "Nanpō bunka seisaku to Tanaka Zenryū". *Nan Shin* 7, no. 4 (1942): 22–28

Nathan, J.E. *The Census of British Malaya 1921*. London: Waterlow & Sons, 1922.

Peattie, Mark R. "The Nan'yō: Japan in the South Pacific, 1885–1945". In *The Japanese Colonial Empires*, edited by Ramon Hawley Myers and Mark R. Peattie, pp. 172–211. Princeton, NJ: Princeton University Press, 1987.

Simpson, Andrew. "Hong Kong". In *Languages and National Identity in East Asia*, edited by Andrew Simpson, pp. 168–86. Oxford University Press, 2007.

Skinner, G. William. "Introduction". In *The Study of Chinese Society*, by Maurice Freedman. Stanford: Stanford University Press, 1979.

Stoler, A. "Epistemic Politics: Ontologies of Colonial Common Sense". *Philosophical Forum* 39, no 3 (Fall 2008): 349–61.

Straits Settlements. *Straits Settlements Miscellaneous Numerical Returns*. Singapore: Straits Settlements Government Press, 1881.

Suzuki, Shogo. *Civilization and Empire: China and Japan's Encounter with European International Society*. London: Routledge, 2009.

Taiwan Ginkō Chōsa-ka. *Kanton Kansei ryōshō shutsuchō hōkoku gaiyō*. Taiwan: Taiwan Ginkō Chōsa-ka, 1923.

Taiwan Sōtokufu. *Taiwan Kanshū kiji* 4, no. 4 (1904).

Trocki, Carl A. *Opium and Empire: Chinese Society in Colonial Singapore, 1800–1910*. Ithaca: Cornell University Press, 1990.

———. *Singapore: Wealth, Power and the Cultural Control*. London: Routledge, 2006.

Vaughan, J.D. *The Manners and Customs of the Chinese of the Straits Settlements*. Kuala Lumpur: Oxford University Press, [1879] 1974.

Vieland, C.A. *British Malaya (the Colony of the Straits Settlements and the Malay States under British protection, Namely the Federated States of Perak, Selangor, Negri Sembilan and Pahang and the States of Johore, Kedah, Kelantan, Trengganu, Perlis and Brunei): A Report on the 1931 Census and on Certain Problems of Vital Statistics*. London: Crown Agents for the Colonies, 1932.

Xu, Jiyu. *Eikan Shiryaku*, translated by Shun'yō Inoue, Tekien Mori, and Ryuōho Mimori. Oōsaka: Tsurugaya Kuheð; Edo: Uchinoya Yaheiji, 1861.

Yen Ch'ing-hwang. "The Response of the Overseas Chinese in Singapore and Malaya to the Tsinan [Jinan] Incident, 1928". In *Overseas Chinese in Asia between the Two World Wars*, edited by Ng Lun Ngai-ha and Chang Chak Yan. Hong Kong: Overseas Chinese Archives and Centre for Contemporary Asian Studies, Chinese University of Hong Kong, 1989.

Yong Ch'ing-fatt. *Tan Kah Kee: The Making of an Overseas Chinese Legend*, rev. ed. Singapore: World Scientific, 2014.

Yong Ch'ing-fatt and R.B. McKenna. *The Kuomintang Movement in British Malaya, 1912–1941*. Singapore: National University of Singapore Press, 1990.

Yung Wing. *My Life in China and America*. New York: Holt, 1909.

12

Chinese Studies in Japan and South Korea: Geopolitics, Local Embeddedness and Knowledge

Claire Seungeun Lee

Interdisciplinary or multidisciplinary programmes like Asian Studies[1] can be found in many universities, particularly those located in Western societies. This is, by and large, a result of a curiosity over Asian "exotic others" and a reflection of colonial tradition to a certain extent. By contrast, Asian universities that have not inherited a Western colonial legacy have no strong tendency to maintain Asian Studies as a separate discipline.[2] However, in part due to the influence of the United States (on the development of area studies)[3] and the colonial legacy in other countries, area studies by region and country exist in Asian universities. In Japan and South Korea, for instance, East Asian area studies by and large started with Chinese language and literature and later embraced regional social sciences. Area studies[4] (地域 [chiki][5] 研究) in Japan started to appear in the 1950s, and the discipline expanded in the 1980s and 1990s. Tokyo University of Foreign Studies was the first university to offer such programmes (Takeuchi 2012, p. 10). In Korea, Hankuk University of Foreign

Studies has language- and area-based departments. Later, the Kim Young Sam government (1993–98) of South Korea, which rapidly embraced a globalization discourse (*sekyehwa*) as an important state agenda, established a set of nine graduate schools of international or area studies[6] in 1997. In addition, the shortage of experts on trade and international political economy provided the impetus to establish more area studies programmes.

There is a rationale for comparing the development of Chinese Studies in Japan and South Korea. First, as neighbouring countries in East Asia, China, Japan and Korea have cultural proximity and shared histories. Second, the region is facing issues of sovereignty over Dokdo/Takeshima Island, which has an impact on relations between South Korea, Japan and China. Japan has been in conflict with both China and South Korea over sovereignty issues involving Diaoyus/Senkaku Island in the South China Sea and Dokdo/Takeshima Island in the East Sea/Japan Sea. Third, relations among the three countries are inevitable; they are economically interdependent. China is the largest trading partner for Japan and South Korea. Fourth, the human flow of Chinese international students and tourists to Japan and South Korea is larger than to any other country (Lee 2014). Therefore, there are strong motivations for Japan and South Korea to know about China.

Under such conditions, "knowing of contemporary China" or "Chinese Studies" — or Sinology[7] — is particularly important for neighbouring countries in the era of rising China. This chapter is limited to the discussion of social science–based Chinese Studies, because its origins, development and relations with geopolitics are different from humanities-based Chinese Studies. This study explores the geopolitically charged relations and genealogies of knowledge with regard to the development and state of Chinese Studies in Japan and South Korea. Local and geopolitical contexts play a significant role in constructing and disseminating Chinese Studies as a particular knowledge in these two Asian societies. The following questions are examined: (1) how the divergent paths of knowledge production of Chinese Studies in Japan and South Korea have been managed in the midst of changing geopolitics in the region, and (2) how Japan and South Korea negotiate different types of knowledge and sources — funding, institutions, governments, public needs — in maintaining and further developing

Chinese Studies as one of the largest area studies disciplines in each of these two countries.

This research explores Chinese Studies as a "knowledge industry" for the institutionalization of knowledge on China in Japanese and South Korean societies. The concept of "knowledge industries" highlights a key characteristic of area studies in general as well as the importance of knowledge about China in these settings. At the societal level, "area studies" is expected to serve the role of providing up-to-date knowledge from the local perspective. Knowledge is produced and constructed in the industries and can be discussed as educational knowledge, institutional knowledge and practical knowledge. Such types of knowledge reinforce and shape how Chinese Studies in Japan and South Korea develop.

The Historical Development of Chinese Studies

Japan

Japan has a long tradition in the study of China as an academic discipline, from Sinology (支那学, *Shinagaku*) to Chinese Studies (中国研究). This could be attributed to the common use by the Japanese and Chinese of the same written text — Chinese characters. Due to the common feature of using Chinese characters (kanji), in particular, Japanese scholars had a better understanding of Chinese characters than scholars from other countries.

Sinology is particularly associated with the literature, history and philosophy of China in the pre-war period of Japan. The transition from Sinology to Chinese Studies was a rather gradual movement. In part due to this, the Japan Association for Modern China Studies (日本現代中国学会),[8] which is the oldest and probably the most comprehensive association in Japan, was established in 1951. The existence of such an organization implies that research on China attracted a substantial number of Japanese scholars at the time and also the continuation of *Shinagaku* from a different research strand. Scholars who benefited from the pre-war research tradition of *Shinagaku* are considered the first generation of the Chinese Studies tradition of Japan.

The second generation consisted of those who had a curiosity about socialist China and went to study in the United States in the 1950s and 1960s. The third generation consisted of those who started studying after Sino–Japanese diplomatic normalization in 1972 (Takagi 2004). In part due to such paths, the development of Chinese Studies in Japan differs from that in South Korea. Although Oksenberg claims that it was the initiation and development by the Japanese PhD graduates from American universities that started Chinese Studies, local training in prestigious Japanese institutions also contributed to the advancement of Chinese Studies. Some of the early scholars, on the other hand, went to the United States, and later some studied in Japan. Also, Communist China made it difficult for them to enter China. This also explains how the initial motivation for Chinese Studies in Japan was to know about Taiwan as one of Japan's colonies.[9]

Likewise, the scholarly training of Japanese researchers of Chinese Studies has a different development path. In the 1980s and early 1990s, the relaxation of tensions between Taiwan and the mainland and the democratization of Taiwan itself, coupled with the return of U.S.-trained PhDs and the rise of a new generation of scholars, had stimulated contemporary Chinese studies in Japan, including the analysis of Taiwan itself.

In the 2000s and 2010s, young scholars went to China or Taiwan to study the Chinese language before continuing their studies in prestigious universities in Japan or abroad. As with the case of South Korea, their scholarly training was diversified. Due to the influx of Chinese students to Japan, an increasing number of Chinese graduate students participated in academic events and published in Japanese and Chinese in the realm of Chinese Studies in Japan. We could observe this trend in South Korea with the inflow of Han Chinese and Korean Chinese students, either to study the Korean language or even to study their own countries in South Korea.

In addition to the impetus to the creation of the discipline in Japan, based on archival and bibliographic research of the Japanese database, it is rather surprising to find that endeavours to examine the overall view of Chinese Studies in Japan are lacking, even in the local language. However, China scholars in Japan working on Chinese Studies appear to focus on specific economics, politics or other issues, and a systematic study of the trajectory of the discipline from the local researchers has yet to be found.

For example, several China scholars have commented on the development of Chinese Studies in Japan. Yan Shanping (2009) made a speech on the future of Chinese Studies in Japan in the context of Japan–China cooperation. Shu (2012), in particular, offers an extensive account of the Japanese Association of Chinese Studies as an example of investigating Chinese Studies in post-war Japan. In contrast to the article by Shu (2012), which is centred on the association, a reflective overall account of Chinese Studies in Japan was offered by Kokubun (2001). Some Japanese scholars have attempted to discuss issues and problems encountered by those studying Chinese Studies in Japan (Ushijima 2008; Yumino 2009). On the contrary, the discipline of area studies in journals focuses on research traditions, methods and practices (Kajitani 2007), but not on the development of Chinese Studies in Japan.

South Korea

In contrast to Japan, Chinese Studies in Korea have been analysed extensively, both in general and with respect to specific subjects. First, general overviews of the discipline of Chinese Studies are investigated by Chun (1998) and Kim and Chun (1996). These two academic contributions observe the origin and development of area and international studies in South Korea. Second, Chinese Studies are well discussed in particular in the context of Political Science or Chinese Politics. This is in accordance with the distribution of Korean scholars who study China. In other words, a large number of such Korean scholars have researched the international and domestic political issues of China. For instance, Chung (2000) and Chung et al. (2005) investigate Chinese political science studies in South Korea by analysing one of the prominent journals on China (in Korean) and English journals based on source, method and writing. Chung (2000), in particular, investigates Chinese political science. In a similar vein, Dohee Kim (2006) explores Chinese Studies vis-à-vis politics in South Korea by interviewing a number of scholars. It is noted that the abstract and title of Kim's article may give the impression that the paper attempts to focus on Chinese Studies in general. However, her discussion is restricted to Chinese politics only, which is in line with the practice of Chinese Studies in South Korea. In a nutshell, at both the macro level of Chinese Studies reviews and in studies on Chinese politics, both strands of research are presented by Korean scholars in the field of "Chinese politics".

Some Korean scholars have also examined Chinese Studies in other contexts which have not been well discussed in the Japanese academia yet. One area would be "Chinese Studies elsewhere" (not in South Korea). Junghee Lee (2000) gives an overview of contemporary Chinese Studies in Western societies. Another interesting area would be the discussions on "Chinese Studies of China" (D.-H. Kim 2010; M.J. Lee 2001; Yu 2010).[10] Yu (2010), in particular, investigates the current situation of Chinese sociology in China, not in South Korea or elsewhere. It is interesting to note that sociology or society-related topics are investigated in the context of China, not in South Korea. Chinese Studies from a sociological angle have not been the focus yet. This clearly elucidates the way in which Chinese Studies in South Korea is institutionalized. Such an inclination towards political science, but not towards sociology, is largely because many scholars who work on China are not interested in society (and culture). Although sociology has its own division of cultural sociology or sociology of culture, some humanities scholars who initially study literature and linguistics tend to extend their fields towards "culture". This is because their own expertise does not sell well in the Korean academy, where there is increasing attention to an interest in culture in general.

The dominance in research traditions, which is concurrent with the development of each cohort, has changed over time. Based on internal and external contextual factors of the development of Chinese Studies in Japan and South Korea, the following is, in chronological order, a summary of the different cohorts of Chinese Studies scholars in South Korea.

The first generation of Korean Sinologists consisted of those who studied in the 1970s (or even earlier). In the 1970s and 1980s, when China was still under the Communists and the socialist regime, and having North Korea as an "enemy" in particular in an ideological sense, it was rather difficult for South Koreans to study China. Along with such sensitivity towards China as a research object, South Korean scholars were encouraged to know about "communist others" — both China and North Korea. This is underlined by the knowledge that we Koreans could be better prepared for our present and future. For that reason, studies in politics and international relations of China were popular and encouraged. During those years, South Korean scholars could only enter the "Free China" (Taiwan) and study in Taiwan. Given the above-mentioned context, among the first and second generations of South Korean scholars, politics and international relations of China and Taiwan were the most frequent areas of study. Economics[11] and sociology (and culture)[12] were likely to be missing. The second generation, in particular, included those who started to conduct research in the mid-1980s, and most of them studied abroad in Taiwan.

In the 1990s, since the diplomatic normalization between China and South Korea, an increasing number of South Korean scholars chose China over Taiwan for their destination of overseas study. Fields of study became more diverse, with the addition of social science disciplines for studying China — economics, politics and also sociology and anthropology. During that period, South Korean scholars studied and conducted research in both Taiwan and increasingly in China. The third generation consists of those who studied in the early 1990s and trained in China, South Korea, the United States, the United Kingdom, or elsewhere.

The number of scholars who began to study in the realm of economics, finance, management and business in the second generation of scholars increased in the third and fourth generations.

Scholars of the fourth generation, those who studied in the 2000s, have a more diverse background than previous generations. In the 2000s, politics and economics were still dominant among Korean scholars. Some started to turn their attention to sociology. A limited number of scholars in the second and third generations studied the society and culture of China in the social science tradition, but they were very few. Even in the 2000s and 2010s, only a small number of researchers have studied sociology or Chinese Studies primarily with a special emphasis on society (and culture, not in the humanities sense).

In recent times, "China" has started to appear as a subject of study, not only among area studies scholars but also in the social science disciplines. For example, some scholars without language training or specific area or country backgrounds also undertook the study of China for their postgraduate degrees. Such scholars have begun to close the gap between scholars originally from country-specific training and those from general social science training.

Taken together, social science–based Chinese Studies has developed to accommodate the needs of government, society and business in Japan and South Korea. The ways in which Chinese Studies are managed in Japan and South Korea have their commonalities as well as differences based on their local embeddedness and political situation.

Managing and Producing Knowledge in Genealogies of Chinese Studies

Knowledge production[13] is often discussed in the context of science and technology studies at one end and sociology of knowledge and education at the other. In relation to science and technology, Fensterheim (2009) investigated China's knowledge production by looking at patents, technology and scientific publications. In the humanities and social sciences, Tewari, Gihar and Qi (2013) compared knowledge production in China and India in the higher education system. Hong (2010) particularly explored the role of a university in knowledge production, transfer and utilization and technological innovation in the context of South Korea.

In Chinese Studies, the ways in which knowledge and sources are managed play a critical role in shaping the discipline in Japan and South Korea. Educational and research institutions like universities and institutes are also important, but the types and sources of knowledge are more significant.

Chinese Studies in the process of disciplinary configuration may need to offer multiple types of knowledge.[14] Types of knowledge in the setting can be highlighted as follows. First, local knowledge forms the foundations of knowledge of China. It has different forms, including language, culture, history and regional affairs. In this regard, learning Chinese is not only for those who are majoring in China-related disciplines and interested in China, but it is also for those who perceive China as a platform for finding jobs and/or enhancing their career path with Chinese. Knowledge and information on Chinese culture, history and regional affairs are equally important to knowing the language. These often function as a lubricant in practice. Second, practical knowledge consists of contemporariness and interaction. With respect to contemporariness, Chinese Studies — like other area studies — needs to remain sensitive to ongoing social changes. The rapidly changing Chinese society and relations with Japan and Korea are highly important for these countries, not only for academic purposes but also for everyday interactions with China and Chinese people. The latter, interaction, illuminates the fact that some mutual understanding is needed in particular in relation to linking the local and foreign. In a related vein, understanding Chinese people in Japan and South Korea and Japanese and Koreans in China is important.

Inherently, knowledge of China from the perspectives of the public, society and the state leans more towards practical (and tacit) knowledge which is applicable to everyday life than to theoretical knowledge. For scholars, the latter can also be important; however, unlike other "pure" soft sciences,[15] knowing a foreign country intrinsically serves for its contemporariness and practicality. Accordingly, the way in which such a body of knowledge is produced, transmitted and managed in the knowledge industry vis-à-vis Chinese Studies is embedded in the characteristics and needs of local societies.

The set of above-mentioned knowledge is largely of the People's Republic of China (PRC) rather than of other Chinese societies. Due to the power dynamics, "particular" knowledge of the PRC society can only be accepted. Most Chinese Studies related courses in Korean universities do not offer or include overseas Chinese societies, not even Hong Kong, Taiwan or Macau, although a large number of full-time faculty members and part-time lecturers studied in Taiwan and Hong Kong. It is important to note that courses on overseas Chinese societies have been offered in recent years in a few universities.[16] In this respect, the backgrounds of the researchers or lecturers do not really matter in the design of the curricula. What is more important in universities is the significance of a particular society — China — to Japan and South Korea rather than a diversity of knowledge of the various Chinese societies.

In light of the above, it is important to delineate what should belong to "China" in the discipline of Chinese Studies. In this respect it is important to note that Chinese Studies[17] in both Japan and South Korea has been oscillating between "the China factor", studying China, and "the Taiwan factor", studying Taiwan, as a result of diplomatic relations with China and the academic backgrounds of scholars.

As such, the case of Taiwan as "particular" knowledge illuminates the power dimension of knowledge production and transmission. First, this is primarily reflected by the Chinese government's "One China, Two Systems" policy as managing genealogies of certain knowledge. As argued earlier, defining "Chinese" Studies as a PRC-based one, in turn, means dislocating Taiwanese Studies in the discipline and public domain.

Second, the colonial relation between Japan and Taiwan, in this sense, may complicate the picture for Japan in dealing with the boundary issue. Fifty years of the colonial nexus between Japan and Taiwan has shaped the direction of Chinese Studies in Japan rather differently. South Korea normalized its diplomatic relations with the PRC in 1992 and consequently had to sever ties with the Republic of China (Taiwan). This change in Korea's diplomatic relations with the two societies configured a new direction of research, focusing on China rather than Taiwan.

In retrospect, the geopolitical factor certainly not only influences the position of Chinese Studies and Taiwan Studies, but it also shaped a new way of managing the discipline recently. In Japan, two divergent patterns of knowledge production and dissemination, which were inherited from social and diplomatic relations, are illuminated. In South Korea, on the other hand, there are no "Taiwan Studies" or any scholars who work primarily on Taiwan. The recent establishment of the Contemporary Taiwan Research Center at Hankuk University of Foreign Studies in 2011 was in order to re-establish the lost connection to Taiwan Studies in South Korea, the launch strategically coinciding with the hundredth anniversary of the Republic of China. The development of the centre and the hosting of an academic conference entitled "Creativity and Vision:

New Tendency on Building Taiwanology" were supported by the Chiang Ching-kuo foundation.[18] This was a "belated" effort to connect Taiwan to South Korea and establish Taiwan Studies in the country. The regaining of the lost connection to the past was based on delayed recognition of the importance of Taiwan in China–South Korea or China–Taiwan relations.

Finally, marketability and the value of such knowledge in Japan and South Korea is highly contextualized and constantly changing. In the case of Japan, local training in prestigious Japanese institutions has been the mainstream approach rather than studying abroad. On the other hand, linking with diplomatic relations, many Korean scholars who are currently faculty members have benefited from their training in Taiwan. Yet, largely due to China's rapid economic growth, there has been tension related to conducting research on Taiwan. There has been a significant change in recent years. Nowadays, most of the Japanese and Korean students choose China instead of Taiwan in the pursuit of their education. This is in line with younger generations of Korean scholars in Chinese Studies going to or being knowledgeable about China rather than Taiwan. Compared to China, Taiwan is small and less important, in particular to Korean students and businesses, whereas Taiwan and Japan have maintained a mutual friendship as a former colony and colonizer. Many Korean companies enter the Chinese market, while Japan has a similar trend in relation to this, in part due to the colonial nexus; some Japanese people and companies continue to choose Taiwan. However, all in all, practically speaking, markets for knowledge and the economy of China are bigger and thus more promising for Japan and South Korea.

In a related vein, by looking back to the decades of Chinese Studies in Japan and South Korea, one can notice changes and continuities which are reinforced by changing dynamics of geopolitics and the international and domestic environments. Considerations of diplomatic relations, of moving on from the communist baggage, and of acknowledging the importance of neighbours have been discussed earlier. The rise of China offers great opportunities for Japanese and Korean scholars to develop and institutionalize Chinese Studies.

Changing Geopolitics, Changing Expectations

Defining Domains of Chinese Studies

In the early days of studying China as a knowledge or *discipline* in foreign countries, a large number of scholars in Chinese Studies in Korea and Japan tended to study literature and linguistics.[19] This led to the creation of departments of Chinese Literature and Linguistics in many universities, rather than departments of Chinese Studies. Chinese Studies tends to include diverse social science disciplines, such as Political Science, Economics, Sociology, Business, Law and so on. Unlike the case of Chinese Literature and Linguistics, the latter with a background on social science could be found in two strands: One is within the China-related departments; another is within the social science disciplines. In the case of Japan and South Korea, Chinese Studies is often associated with the former — such a tradition of the area-focused one exists rather predominantly, as most of the social science departments primarily centre on studying local societies in the home countries.

The Chinese Studies which can be classified into area, regional, or even international studies has been affected by the geopolitical, international and domestic environments. Studying other nations reflects such changes over time. Japan and South Korea have been witnesses to the transformations of their neighbour China as it underwent dramatic changes and economic upgrading. Thus, these two countries are not only in a good position to study China, but, more importantly, have a great interest and need to put much emphasis on the knowledge. The most recent example from the geopolitical situation between China and South Korea is South Korea's decision to deploy the Terminal High Altitude Area Defense (THAAD) system in the Korean Peninsula. This reshapes how South Korea should perceive and deal with China, and vice versa, and how and what kinds of knowledge Chinese Studies in South Korea needs to produce.

Reflecting such contexts, the way in which the two main areas of Chinese Studies are organized is by the internal and international surroundings of China. In particular, research on China was inherently considered as placing importance on one of the "communist" countries, which has led scholars to focus on the politics and diplomacy of China. In the early 1950s and 1960s, foreigners could not go to Communist China, and the only choice was for them to go to Taiwan. In the case of Japan, the tradition of studying China started earlier than in South Korea. The normalization of Sino–Japanese relations in 1972 also contributed to Japanese interest in China. In contrast to Japan, prior to its diplomatic normalization with China, for South Korea, because of the tension and ideological disparity between the two Koreas, travelling to China was not possible. As those who attempted to read or possess documents on communism could be seen as "anti-democracy" or "anti-government", it was only after the establishment of the diplomatic relationship between South Korea and China in 1992 that Koreans were able to go to China to study. This gave South Koreans not only the liberty to travel to China but also the freedom to conduct research on the country.

Such changes and discussions are documented in local academic traditions in both Japanese and Korean, but not all of such works have been accessed or are accessible to international scholars. Chinese Studies, or studies of China, in Japan and Korea intrinsically have been affected by Sino–Japanese and Sino–Republic of Korea relations. The diplomatic relations and surrounding geopolitical settings reinforce these interacting relations and shape the possible directions of where to go and what to study. This section, accordingly, presents an overview of Chinese studies in these two countries.

Practising Chinese Studies as Knowledge

As discussed earlier, Chinese Studies has started to exist as a discipline in Japan and South Korea. In these societies, Chinese Studies existed as linguistics and literature, and later social science–based Chinese Studies made an appearance. This trend was more prevalent in South Korea than in Japan. While many Japanese universities still keep Chinese Language and/or Literature as a department's name, many Korean universities have tried to position the majority of

Chinese Studies programmes to study China from a practical lens, and thus offer more opportunities for students in the job markets. Thus, the department names of Chinese Studies have moved towards names with a focus on area studies or a social science background, such as the Department of Chinese Studies or the Department of Chinese Business. By taking this approach, the Chinese Studies programmes in Korean universities address more explicitly practical knowledge than the original focus on language and literature (Lee 2017). As such, producing educational knowledge for Chinese Studies is interrelated to institutional knowledge.

In the process of changing the names of departments, the institutional settings for Chinese Studies have changed at the university level as well as at the research level. In Japan and South Korea, China has been, on the one hand, the most significant partner for trade and, on the other, for politics and diplomacy. The Japanese and Korean governments have semi-governmental research organizations such as the Japan External Trade Organization (JETRO n.d.) and the Korea Trade-Investment Promotion Agency (KOTRA n.d.). These quasi-research and trade-support organizations for Japanese and Korean companies play an important role in producing practical knowledge based on societal needs.

It is important to address how local embeddedness and geopolitical contexts affect the ways in which Chinese Studies is viewed and practised and how it is expected to be a significant knowledge producer for society. The most recent example is South Korea's decision to deploy the THAAD on the Korean peninsula in July 2016, which worsened the geopolitical situation between China and South Korea. It also reshapes how South Korea should perceive and deal with China, and vice versa, and what kinds of knowledge Chinese Studies in South Korea needs to produce. A new way of thinking about China and of coping with the geopolitics-led economy, trade, culture and societal issues has emerged in South Korea. For instance, scholars, along with government officials, have opened discussions about how to solve this problem wisely, and business leaders and business partners have addressed their concerns over this issue. Thus, Chinese Studies as a discipline and knowledge is positioned and expected to keep up with societal needs for educational, institutional and practical knowledge.

Concluding Remarks: A Tale of Developing Chinese Studies in Two Societies

This chapter has traced the developments of Chinese Studies in neighbouring countries to China — Japan and South Korea — by exploring geopolitics, research and knowledge management. As the largest trading partner for both Japan and South Korea and as their neighbour, China is important not only at the state level but also at the societal level. I argue that these states perceive Chinese Studies, along with other area studies, as "knowledge industries" for institutionalizing and accumulating knowledge on China by reflecting their own geopolitical and societal contexts to the discipline.

Chinese Studies in both South Korea and Japan by and large started from studies on language and literature and expanded its scope to the social sciences. This commonality in these two countries stems largely from learning from the experience and research traditions of other countries, as well as needs at the public and state levels. The key points of this chapter can be summarized as follows. First, in terms of the *development of the disciplinary configuration* of Chinese Studies in Japan and South Korea, geopolitical relations and institutional support have developed a basis for knowledge production and the dissemination of Chinese Studies in these societies.

In the case of Japan, Chinese Studies started earlier than in South Korea, which reflects the longer period of Sino–Japanese relations. In South Korea, due to the ideological gap, studying China was difficult prior to normalization. For both countries, the discipline of studying China has witnessed both change and continuity, as well as an increase in the number of researchers and institutions. Second, the *geopolitics and scholarly traditions* (training, choice of country to study abroad) differ between Japan and South Korea. In Japan, local training in prestigious Japanese institutions and in the United States has been the mainstream, rather than studying in China. For South Korea, geopolitical relations are well represented in the backgrounds of scholars. In other words, linking with diplomatic relations, many Korean faculty members have benefited from their training in Taiwan. Yet, largely due to China's rapid economic growth, there is a tension related to conducting research on Taiwan. Third, from a perspective of *knowledge production and the knowledge industry*, knowledge which is produced and constructed in the industries can be discussed as educational knowledge, institutional knowledge and practical knowledge. As for educational knowledge, many universities started Chinese Studies programmes to teach Chinese literature, languages and linguistics, but the focus later changed, with humanist-based Chinese Studies coexisting with or even being replaced by practical knowledge on China. With this change, the institutional settings for Chinese Studies have developed not only at the university level but also at the levels of government and research. Practical knowledge has, consequently, developed within such institutional contexts in line with societal needs, with the modern perception now being that the study of China is a more apt and practical discipline.

In a nutshell, developments of Chinese Studies in Japan and South Korea show the ways in which knowledge is produced and managed in line with geopolitical and local factors. The growth of the knowledge industry of contemporary China in these countries will be sustained and even expanded as China continues to rise.

Notes

1. See Goh (2011) on Southeast Asian Studies.
2. It is noted that research institutes on Asia in general are available.
3. In this regard, the British tradition of Developmental Studies is noted here as a similar reasoning.
4. Area studies started in the 1950s in the United States during the Cold War era.
5. 地域 in Japanese refers to area and region.
6. The Kim Young Sam government started to embrace a "segyehwa" (globalization) discourse, which resulted in several graduate schools of international or area studies in South Korea. There are now nine graduate schools on international/area studies: Chungang University, Ewha Woman's University, Hankuk University of Foreign Studies, Hanyang University, Seoul National University, Sogang University, Korea University, Kyunghee University and Yonsei University. The first round to establish these graduate schools took place in 1997, with subsequent government funding support for five years.
7. In this chapter I prefer to use "Chinese Studies", as most departments in Japan and Korea use this term rather than "Sinology". This is in line with the convention of naming other area-specific disciplines.

8. The Japan Association for Modern China Studies <http://www.genchugakkai. com/gakkaigaiyou.html> (in Japanese; accessed 15 September 2013).

9. The scope of this research is restricted to Chinese Studies. I do not explicitly pay attention to Taiwan as a separate subject of study. Yet, there is a difference in treating Taiwan as a subject of study in the context of Japanese and South Korea academies, which stems from their geopolitical relations and the local academic cultures. In Japan, Taiwan, as a former colony of Japan, has been continuously studied to a certain extent. In South Korea, although many scholars went to Taiwan to study largely due to the lack of access to China, they have a tendency of studying China through the lens of Taiwan.

10. It is noted that Minja Lee is a political scientist on China, but she writes on sociology.

11. For convenience, the term "economics" here encompasses economics, business, commerce and finance.

12. I do not intend to discuss here studies on Chinese culture in literature and linguistics with the advent of the "cultural turn". In this respect, culture is often perceived as rather "soft" to deal with. Researchers working on culture from the perspective of sociology and those from humanities have different traditions.

13. One of the significant works in knowledge production is Gibbons et al. (2010).

14. I will not attempt to investigate the aspect of teaching in the discipline, as it is beyond the scope of the chapter.

15. The reference point here is "natural science in hard science".

16. For example, Chungang University, Hankuk University of Foreign Studies, and Incheon University offer overseas Chinese modules.

17. Throughout this chapter, "Chinese Studies" is limited to contemporary studies (unless otherwise specified).

18. Interview with the director of the centre, May 2011, Seoul, South Korea.

19. It is noted that this is a general trend in other area studies disciplines in Japan and South Korea.

References

Arita, Kayoko. "Facilitating Discussion of Controversial Issues in Japanese Language Classes: 'Deterioration in Japan–China Relations' as an Example" (in Japanese). *Literacies* (2007): 113–30.

Barnds, William J. "Japan and Its Mainland Neighbours: An End to Equidistance?" *International Affairs* 52 (1976): 27–38.

Beer, Lawrence W. "Some Dimensions of Japan's Present and Potential Relations with Communist China". *Asian Survey* 9 (1969): 163–77.

Boyd, R.G. "China's Relations with Japan". *Australian Outlook* 14 (1960): 50–68.

Chiang, Y. Frank, and Kazuomi Oochi. "The Status of Taiwan in International Law and Japan–China Relations" (in Japanese). *Revue de droit compare* 44 (2010): 39–80.

Chun, Seon-Heung. "Korea's Chinese Studies: Trends and Issues" (in Korean). In *Korea's Area Studies: Trends and Issues*, edited by Sangsup Lee and Taehwan Kwon, pp. 3–41. Seoul: Seoul National University, 1998.

Chung, Jaeho, ed. 중국정치연구론: 영역, 쟁점, 방법 및 교류 [Researching Chinese politics: areas, issues, methods and interactions]. Seoul: Nanam, 2000.

Chung, Jae Ho, Chi-young Ahn, Man-joon Park, Yoon-mi Chang, Changhoon Cha, and Byung-kwang Park. "한국에서의 중국정치 연구의 재 고찰: 자료, 방법론 및 담론을 중심으로" [Reassessing Chinese political studies in Korea: On source materials, methodologies, and discourse structures]. 국제정치논집 [International Politics Studies] 45, no. 2 (2005): 103–29.

Fensterheim, Devein Robert. "Knowledge Production at the Global Frontier: The Case of China". MA thesis, Massachusetts Institute of Technology, 2009.

Gemba, Koichiro. "Japan–China Relations at a Crossroads". *Diplomatic Insight*, 31 December 2012.

Gibbons, Michael, Camille Limoges, Helga Nowotny, Simon Schwartzman, Peter Scott, and Martin Trow. *The New Production of Knowledge: The Dynamics of Science and Research in Contemporary Societies*. London: Sage, 2010.

Goh, Beng-Lan, ed. *Decentring and Diversifying Southeast Asian Studies: Perspectives from the Region*. Singapore: Institute of Southeast Asian Studies, 2011.

Hangström, Linus. "Relational Power for Foreign Policy Analysis: Issues in Japan's China Policy". *European Journal of International Relations* 11, no. 3 (2005): 395-430.

Hatoribe Ryuji (服部, 龍二). "Japan–China, Japan–U.S. Relations over the Senkakus" (in Japanese). 外交 [Diplomacy] 15 (2012): 35–47.

Hayakawa, Iwao. "The Fundamental Truth of Economics Calculation: Japan, China, and United States Relations". *Bulletin of Aichi Institute of Technology. Part B* 24 (1989): 103–7.

Hayakawa, Tetsuo. "The Outlook for the Japan China Trade for Normalizing Relations". *Kyoto Sangyo University Essays. Social Science Series* 2 (1973): 104–113.

He, Yinan. "Remembering and Forgetting the War: Elite Mythmaking, Mass Reaction, and Sino–Japanese Relations, 1950–2006". *History and Memory* 19 (2007): 43–74.

Hellmann, Donald C. "Japan's Relations with Communist China". *Asian Survey* 4 (1964): 1085–92.

Hoadley, J. Stephen, and Sukehiro Hasegawa. "Sino–Japanese Relations 1950–1970: An Application of the Linkage Model of International Politics". *International Studies Quarterly* 15 (1971): 131–57.

Hong, Heung-deuk. 대학의 과학기술지식 생산 및 유통의 구조적 특징에 관한 사례분석 [Structural characteristics of universities' science technological knowledge production and dissemination]. 사회과학연구 [Social Studies Research] 49, no. 2 (2010): 319–52.

Hsiao, Gene T. "The Sino–Japanese Rapprochement: A Relationship of Ambivalence". *China Quarterly* (1974): 101–23.

Hsieh, Kuan-Yu, and Yuri Sadoi. "Changes in Triangular Economic Relations between Japan, China and Taiwan in the 21st Century" (in Japanese). 名城論叢 13 (2012): 1–18.

Hung, Chang-Tai. "The Fuming Image: Cartoons and Public Opinion in Late Republican China, 1945 to 1949". *Comparative Studies in Society and History* 36 (1994): 122–45.

Ichirou, Inoe. "Chinese Foreign Policy Decision Making in the Case of 2005 Anti-Japanese Protests: Levels of Analysis Approach" (in Japanese). *Journal of Policy Studies* (2012): 1–13.

Imai, S. "Japan's Understanding of China and Chinese Studies in the Twentieth Century" (in Japanese). *Chinese Studies* 53, no. 1 (1999): 36–53.

Japan External Trade Organization (JETRO). n.d. <https://www.jetro.go.jp>.

Jerden, Bjorn, and Linus Hagström. "Rethinking Japan's China Policy: Japan as an Accommodator in the Rise of China, 1978–2011". *Journal of East Asian Studies* 12, no. 2 (2012): 215–50.

Jiang, Hong (姜, 弘). "Ohira Masayoshi's Impression of China and Foreign Policy toward China: To Build Japan–China Relations with Mutual Trust" (in Japanese). 国際文化学研究: 神戸大学大学院国際文化学研究科紀要 (2012): 1–15.

Kajitani, K. "Thinking About Area Studies in Globalization" (in Japanese). In *Rethinking "Area Studies" in Globalization: The New Perspective of Modern China Studies*, Contemporary Chinese Studies no. 21, edited by Shigeo Nishimura and Tanaka Hitoshi, pp. 130–39. 2007.

Kan, Hideki. 石田正治教授 上田國廣教授 退職記念論文集 [The Nixon administration's initiative for U.S.–China rapprochement and its impact on U.S.–Japan relations, 1969–1974]. 法政研究 78 (2011): 644–82.

Katayama, Kazuyuki. "Development of Japan–China Relations since 1972". *International Journal of China Studies* 2 (2011): 647–79.

Kim, Dohee. "The Chinese Studies of Korea: Issues and Idea" (in Korean). *East Asia Studies* 50 (2006): 55–89.

———. "Chinese Studies of China: Catch Up and Get Over the Chinese Studies of America" (in Korean). *Contemporary Chinese Studies* 12, no. 1 (2010): 1–29.

Kim, In, and Byungkon Chun. "The Current Situation and Issues of Chinese Studies". In *The Current Situation and Issues of Area Studies*, edited by Area Studies of Hankuk University of Foreign Studies. Seoul: Hankuk University of Foreign Studies Press, 1996.

Kokubun, R. "Four Contradictions of Chinese Studies of Japan" (in Japanese). *World* 685 (2001): 117–21.

Korea Trade-Investment Promotion Agency (KOTRA). n.d. <https://www.kotra.or.kr>.

Langer, Paul F. "Japan's Relations with China". *Current History* 46 (1964): 193–93.

Lee, Claire Seungeun. "China's Leap Forward from 'Brain Drain' to 'Brain Gain': Its International Student Recruitment Strategy and the Decision-Making Process of Students" (in Korean). *Contemporary Chinese Studies* 14, no. 2 (2013): 321–61.

———. "Methodological Explorations for Understanding Contemporary Chinese Society: The Chinese Social Survey as Method". *Journal of Chinese Studies* 80 (2017): 177–202.

Lee, Dong-Ryul. "The Strategic Implications of 'Responsible Power' in China" (in Korean). *East Asian Studies* 50 (2006): 344–76.

———. "China's Strategy to the North Korea and China–North Korea Relations: Kim Jong-il's Visit to China in 2010" (in Korean). *Studies of Area Studies* 29 (2010*a*): 297–320.

———. "Chinese Diplomatic Strategy and Challenges for Its Rise as a Global Power" (in Korean). *National Defence Studies* 53 (2010*b*): 1–24.

Lee, Junghee. "Subject and Methodology of Area Studies: Contemporary Chinese Studies in English-Speaking Countries". Paper presented at the Korean Sociological Association, 2000.

Lee, Min-Ja. "China's Chinese Studies: Focusing on Sociology". *China–Soviet Union Studies* 91 (2001).

Liu, Ts'ui-jung. "Taiwan Studies in the Mainland China". *Chang Gung Journal of Humanities and Social Sciences* 5, no. 2 (2012): 229–62.

Lu, Xijun. "China's Diplomatic Choices during the Japan–China Crisis of 1931–1932: A Study of the Nationalist Government's Decision to Re-establish Diplomatic Relations with the Soviet Union (in Japanese). *Hitotsubashi Review* 117 (1997): 141–67.

Morino, Tomozo. "China–Japan Trade and Investment Relations". *Proceedings of the Academy of Political Science* 38 (1991): 87–94.

Nish, Ian. "An Overview of Relations between China and Japan, 1895–1945". *China Quarterly* (1990): 601–23.

Nishimura, S., and H. Tanaka Nishimura, Shigeo (西村成雄) and Hitoshi Tanaka (田中仁). "Chinese Studies in Post-war Japan" (in Japanese). *Contemporary Chinese Studies* 7 (2007): 1–33.

Nomura, Kouichi. "Chinese Studies and Understanding of China" (in Japanese). *Chinese Studies* 54, no. 11 (2000): 37–53.

Oksenberg, Michael C. "The American Study of Modern China: Toward the Twenty-first Century". In *American Studies of Contemporary China*, edited by D. Shambaugh, pp. 315–43. Washington, DC: Woodrow Wilson Center Press/Sharpe, 1993.

Ouyang, Wei (欧陽維). "The Asia Pacific Security Situation and the Japan–China Security Relations" (in Japanese). *Defense Studies* (2011): 123–27.

Przystup, James J. "Japan–China Relations: Looking for Traction". *Comparative Connections* 13, no. 1 (2011): 119–28.

––––––. "Japan–China Relations: Happy 40th Anniversary…?" *Comparative Connections* 14, no. 1 (2012*a*): 117–28, 154–55.

––––––. "Japan–China Relations: Happy 40th Anniversary…? Part 2". *Comparative Connections* 14, no. 2 (2012*b*): 105–18.

––––––. "Japan–China Relations: 40th Anniversary". *Comparative Connections* 14, no 3 (2012*c*): 109–24.

Qiu, Lizhen (邱麗珍). "Japan's Economic Diplomacy to China after the Normalization of Sino–Japanese Diplomatic Relations (2) Yoshihiro Inayama and the Japan–China Long-term Trade Agreement" (in Japanese). *Hokkaido Law Review* 61 (2010): 53–107.

Qureshi, Khalida. "The Far Eastern Detente: The Normalization of Sino–Japanese Relations". *Pakistan Horizon* 26 (1973): 54–67.

Rose, Caroline. "'Managing China': Risk and Risk Management in Japan's China Policy". *Japan Forum* 22, nos. 1–2 (2010): 149–68.

Schubert, Gunter. "Contemporary Taiwan Studies in Europe: More Institutional-ized, More Vital". *Journal of Current Chinese Affairs* 41, no. 3 (2012): 3–6.

Sendo, Yoshiki (仙頭佳樹) and Mingyu Wu (呉明宇). "A Study on Complementary Relations of Japan–China Trade" (in Japanese). *Kobe City University Journal* 59 (2008): 1–8.

Shambaugh, David, ed. *American Studies of Contemporary China*. Armonk: Sharpe, 1994.

Shu, Huhong (瀬戸宏). "Chinese Studies in the Second World War: Focusing on the Contemporary Chinese Association of Japan" (in Chinese). 2012 <http://www.qstheory.cn/zz/hwxs/201208/t20120822_177103.htm> (accessed 29 August 2013).

Sullivan, Jonathan. "Is Taiwan Studies in Decline?" *China Quarterly* 207 (2011): 706–18.

Takagi, Seiichiro. "Chinese Studies in Japan: Developments and Issues" (in Korean). n.p. 2004.

Takeuchi, Shinichi (武内進一). "Area Studies and Discipline: The Perspective from Africa" (in Japanese). *Asia Economy* 53, no. 4 (2012): 6–22.

Tewari, D.D., Sandhya Gihar, and Jianhong Qi. "Knowledge Production in China and India: A Look at the Higher Education Sectors and Intended Changes of Indian Higher Education System". *Journal of Social Science* 34, no. 2 (2013): 155–64.

Tsuchiya, Masaya. "Recent Developments in Sino–Japanese Trade". *Law and Contemporary Problems* 38 (1973): 240–48.

Ushijima, Yuuko (牛嶋憂子). "Contemporary Chinese Studies: The Current Stage and Prospects" (in Japanese). *Asian Culture* 30 (2008): 90–98.

Vogel, Ezra F., Yuan Ming, and Tanaka Akihiko, eds. *The Golden Age of the U.S.–China–Japan Triangle, 1972–1989*. Boston: Harvard University Press, 2002.

Wakaizumi, Kei. "Japan's Role in a New World Order". *Foreign Affairs* 51 (1973): 310–26.

Weston, Stephanie A. "Reframing the New Normal in U.S.–Japan–China Relations". *Fukuoka University Review of Law* 57 (2012): 95–161.

Yan, Shanping. "日本の中国研究の今後を考える". 2009 <https://www1.doshisha.ac.jp/~shyan/200901forSCMS.htm> (accessed 17 March 2014).

Yin, Yanjun (殷燕軍). "Normalization of Japan–China Relations and Taiwan Regime" (in Japanese). *Quarterly Journal of Economics* 222 (2005): 16–36.

Yu, Jeong Won. "Sociology in China: A Survey on Research Group and Research Subject of Sociological Studies" (in Korean). *Chinese Studies* 49 (2010): 517–42.

Yumino, Masahiro (弓野正宏). "Contemporary Chinese Studies: China's Present and China's Turning Point" (in Japanese). *Waseda Asia Review* 6 (2009): 90–93.

Zhao, Quansheng. "Sino–Japanese Relations in the Context of the Beijing–Tokyo–Washington Triangle. In *Chinese–Japanese Relations in the Twenty-first Century: Complementarity and Conflict*, edited by Marie Söederberg, pp. 32–51. London: Routledge, 2002.

Index

Note: Page numbers followed by "n" denote endnotes

A

AAS. *See* Association for Asian Studies (AAS)

abangan, 106–8, 111, 112, 114

Abhijnanashakuntala, 199

Acharya, Amitav, 8, 37

AFMLTA (Australian Federation of Modern Language Teachers Associations), 57

"Afro-Asian", 212

Ahern, Emily
  Cult of the Dead in a Chinese Village, The, 147

Al-Zarkawi, Abu Muzab, 114

Amazon Books website, 66

American foreign policy, 88

American geopolitical interest, 81

American imperialism, 126

American orientalists, 22

American Oriental Society, formation of, 22

American scholarship, on Javanese religion
  Beatty, Andrew, 102, 107, 116n4, 117n12
  Geertz, Clifford, 101–2, 104–7, 112–14

Hefner, Robert, 106–9, 115
  influence of communism in Asia, 104
  interest towards Islam, 105–6
  Ricklefs, Merle C., 109–14, 117n19

Ang, Ien, 57–58

Anglo-French orientalism, 31

Anglo–Japanese alliance, 232

Anquetil-Duperron, Abraham-Hyacinthe, 27

Appadorai, A., 224

Arabic Studies, 26

Arai Kanpo, 216

Arao Sei, 241

"area studies" approach, 226
  criticism of, 144

ASEAN (Association of Southeast Asian Nations), 77, 176, 179, 180

ASEAN–Russia Dialogue partnership, 180

ASEAN–Russia: Foundations and Future Prospects, 180

Asia, geopolitical construction of
  Association for Asian Studies' logo map of, 86
  books and journals covers, 64–66, 74

cartographic definition of, 78, 79
contested "Asia", 8–10
European colonial empires in, 76,
    77
ongoing reframing of, 75
overview, 64–67
pan-Asianism and, 76
social construction of, 83–88
specific boundaries of, 74
"Asia is not one", 8
Asian Affairs: An American Review, 79
Asian-African Conference (1955), in
    Bandung, 77
"Asian Asia", 75, 80
"Asian Century", 76, 89
Asian Journal of Political Science, The,
    78
Asian languages, 26, 38, 46, 60
"Asianness", idea of, 14
Asian Relations Conference (1947),
    77, 212, 224
Asian Security, 78
Asian Survey cover map, 78, 82
Asiatic Academy, 192
"Asiatic Asia", 77, 80
Asiatic languages, 25, 27
Asiatic Museum, 192
Asiatic Society (Academie Asiatique),
    192
Asiatic Society of Bengal, 28–33
Association for Asian Studies (AAS),
    5, 65, 76, 79, 80, 82
Association of Southeast Asian
    Nations (ASEAN), 77, 176, 179,
    180
"Atlas Asia", 77, 80, 84
"Atlas South Asia", 84
Auchmuty Report (1971), 45, 46
Australia
    "Asia literacy" programme, 9
    education system, 46

federal legislation, 56
Fraser government (1975–83), 56
geo-political location, 50
"multicultural Australia", 56
*Australia in the Asian Century: White
    Paper,* 45
Australian Federation of Modern
    Language Teachers Associations
    (AFMLTA), 57
Australian National University, 54
Australia's "Asia literacy"
    as sociocultural practice, 56–59
    as spatial practice, 47–52
    Asian languages education, 46
    Asian Studies education, 46
    Auchmuty Report (1971), 45, 46
    conceptualization of, 49
    cultural categories, 44
    "distant proximity", 56
    economic and commercial systems,
        47
    education system, 44–45
    geography and education, 53–55
    Ingleson, John, 50
    multiculturalism, 56–58
    overview, 44–45
    programmes, 44, 45
    rationale and goals, 45–47, 56
    social framings of, 46
    spatial rationale for, 50

B
Baba Chinese, 234, 238, 239, 247
Bachtiar, Harsya, 105
Badawi, Datuk Abdullah Ahmad, 48
Bagchi, P.C., 219
Bakunin, Mikhail
    *Tropical Holland: Five Years on the
        Island of Java,* 170
Bandung Conference (1955), 77, 124
Bank of Taiwan, 242

Bayard, Pierre, 134
Beatty, Andrew, 102, 107, 116n4
  Shadow Falls in the Heart of Java, A, 117n12
Beeson, Mark
  Routledge Handbook of Asian Regionalism, The (Beeson & Stubbs), 82
Bering, Vitus, 168
Berzin, Eduard, 172, 175
Bezzenberger, Adalbert, 195
Bhabha, Homi, 57
Bhagavadgita, 197
Biblical Studies, 194
"biliterate trilingualism", 248
Bolshevik Revolution, 190
book and journal covers, 64–66, 74
Bopp, Franz, 27, 196
Borodin, Michael, 222
Bose, Nandalal, 216
Bose, Phanindranath, 219
Bose, Subhash Chandra, 222–23
Brandt Commission Report on International Development, 69–70
British
  and Asiatic Society of Bengal, 28–33
  and Japanese classification systems, 233, 234
  authority of Straits Settlements, 234
  colonial status quo, 233, 247
  colonial system, 234
  decennial census reports, 236
  free-trade imperialism, 231
British Crown Colony, 234
Burhani, Najib, 117
Burma, 174
  flag of, 87
  relations with European powers, 169
Burstein, Daniel, 130–31
Bush, George W., 110

C
Cambodia
  academic reports on, 129
  American Cambodians, 127–29, 135
  American interest towards, 128
  auto-genocide, 122
  "Cambodia problem", 133
  French colonization, 124, 125
  French interest towards, 127–28
  (auto)genocide in, 121, 122
  genocide, 11, 121, 122, 129–34, 138n2
  Khmer Rouge movement, 123–26
  media reporting on Cambodian affairs, 129–34
  "mediatization" of practices, 120, 121
  Pol Pot, 124
  post-colonial history, 123–26
  refugee resettlement process, 134–36
  refugees, 127–29
  Standard Total View (STV), 131–32
  Vietnamese intervention, 133
  Vietnamese invasion of, 126, 130
Cambodian Genocide Program, Yale University, 121
"cartographic aggression", 73
Castell, Edmund, 25, 40n4
CCKF (Chiang Ching-kuo Foundation), 154, 263
Chambers, Michael R.
  South Asia in 2020: Future Strategic Balances and Alliances, 88
Chandler, David, 129
Chatterji, Suniti Kumar, 219
  Balts and Aryans in Their Indo-European Background, 202
Cheah, Pheng, 145
Chiang Ching-kuo, 154, 155
Chiang Ching-kuo Foundation (CCKF), 154, 263
Chiang Kai-shek, 217

China
  and Japan, 75
  and Peranakan Chinese, 235
  anti-Japanese movements, 232,
    233
  anti-Manchu republican revolution,
    241
  Cultural Revolution, 147
  foreign-born Chinese, 237
  literature and linguistics, 264
  languages of, 237, 238
  nationalism, 233, 239, 247
  one-China principle, 154
  "One China, Two Systems" policy,
    262
  Portuguese interest in, 26
Chinese Advisory Board, Malaya,
  235
Chinese Studies, 253, 255, 269n9
  domains of, 264–65
  in Japan, 254, 255–57
  in South Korea, 254, 257–60
  knowledge production, 260–63
  perspectives on Taiwan, 143
  practising, as knowledge, 265–66
  social science–based Chinese
    Studies, 260
  to teach Chinese literature, 268
Chodzko, Alexander, 193
Choudhury, Maitreyee, 8–9
Chulalongkorn, 169, 170
Clementi, Cecil, 239, 249n1
Clodius, Johann Christian, 26
Cohen, Stephen Philip
  Security of South Asia: American and
    Asian Perspectives, The, 87
Cochin-Chinese, 235–36
Cold War, 39, 53, 77, 84
  end of, 3, 36
  geopolitical context, 166
  Java and American scholarship in,

102–6
Colebrooke, Henry Thomas, 25
Committee of Concerned Asian
  Scholars, 144
Communist International, 171
Communist Party of India (CPI),
  201
Contemporary Taiwan Research
  Center, 262
Cowan, Robert, 195
CPI (Communist Party of India),
  201
"Creativity and Vision: New
  Tendency on Building
  Taiwanology", 262–63
cultural diversity, 57, 75
cultural relativism, 21
Czartoryski, Adam Jerzy, 192

D
Dai Jitao initiative (1891–1949), 217
Dalai Lama, 87
"Death Traffic in Opium, The", 215
Democratic Progressive Party, 159
Den Kenjirō, 242
de Sacy, Silvestre, 25, 27
diaspora, concept of, 57
"distant proximity", concept of, 56
Drugov, Alexei, 176
Duara, Prasenjit, 231
Dutch colonies, of Indonesia, 26
Dutt, V.P., 225

E
EASAS (European Association for
  South Asian Studies), 86
East, W. Gordon
  Changing Map of Asia, The (East &
    Spate), 75
EATS (European Association of
  Taiwan Studies), 152, 156

Ecole Française d' Extreme-Orient
    (EFEO), 28, 128
École spéciale des langues orientales
    vivantes, 27
Edwards, Penny
    Cambodge: The Cultivation of a
        Nation, 127
EFEO (Ecole Française d' Extreme-
    Orient), 28, 128
"embedded statism", 55
Engels, Friedrich, 173
Ethnogeographic Board, 53
Europe
    romanticism, 30, 31, 34, 35
    Taiwan Studies in, 152–56
European Association for South Asian
    Studies (EASAS), 86
European Association of Taiwan
    Studies (EATS), 152, 156
European colonialism, 76
European languages, 51, 237
Europe–Asia dichotomy, 220
Evans, Gareth, 48
"extreme orient", 28

F
"Far Eastern Association, The", 82
Far Eastern Quarterly, 82
Federated Malay States, 237
Felski, Rita, 58
FitzGerald, Stephen, 46
"Folklorists' case", 205
framing, concept of, 1–2, 67–74
France
    and Cambodia, 121, 130, 132
    Cambodian refugees in, 127–29
    Oriental Studies, 27
"Free China", 147, 259
Fujita Toyohachi, 244
Fulbright Program, 148

G
Gaidamak, 170
Gandhi, Indira, 201
Garnaut, Ross, 51
Geertz, Clifford, 11, 101, 114
    Agricultural Involution, 105
    anthropological study, 112
    Bali cockfight, essay on, 113
    invention of abangan, 112, 114
    perception of Islam, 106
    Religion of Java, The, 101–2, 104–5,
        112, 115n1
    religious variants, 107
geographical determinism, 49
"geo-graphing", process of, 49, 50
geography, and education, 53–55
Geopolitics
    as subject of study, 10
    Asian cartography, post-war, 81–82
    biases in maps, 73–74
    changing dynamics of East Asia,
        264–65
    Cold War framing, 5, 84, 104, 166,
        176–77
    concept of, 1, 10
    construction of Asia, 64–66
    "critical geopolitics" applied to
        Asia literacy, 48–51
    framing of Western discourses, 10
    "geopolitical Asia", 84, 87
    "geopolitical South Asia", 87
    post–Cold War reordering, 108,
        143–44, 166
    U.S. priorities in South Asia, 88
    War on Terror framing, 102
German theosophy, 197
German orientalism, 27, 31
German romanticism, 40n5
Ghadar Party, 217
Ghosh, Aurobindo, 213–15
Gibb, H.A.R., 33

Gimbutas, Marija, 207n3
Ginsburg, Norton
    Pattern of Asia, The, 75, 84
globalization, 3, 144
Goffman, Erving, 67
Gold, Thomas
    State and Society in the Taiwan
        Miracle (Gold), 149
Golitsyn, Alexander, 193
"Greater East Asia Co-Prosperity
    Sphere", 77
Greater India Society, 219
Great October Socialist Revolution
    (1917), 32
"G 30 S event", 107, 111, 112
Guber, Alexander, 174, 175, 178
    Indonesia: Socio-economic Essays, 174
    Jozé Rizal (Guber & Rykovskaya),
        174
    Philippines, The, 174
Gunn, Geoffrey C.
    Cambodia Watching Down (Gunn &
        Lee), 121

H
Hai San Street, 235
Hall, Daniel George Edward, 175
    History of Southeast Asia, 175, 183n8
Hankuk University of Foreign
    Studies, 253–54, 262
Harley, J.B., 68
Harvard Taiwan Studies Workshop,
    151
Hastings, Warren, 29
Haushofer, Karl, 10
Hefner, Robert, 11, 109, 116n3
    Civil Islam: Muslims and
        Democratization in Indonesia,
        108
    Hindu Javanese: Tengger Tradition and
        Islam, 102

Islam in Indonesia, 115
    Javanese religion, study of, 106–8
Henri-Lévy, Bernard, 130
Higashi Honganji, 242
Hindi films, 228
Historical Review, Olarovsky's
    research on Siam, 170
Ho Chi Minh, 171
Hobart, Mark
    Java, Indonesia and Islam, 102
"Hokkien racial trait", 243
Hong Kong, 261
Hourani, Albert, 24
Hughes, Kirrilee, 9
Huntington, Samuel
    Clash of Civilizations, 108, 115,
        117n15
Husserl, Edmund, 67
hybridity, concept of, 55, 58, 59

I
ICAS (International Convention of
    Asian Scholars), 4, 76
Ide Kiwata, 244, 245, 249n3
IIAS (International Institute for Asian
    Studies), 4, 80
Imperial Academy of Sciences, 171
INALCO (Institute national
    des langues et civilisations
    orientales), 27
India
    and China, 85
    and Pakistan, 83
    and South Asia, 82
    Indian civilization, 211, 224
    Indian Peninsula, 83
    Indian philosophy, German
        translations of, 197
    Indian texts, literary production, 197
    Indian Union, 65
    Jammu and Kashmir in, 65

India–China Friendship Association,
    217
Indian National Army, 222
Indian School for International
    Studies, 224, 225
Indian Studies, 13–14
Indian understandings of Asia,
    211–12
    cartographic/intellectual
        boundaries, 212
    geostrategic compulsions, 213
    Ghose, Aurobindo, 213–15
    Greater India Society, 219
    Nehru, Jawaharlal, 223–24
    Roy, M.N., 213
    Sarkar, Benoy Kumar, 219–21
    Tagore, Rabindranath, 213, 215–17
    Visvesvaraya, M., 218
India–Soviet Cultural Society
    (ISCUS), 202
Indology, 27, 37, 41n6
Indonesia, Dutch colonies of, 26
Indonesian Communist Party,
    demolition of, 115
Ingleson, John, 50, 61n6
Ingram, David, 57
Inoue Kiyoshi, 231
Inoue Masaji, 241, 242
Institute for Regional Studies (IRS),
    28n8
Institute national des langues
    et civilisations orientales
    (INALCO), 27
Institute of Far Eastern Studies, 172,
    180
Institute of Oriental Languages,
    32–33
Institute of Oriental Studies, 26, 32,
    35, 171, 172, 175, 179, 192
Institute of Pacific Relations, 82
Institute of World Economy, 172, 179

institutionalization
    of European Taiwan Studies, 153
    of Southeast Asian Studies, 172–73
Inter-Asia Cultural Studies project,
    159
inter-Asia gazes, 14–16
International Convention of Asian
    Scholars (ICAS), 4, 76
International Institute for Asian
    Studies (IIAS), 4, 80
international relations, 172, 179
    world regional studies and, 179–82
Inter-University Program for Chinese
    Language Studies, 148
inward orientalism, 14, 195–98, 206
Isaacs, Harold, 69
ISCUS (India–Soviet Cultural
    Society), 202
Islam, in Java, 109–14
    abangan, 106–8, 111, 112, 114
    domination of, 106
    putihan, 111, 112
    Ricklefs' views on, 109–10
    santri, 106–9, 112, 114, 115
    underestimation of, 105

J
Jacoby, Neil H.
    US Aid to Taiwan, 147
James, William, 67
Japan, 253, 263
    anti-Japanese nationalism, 232, 239
    Azuchi Momoyama period, 240
    China and, 75
    Chinese Studies in, 254, 255–57
    daimyos, 240
    diplomatic normalization with
        China, 265
    dramatic rise of, 34
    early Tokugawa period, 240
    Japan–China relations, 241, 257

Japanese classification system, 15,
    233, 234
Japanese pan-Asianism, 232, 241
Ministry of Education, 225
pan-Asianism in Japan, 232
rival to Russia, 168
strength, 216
Japan Association for Modern China
    Studies, 255
Japan External Trade Organization
    (JETRO), 266
Japan Foundation, 225
Jaskūnas, Valdas, 13–14
Java, 11
    Islam in, 105–6, 109–14
    Japanese occupation, 103
    religion in. *See* American
        scholarship, on Javanese
        religion
Jones, William, 10, 25, 28, 29, 41n7,
    192
    *Asiatic Researches: History and
        Antiquities, the Arts, Sciences
        and Literature of Asia*, 31
Journal of Asian Studies, 79, 82
*Journal of South Asian and Middle
    Eastern Studies, The*, 72, 73

K
Kahin, George, 104
Kalashnikov, Nikolay, 176
Kalidas Nag, 219
Kennedy, John F., 128
Khaldin, Mikhail, 174
Khmer Rouge, 120, 138n4
    aim of, 123
    "anomaly of nature", 132
    genocide, 121, 122
    in United States, 131
    media attention towards, 129–34
    "pure Khmer", 122, 125–26

Standard Total View, 131–32
    under Pol Pot, 124
Khrushchev, Nikita, 201
Kiernan, Ben, 132
Killing Fields, The, 122
Kim, Dohee, 257–58
Kimura Matsutarō, 243
Kim Young Sam, 254, 268n6
Kingsbury, Robert
    South Asia in Maps, 86
Kissinger, Henry, 149
Klaproth, Julius, 192
Klinghoffer, Arthur, 67
Knapp, Ronald G.
    "Geographer and Taiwan, The",
        149
"knowing Asia", 45
knowledge-based studies, 26
knowledge production, 145, 260–61
    knowledge industries, 15, 255, 267
    knowledge networks, 6
    local knowledge production, in
        area studies, 145
Kobayashi Shinsaku, 244
Kodama Gentaro, 241
Koku Ryōgo, 243
Koldunova, Ekaterina, 7, 13
Korean language films, 228
Korean Studies, 153
Korea Trade-Investment Promotion
    Agency (KOTRA), 266
Koriander, Emil, 170
KOTRA (Korea Trade-Investment
    Promotion Agency), 266
Kowalewski, Józef (Osip), 193
Krusenstern, Ivan, 168
Kuo, Huei-Ying, 15
Kuomintang (KMT) government,
    Taiwan, 147, 149–50, 222
Kuwabara Jitsuzō, 244
Kuwata Rokurō, 245

L
Lajpat Rai, Lala, 222
Languages Other Than English
 (LOTE), 46
language-training programmes, 226
Langues O, 27
Latham, Michael
 Modernization as Ideology, 117n18
Lee, Claire Seungeun, 15
Lee, Jefferson
 Cambodia Watching Down (Gunn &
 Lee), 121
Lenin, Vladimir, 173
Lewis, Martin W., 45, 48, 49, 51, 52,
 55, 59, 75
 Myth of Continents, The (Lewis &
 Wigen), 48
Lithuania
 educational policies, 191
 inward orientalism, 14, 195–98
 Indian studies in, 13–14, 189
 Lithuanian–Indian Friendship
 Society, 200–205
 Mironas, Ričardas, 198–200
 nation-state debate, 189
 Oriental Studies, 191–95
 parallel society, orientalism of,
 205–7
 political life, collapse of, 190
 Soviet annexation of, 190
Lithuanian Council, 190
Lithuanian–Indian Friendship Society,
 191, 200–205
Lithuanian–Indian society, 203, 206
Lithuanian Roerich Society, 206
Lithuanian Society for Friendship and
 Cultural Relations with Foreign
 Countries, 201, 202
Lombard, Denys, 105, 116n5
 Nusa Jawa: Silang Budaya, 102
Loscher, Gil, 114

LOTE (Languages Other Than
 English), 46
Ludden, David, 29n20, 81

M
Mackinder, Halford, 10
Mahan, Alfred Thayer, 10
Majumdar, R.C., 219
Maldive Republic's flag, 79
Maletin, Nikolay, 176
Mandarinization, 238, 248
Mao Zedong, 222
maps
 framing of, 67–74
 "mental maps", 69, 89
 Mercator projection, 69
 on journal covers
 Asian-content journals, 78
 Asian Security, 78
 Asian Survey, 78, 79
 India-centric South Asia, 72
 *Journal of South Asian and Middle
 Eastern Studies*, 72
 professional journals, 73
 Regional Studies, 72
 Peters projection, 69–70
Marshall Plan, 34
Marx, Karl, 173
McCracken, Ellen, 74
Memorandum, 82
Mendeleyev, Dmitri, 169
Mercator projection, 69
Merewether, E.M., 236
metageography, 9
 concept of, 45, 48, 49, 51
metamorphosis, of Western mind,
 33–39
MGIMO University, 176, 178, 180,
 183n5
Mickevičius-Krėvė, Vincas, 197
Miller, Alice, 80, 81

Millikan, Max, 116n7
Mironas, Ričardas, 195, 204, 207n4
    legacy of, 198–200
Mohan, Raja
    *Crossing the Rubicon: The Shaping of
        India's New Foreign Policy*, 65
Mojeyko, Igor, 172
Molotov–Ribbentrop Pact, 190
Morskoi Sbornik (Maritime Journal),
    170
Moscow State Institute of
    International Relations, 172
Moscow University, 167
Moskovskii Telegraf (Moscow
    Telegraph), 169
Muchliński, Antoni, 193
"multicultural education", 56
multiculturalism, 56–58
    "mode of sharing", 57
Muslims, in Java, 105
    abangan, 106–8, 111, 112, 114
    putihan, 111, 112
    santri, 106–9, 112, 114, 115
Myscliewic, Eva, 134

N
Nadejda, 168
Naitō Konan, 243
NALSSP (National Asian Languages
    and Studies in Schools Program),
    46, 47
nanban bōeki, 240
Nan'pō Dozoku, 244
Nanyō Nihon machi, 340
Nathan, J.E., 237, 238
National Asian Languages and
    Studies in Schools Program
    (NALSSP), 46, 47
National Defence Education Act
    (1958), 53

National Defense University (NDU),
    66
National Geographic Geopolitical
    Map of Asia, 28n11
National Palace Museum, 147
NATSA (North American Taiwan
    Studies Association), 156
Nayar, Baldev Raj, 65
NDU (National Defense University),
    66
Nehru, Jawaharlal, 213, 223–24
Netherlands, Oriental/Asian Studies
    in, 26
Neva, 168
New Order (1970–2000), Islam under
    and after, 106–9
Nicholas II, 170
9/11 attack (2001), 3, 110
Nixon, Richard, 149
Non-Aligned Movement, 124
North American orientalists, 22
North American Taiwan Studies
    Association (NATSA), 156

O
"objectivity" of maps, 68
Ohlendorf, Hardina, 12
Okakura Tenshin, 216, 217
    Awakening of Japan, The, 216
    Ideals of the East, The, 216
Oksenberg, Michael, 256
Olarovsky, Alexander, 170
Orient, 2, 22–25, 27, 28, 31
orientalism, 76
    Anglo-French, 31
    inward, 14, 195–98, 206
    parallel society, 205–7
    Said's views on, 8, 23, 24
Oriental Studies, 21–22
    distinctive traditions of, 25
    generic concept of, 37

humanistic approach prevalent in, 22
in Europe, 23–28
in late sixteenth century, 25
in Lithuania, 191–95
in Portugal, 25
nature of, 23
Orient and, 23, 28
pre-revolution Russia, 32
to Asian Studies, 33–39
Osaka Mercantile Steamship Company, 242

P
paganism, Lithuanian, 197
Pakistan
  Azad Kashmir, 65
  civil war (1971), 85
  territory, 65
Pakistan American Foundation, 72
Panchatantra stories, 199
Panikkar, K.M., 224
  Asia and Western Dominance, 224
parallel society, orientalism of, 205–7
Paris Peace Accords, 139n6
Patnaik, Janaki Ballav, 203
Patnaik, Sarat, 203
Paul, T.V.
  India in the World Order: Searching for Major-Power Status, 65
Peace Corps programme, 128
People's Republic of China (PRC), 15–16, 87, 149, 224, 261–62
Peter I (Russian emperor), 168
Peters, Arno, 69
Peters projection, 69–70
Pickering, William A., 234, 235
Pilger, John, 133
  Year Zero: The Silent Death of Cambodia, 122, 133
Pococke, Edward, 25, 40n4

Polish–Lithuanian Commonwealth, 191
politico-civilizational frameworks, 49
Pollock, Sheldon, 195
Ponchaud, Francois, 129
  Cambodge: Année Zéro, 121, 129, 130
Portugal, Oriental / Asian Studies in, 25–26
postmodern social theories, 68
Pountney, A.M., 237
Pratjekabuda, 197
Prevost, Antoine François
  General History of Voyages, The, 167
Primakov, Yevgeny, 35, 178–79, 182
"primitive ethnographies", 23
priyayi, 109, 112
professional associations, logos of, 89
Purcell, Victor, 248
"pure Khmer", ideology of, 122, 125–26
putihan, 111, 112

Q
"qualified knowledge", 232, 233
Quanzhou Hokkien, 243

R
radical humanism, 222–23
Rafael, Vincente, 159
Raja Mohan, C., 65
Ramuva, 205
Rath, Rathanath, 202
"received metageographical categories", 52
Reclus, Elisée
  Earth and Its Inhabitants, The, 74
"Red China", 147
refugee resettlement process, Cambodia, 134–36
Regional Studies, 72
Reiske, Johann Jakob, 26

Renaissance, 24
Renan, Ernest, 89
Ricci, Matteo, 40n4
Richter, William L., 7, 9–10
Ricklefs, Merle C., 11, 117n19
    abangan and putihan, 111, 112
    Islam in Java, 109–14
    Islamisation and Its Opponents in
        Java, 102, 110
    "Jogyakarta under Sultan
        Mangkubumi, 1749–1792", 110
    Polarizing Javanese Society, 109
Rigveda, 197, 199
Rolland, Romain, 216
romanticism, 30, 31, 34, 35
Roosevelt, Theodore, 10
Rose, Leo, 179
Roth, Rudolph, 27
Royal Asiatic Society, Malayan
    Branch of, 235
Royal Asiatic Society of Great Britain
    and Ireland, 32
Roy, M.N., 213, 222–23
    Revolution and Counter Revolution in
        China, 222
Rudd, Kevin, 60n2
    Asian Languages and Australia's
        Economic Future, 47
Rudd Report (1994), 47, 60n2
Rudzinskaitè-Arcimavičienè, Marija,
    194
Russian-American Company, 168
Russian Humanitarian Science
    Foundation, 180
Russian orientalists, 32
Russian State Library website, 181
Russia, Southeast Asian studies in,
    165
    asymmetry in Russian foreign
        policy, 177–79
    books and articles publication, 173

colonial competition, 168–69
emergence of, 174–76
geopolitical factors, 166
growing interest in, 167–68
historical roots of, 167–71
institutionalization, 172, 176
Russia's interest in Southeast Asia,
    167
Russo–Siamese relations, 169–70
Soviet period, 171–77
world regional studies, 179–82
Russo–Siamese relations, 169–70

S
SAARC (South Asian Association for
    Regional Cooperation), 77, 86
Said, Edward, 8, 23–24, 31, 32, 34, 36,
    195
    Orientalism, 8, 23, 24
Saint Petersburg State University, 172
Sanskrit and Comparative
    Linguistics, 27
Sanskrit language, 198–99
santri, 106–9, 112, 114, 115
santrinization, in Indonesia, 115
Sarkar, Benoy Kumar, 219–21
    Futurism of Young Asia, The, 220
Sarkar, Jadunath, 219
Sartre, Jean-Paul, 130
SASA (South Asian Studies
    Association), 87
Scalapino, Robert, 179
Schlegel, August Wilhelm, 25, 27
Schmidt, Karl
    Atlas and Survey of South Asian
        History, 86
School of Oriental and African
    Studies (SOAS), 32, 155
"School of Oriental Languages", 54
Schutz, Alfred, 67
Schwartzberg, Joseph

Historical Atlas of South Asia, The, 85
Senn, Alfred, 195
Severnyi Arkhiv (Northern Archive), 169
Shah, Mangaldas Jagjivandas, 202
Shambaugh, David
    International Relations of Asia (Shambaugh & Yahuda), 82
Shapira, Khaim-Nakhman, 194, 207n2
Sharpe, M.E., 151
Shellabear, W.G., 237
Shiga Shigetaka, 240
Shinagaku, 255
Siam–Russia relations, 169–70
Sihanouk, Norodom, 124
Simonia, Nodari, 172
Singapore
    Chinese communities in, 233
    Institute of Southeast Asian Studies, 180
    Japanese occupation of, 246
Sino–American relations, 148–49
Sino–Indian conflict, 202
Sino–Japanese relations, 267
    normalization of, 256, 265
Sinology, 254, 255
Sękowski, Józef, 193
SOAS (School of Oriental and African Studies), 32, 155
social construction, 67–74, 77, 89
social disobedience, 205
"societies of friendship", 204
Society of Soviet–Indian Cultural Relations, 201
"sociology of knowledge", 5
South Asia
    Afghanistan in, 89
    American interests in, 88
    construction of, 83–88
    geopolitical core of, 88
    regionalism, 82

Tibet and, 87
South Asian Association for Regional Cooperation (SAARC), 77, 86
South Asian Studies Association (SASA), 87
Southeast Asia
    Afghanistan in, 78–80, 82, 84–89
    in post-war years, 231
Southeast Asia in World History, 175
Southeast Asian Studies, 13
South Korea
    Chinese Studies in, 253–54, 257–60
    companies, 263
    geopolitical relations, 267
South Sea Association (SSA), 242
South Seas Chinese, 15
    anti-Japanese movements among, 232
    British colonial censuses, 232–33
    Chinese "race", 240–46
    Japanese surveys of, 240
    Straits-born Chinese, 236–38
Soviet cultural diplomacy, 200
Soviet–Indian friendship, 201, 204
Soviet Union, 166, 182
    annexation of Lithuania, 190
    collapse of, 108
Soymanov, Theodore, 168
Spate, O.H.K.
    Changing Map of Asia, The (East & Spate), 75
"spatial vocabulary", 52
"Speak Mandarin Campaign", 248
Special Broadcasting Service (SBS), 56
SSA (South Sea Association), 242
SSI (Strategic Studies Institute), 66
Stanford Program, 148, 151
Stoler, Ann, 232
Storostas-Vydūnas, Vilhelmas, 197, 198
Straits Settlements, 234, 235

British census report of, 235
Chinese population of, 235
Strategic Studies Institute (SSI), 66
Stubbs, Richard
  Routledge Handbook of Asian
    Regionalism, The (Beeson &
    Stubbs), 82
"Subaltern Studies", 38
Sukarno, 103, 174
Sumsky, Victor, 176
Sunda Strait, 168
Suparlan, Parsudi, 112
Suzuki Keikun, 340

T
Tagore, Rabindranath, 213, 215–17
Taikan, Yokoyama, 216
Taiwan, 256, 259, 261, 263
  colonial relation between Japan
    and, 262
  "de-sinicizing", 159
  Japanese colonial survey, 242
  "Taiwan Academies", 158
  "Taiwan in the Modern World" (book
    series), 151
Taiwan Studies, 12, 146, 262
  as area study, 159
  at School of Oriental and African
    Studies, 155
  Chiang Ching-kuo Chair of, 155
  emergence of, 142
  expansion of, 146
  in Europe, 152–56
  in United States, 146–52
  local knowledge production, 145
Tanaka Zenryū, 241–42
  Taiwan to minami Shina, 241
Tan Chung, 225
Tankha, Brij, 14–15
Tan Yunshan, 217

Taryba, 190
Teo Eng Hock, 239
Terminal High Altitude Area Defense
  (THAAD) system, 264, 266
Tibetan independence movement, 87
Tirtosudarmo, Riwanto, 11
Title VI Act, 54
Tokyo University of Foreign Studies,
  253–54
traditional Orientalist, 33
"tribes", concept of, 236
Trinkūnas, Jonas, 202, 205, 207n4
Truman Doctrine, 34
Tsyganov, Vladilen, 174
2-28 Incident, 148, 149
Tyurin, Vladimir, 172
Tzeng, Albert, 5
  world system of knowledge
    network, 6

U
Uchida Kakichi, 242
Union of Soviet Societies for
  Friendship (USSF), 200–202
United Nations Transitional
  Authority in Cambodia
  (UNTAC), 139n6
United States
  Cambodian refugees, 127–29
  foreign policy, 148
  post–World War II geopolitics, 9
  refugee resettlement in, 135
  Taiwan Studies in, 146–52
USSF (Union of Soviet Societies for
  Friendship), 200–202
USSR, 32, 176
  geopolitical centres, 166
USSR–India friendship symposium,
  204
Uvarov, Sergey Semionovich, 192

V

Valverde, Estela, 51
van Dijk, Kees, 105
Variation of Javanese Religion: An Anthropological Account, The (Beatty), 102
Varisco, Daniel Martin, 24
Vaughan, Jonas Daniel, 235
Vickery, Michael, 131–32
Vieira de Mello, Sergio, 114
Vieland, C.A., 238
Vietnam, 174, 180
  invasion of Cambodia, 126, 130
Vietnamese Academy of Social Sciences, 180
Vilnius University, 191, 202
  academic life at, 193
  history of Oriental Studies in, 192–94
Visvesvaraya, M., 218
Vivekananda, Swami, 218
Vladivostok, 176
Vokrug Sveta (Around the World), 169, 170
Vremia (Time), 170

W

Walker, Richard L., 150
Warraq Ibn, 24
Western mind, metamorphosis of, 33–39

X

Xu Jiyu, 340
Xu Songshi, 245

Y

Yahuda, Michael
  International Relations of Asia (Shambaugh & Yahuda), 82
Yan Shanping, 257
Ying Huan Zhi Lue, 340
Yung Wing, 241

Z

Zabulis, Henrikas, 202

"White Australia" policy, 56
White, Benjamin, 103, 1116n7
Whorf, Benjamin, 37
Wich, Richard, 80, 81
Wigen, Kären E., 45, 48, 49, 51, 52, 55, 59, 75
  Myth of Continents, The (Lewis & Wigen), 48
Wijers, Gea, 11–12
Wolters, O.W., 110
Wood, Denis, 68
Woodward, M., 105, 116n9
"world system of knowledge network", 6
World War II, 81, 128, 171
  geopolitics of, 52